Baily's Hunting Companion

Supporting The BFSS Campaign
for Hunting

THE BFSS CAMPAIGN FOR HUNTING

Baily's, Chesterton Mill, French's Road,
Cambridge
CB4 3NP
Tel 0223 350555

We are grateful to the following for supplying photographs:

Virginia Beard	Pages 6, 9, 11, 16, 19, 41, 64, 76, 94, 100, 101, 159, 179, 181, 198, 199, 207, 256
Jim Meads	Pages 44, 52, 55, 82, 87, 95, 98, 104, 109, 120, 127, 141, 152, 155, 167, 183, 186, 188, 193, 217
Cork Examiner	Page 28
John Mennell	Page 102
Gordon Franks	Page 103
Sophie Hill	Page 106
John Barrow	Page 133
Rachel Green	Page 189
Joan Slaughter's Rogue's Gallery	Page 220
Barbara Thomson	Pages 223 and 225
Pierre Rocton	Page 233

We are grateful to *The Sunday Telegraph*, David & Charles Ltd, and *The Daily Telegraph* for permission to reproduce the extracts on pages 46, 109 and 256 respectively.

We are also indebted to Sir Raymond Carr for many cryptic comments taken from *English Fox Hunting*.

ISBN 0 9523628 1 3

Edited and compiled by Barney White-Spunner

Published by Baily's 1994
© Pearson Publishing Limited 1994
Printed and bound by BPC Wheatons Ltd, Exeter

Contents

Part 3

Foxhunting

Introduction

The aims of *Baily's Hunting Companion* are three-fold – first to articulate the various arguments in support of hunting of which I feel all our supporters should be aware; secondly to show the diversity of hunting that exists in the British Isles and in many other countries worldwide; and, lastly, to give an insight into the complexities of running the sport at the end of the twentieth century. We hope it will be of interest to everyone who supports hunting, whether they actually follow hunts or not. I would emphasize that it is not a hunting directory; Baily's already publish an excellent one – *Baily's Hunting Directory*.

In the UK alone there are over 340 registered hunts providing 22 500 hunting days annually. Without the demand from those who wish to follow hounds there would not be the promotion of so many hunting days.

That, though, is not to say that hunting does not have its threats and problems. They have always existed and no doubt in some form or other always will. The appreciation of these threats to hunting led to the formation of the Campaign for Hunting in December 1991 prior to the McNamara Private Members Bill in February 1992. In its first two years the Campaign has unified the hunting lobby under the umbrella of the British Field Sports Society (BFSS); has produced realistic material addressing the issues; has helped finance a national and regional public relations structure and created a number of pro-active initiatives, and has fought for hunting at every level of attack.

The aim of the Campaign for Hunting is to achieve a better public understanding of hunting and hence a more tolerant attitude to it with the ultimate objective of removing hunting from any of the political parties manifestos.

Direct opposition is hunting's most obvious problem. It has been so since 1891 when two Fabian pamphleteers, both active in the RSPCA, formed the Humanitarian League and targeted the Royal Buckhounds and the Eton Beagles – perhaps the first smacks of class warfare aimed at hunting. Today, the opposition is lead by the League Against Cruel Sports, backed by the RSPCA, The International Fund for Animal Welfare, The Hunt Saboteurs Association and other animal rights groups who together form a determined, highly motivated and extremely well funded enemy. Their principal method is to set public opinion against hunting using the media, advertising, propaganda and emotive issues.

The animal rights movement is the 'in thing' for the nineties and the focus of their attack is foxhunting. However, we regularly see assaults on other field sports, equestrian events and country life in general. If the animal rights movement ever gets on a roll no-one will control its agenda.

Greater numbers of main roads and urbanisation due to the development of market towns and villages has resulted in the loss of huntable country. This is an ever-increasing problem which will have to be continually addressed in the future. A more abstract problem of the misunderstanding of hunting has been created by the change in the social structure of the countryside. The farm labour force of rural people used to living and working with animals has largely been replaced by a retired or commuting urban-based population, who have no experience of the natural world of predators and raptors and little appreciation of maintaining the essential balance of wildlife which is such an important part of our heritage.

Hunting has discovered to its cost that hunt incidents, be they accidental, set-up, created by inconsideration of followers or at the worst the result of bad practice, are more than a problem – they are a liability.

Money, no doubt, has always been a problem. Hunt committees are not renowned for efficient budgeting, and a great many hunters have cherished their ability to pay the minimum for their sport, but latterly, thanks to the generosity of certain hunting families and individuals, and the example of most hunts, the Campaign is being effectively funded. Even so, it must be appreciated that at least ten times more money is being spent against hunting than is being spent for it.

Ultimately the future of hunting or any other field sport will be decided in the Houses of Parliament. Since the war we have seen various attempts by Labour MPs to introduce anti-hunting bills – all have been thwarted. The actual hunting battle is set in the arena of public opinion. As Enoch Powell stated, "Public opinion, and we are all part of public opinion, is the Master of the House of Commons".

The achievements of *Baily's Hunting Companion* can be three-fold – to illustrate the strength of support that exists for hunting; to create a better understanding of hunting; and help, through sales, to finance the battle for its future.

As the Director of the Campaign for Hunting I would like to express my gratitude to Barney White-Spunner for putting all the articles together, and all the hunting enthusiasts for their contribution; without their unselfish efforts we could not have produced a word. I would emphasize that we asked people to write about a particular aspect of the sport in their own way and we have therefore kept editing to a minimum.

You will see that the book is divided into four parts. The first part covers the hunting debate. In the second we discuss how hunting is conducted as the twentieth century draws to its close. In the third there is a brief survey of the many different packs of hounds currently hunting both in the United Kingdom and abroad. Sadly we cannot mention all packs by name, and I am conscious that we have gone into more detail about foxhunting than hare hunting but sadly we just did not have space to write about everyone. Lastly, part four provides you with maps and some useful information, such as addresses, and the Hunting Code of Conduct is reproduced. Stories and comments relating to hunting have been added throughout the book.

Finally, remember that The BFSS Campaign for Hunting benefits directly from the book's sales.

Brian Fanshawe
Director of The BFSS Campaign for Hunting

The Case for Foxhunting

Brian Fanshawe

In recent years there have been many alterations in farming practices and the social structure of the countryside but, despite these changes, the seasons and the laws of nature continue the same.

For centuries man has hunted wild animals for food, clothing, sport and perhaps paradoxically, for the conservation of the hunted species. Hunting with hounds remained an integral part of rural life.

After 300 years of hunting the British fox is in very good shape and is a perfectly preserved species. Unlike the fox on the continent, feared and shunned because of rabies, the British fox commands the respect of the countryman. However, the fox as the senior wild predator and often a ruthless killer, is capable of inflicting great damage. No-one disputes that fox numbers have to be controlled for which there are various methods. Overall, the highest numbers are accounted for by gamekeepers and motorists. Snaring is effective but not selective, lamping with rifle shooting is effective but not practical other than in remote and unpopulated areas. Shot-gun shooting is widespread but leaves many foxes wounded. Other methods such as trapping, gassing and poisoning are all illegal. The proportion of foxes killed by hounds varies across the country; there are many areas close to suburbia, motorways or electric railways where hunting is impractical but in parts of Wales, the Fells and many other hunting counties, hunting with hounds is the principal method of control. By its very nature, hunting kills the weak, the old and the injured and it is also the most effective means of dispersing unacceptably large concentrations of foxes. The hunted fox either makes his escape or is killed instantly. If it is accepted that hunting is the least cruel method of control and supposing only 1 per cent of foxes killed are killed by hounds then the case for hunting is totally sustainable.

There is no doubt that without hunting other methods of fox control would proliferate. In 1949 the Labour Party commissioned the Scott Henderson Report, an Independent Committee of Inquiry, to look into cruelty to wild animals including the issue of hunting. The Committee concluded, "Any field sport which has a reasonable measure of support and is a traditional activity of the countryside and which has some utilitarian value should not be interfered with except for some very good reason."

Interference on the grounds of cruelty would be justified only if it was shown that the amount of suffering involved was excessive or unreasonable. Foxhunting makes a very important contribution to the control of foxes and involves less cruelty than most other methods of controlling them. It should therefore be allowed to continue." That judgement remains entirely relevant today.

The British countryside is not a natural one. Our rich heritage of fauna and flora has survived better than in any other European country because of the dedication of generations of farmers, country people and sportsmen. Hunting has played a central role in this process. The woods, spinneys, fields, hedges, walls, lakes, ponds and moors were fashioned and are preserved by the pattern of country sports. It is in the interest of the field sportsman to maintain the woodland habitat. The Farming and Wildlife Advisory Group recognises that hunting makes a significant contribution to conservation, "The conservation element is inseparable from the provision of hunting."

Both socially and economically hunting is deeply ingrained in rural life. Point-to-points, puppy shows, supporters clubs suppers, dances, hunter trials and other fundraising events are central to the countryside calendar and bring together the rural community. Hunting has created and sustains many jobs in local areas, not only in direct employment but also through associated trades and professions – farriers, vets, feed merchants, saddlers, tailors, boot makers, livery yards, hotels and garages.

With more and more people having leisure time on their hands it is vital that all sporting activities rooted in the countryside are preserved. The access to the countryside engendered by hunting is unique.

Hunting provides immense pleasure to hundreds of thousands of followers, some mounted, some in motor cars, and some on foot. They derive their pleasure for numerous different reasons and each day that reason itself may vary. They hunt for the thrill of riding a good horse across country over unknown territory, they hunt to watch the venery – the skill of the hounds and their huntsmen pitting their combined wits against the wiles of the fox. They hunt for fresh air and exercise, the company, and yes, for the gossip. Their role in the chase is that of the audience in the theatre – the hounds and the hunt staff are the actors on the stage who together with the Masters have the added responsibility of managing the fox population in the country available for hunting. Almost without exception the followers keep, love and care for animals.

Hunting is governed by the Masters of Foxhounds Association and is conducted under a strict code of conduct and rules. There is no better monitor of the rules than the followers themselves who as animal lovers will not tolerate any unacceptable practices.

One has to ask what is the future of the country fox without hunting? The sportsman will always remain the most proficient conservationist. The case for hunting stands.

Brian Fanshawe, a former Master and Huntsman of the Cotswold, the North Cotswold, the Warwickshire, the County Galway and the Cottesmore, is Director of the Campaign for Hunting.

Hunting as a Contribution to Conservation

Barney White-Spunner

Preserving the beauty and character of the British countryside is in the national interest. Apart from a few extremists there are no major groups opposed to policies that contribute to this conservation in principle. Motives may vary – some want conservation because it helps the tourist trade; others because it fits in with their concept of natural living. Interpretations may be different such as between The Department of Transport and the protesters at Twyford Down, but preserving our rural heritage is one of the few matters in this country about which we appear to have a general consensus. The Government White Paper *This Common Inheritance* refers specifically to the importance of maintaining environmentally healthy rural communities. The recent interest in green policies and the care which manufacturers now take to ensure that their products are environmentally friendly demonstrates a new awareness of our environment and the realisation that we must work to preserve it. Hunting plays two key roles in nature conservation: one is obvious but the other less so. Both apply equally to all field sports and both need emphasising.

First, hunting directly contributes to preserving the traditional face of the British countryside and it must be remembered that this face is man-made and not a natural one. Hunting people plant hedges, which they like to jump in preference to barbed wire. Hedges do not have much agricultural value and can be a bore for farmers to maintain. Hunts not only actively encourage their propagation but also their management. Crafts like cutting and laying are preserved which might otherwise disappear. This husbandry benefits not only hunting people but also the many other users of the countryside both animal, in the form of partridges and butterflies for example, and human, such as ramblers who have nice hedges to ramble past and who would probably not derive much pleasure from a hike through a Somme-like mass of wire. British Heritage give generous grants of tax payers' money to a select few to preserve hedges but what other groups spend large amounts of their own money in caring for our hedgerows? And it is not just hedges; hunts keep our bridleways clear and preserve our woodlands, carefully replanting coverts with traditional British trees which provide snug homes for many other animals apart from foxes. Small coppices and areas of natural scrub which might otherwise have been bulldozed have been preserved as fox coverts. "A good example of this", to quote The British Field Sports Society, "is in the country hunted by the Warwickshire foxhounds where 55 woodland areas have been planted specifically for the purpose of hunting and of making coverts for foxes". Many such woods were planted specifically for hunting as a glance at any Ordnance Survey Map will show. Respected conservation groups, such as The Badminton Conservation and Education Trust for the Countryside, actively encourage hunting as they realise that it directly benefits our native woodlands and the wildlife they support. Writing in their recent brochure the Trustees say "Though some of our woodland is ancient, much of it dates from the eighteenth and nineteenth centuries, the Age of Elegance, when a love of the chase and of shooting led sportsmen to plant hedges, woods and spinneys. This they often did in what previously had been featureless or bare countryside. As true sportsmen they understood that the environment that best suited their sport also encouraged all other forms of wildlife".

Hunts also help in many less obvious ways. They lobby for wide headlands to be left around arable fields which again benefits many other users of the countryside; they put in proper old wooden gates, take down barbed wire, and hunting people leave their fields in grass if they can afford to, although sadly there are some notable exceptions.

Similarly hunting helps preserve our wild animals. This aspect of hunting is well covered elsewhere in this book but the point must be emphasised in any discussion of conservation issues. Those who oppose foxhunting find it difficult to understand the apparent paradox in preserving an animal only to kill it later and this lack of comprehension is largely due to a failure to understand the laws of nature. There are many highly principled and moral people who oppose hunting because they do not realise that it is the natural and selective method of controlling foxes. Yes, of course it would be more effective to shoot or gas them in large numbers and a few farmers want just that but then we would have none left and that part of our ecosystem which depends on foxes would disappear. The anti-hunting lobby have no effective response to this. Perhaps it is their distaste for seeing man as a hunter and part of the natural order, pursuing animals on their terms and not resorting to those methods in which his civilisation gives him such an advantage, such as, the bullet or cyanide. Effective as they may be, most countrymen will tell you that these methods are intrinsically more cruel and I've never quite understood why foxes are supposed to have such a preference for suffocating or dying of gangrene from a bullet wound.

This is all obvious to those who live and work in the country although sadly many contributors to the hunting debate comment without experiencing these realities. What is less obvious is the role that hunting plays in the rural community both socially and economically. It is as important to preserve the way of life in the countryside as it is to preserve the countryside itself for the one would be destroyed without the other. In the past many hunting people have replied, when questioned as to the value of hunting to the rural economy, "Oh, it's obvious; I wouldn't live in Barbourshire if I didn't hunt". Such arguments, although sensible enough to those connected with the sport, are less convincing to the sceptics. Now, however, two excellent reports enable us to quantify exactly what contribution hunting does make. The first of these was drawn up by Cobham Resource Consultants in 1990. It estimates that direct expenditure on hunting in that year amounted to £148 m with indirect expenditure at £287 m, and that 9500 people were directly employed as a result of hunting. A further 7000 were employed in directly associated jobs such as grooms in livery stables. According to Stephen Daniels and Charles Watkins, both lecturers in the Department of Geography at the University of Nottingham, writing in *The Geographical Magazine*, "based on these figures, hunting employs more people than do the gas, electricity and water supply industries in rural areas". However, The Cobham Report also estimated that a further 23 200 people were employed nationwide in professions which relied on hunting for their businesses. The report lists a total of 34 categories including farriers, horse feed suppliers and saddlers. Interestingly it also estimates that field sports as a whole contributed £1.4 billion to the British economy in 1991; showing an increase of 40 per cent from 1982.

The second survey was carried out by The Royal Agricultural College at Cirencester for The National Trust to investigate Staghunting on Exmoor. It concluded that 276 jobs, which is just over one per cent of the economically active population of west Somerset, were associated with staghunting and that the total expenditure on stag hunting in the local economy was about £4 m. "The great majority [of the subscribers] lived locally", commented Daniels and Watkins, "and came from all age groups; around a quarter were less than 20 years old and a fifth were over 60. The number of days spent hunting varied enormously; as many as a quarter of households reported 30 or more hunting days in the season and a similar proportion reported 30 or more days following the hunt by car. The survey found that the social activities linked with hunting provided many opportunities for people from isolated areas to get together. There was a strong sense of social cohesiveness among the group". Although this report was written about the West Country, it is equally true for many other areas of Britain and especially North Wales, the Fells and the north east.

This survey provides useful evidence that confirms what hunting people have always known, namely that hunting has a key role to play in the rural community. It also, as this report demonstrates, unites those from different age groups and, most importantly in a society that is rapidly becoming polarised by income level, it crosses the divide created by background and profession in a way which few other sports or ways of life can do. "There is", commented The Cirencester Report, "a sense of community which is based on shared activities as well as shared values." Yet the argument goes even further than that. Many of those who now move to the country do so to get away from the crowds and pollution of the cities. They want to bring their children up in a cleaner, more relaxed and friendly environment. Those who see themselves as the guardians of the rural idyll and who have been born and bred in a particular shire sometimes resent newcomers with their money and their commuting lifestyle but they make a mistake.

The British countryside has always been open to all and should and will remain so. Those now moving out of towns are, afterall, only the great-grandchildren of those who migrated the other way during the Industrial Revolution. These newcomers have an all important vote in rural constituencies just as everyone else does and they do spend money locally. What needs emphasising is that the life to which they aspire is heavily dependent on the countryside retaining its traditional character and that is in turn largely dependent on the continuation of sports such as hunting with its associated activities like pony clubs, horse shows and point-to-points. The Cirencester Report estimated that 56 per cent of horses and ponies are kept for hunting or directly as a result of hunting. "The irony is," to quote Daniels and Watkins again, "that hunting, one of the most potent symbols of this country life, is increasingly threatened." Field sports are also a useful way to get them to spend their money in the countryside. "At a time", said a Minister for the Environment in a speech in 1990, "when there is much emphasis on the diversification of the rural economy, many country sports provide growing opportunities for new sources of income."

British society has in the hunting community a microcosm of people who care deeply about their environment, who enjoy an open invitation to cross land that is normally precluded to other groups and who consequently penetrate deeper into the countryside than most. They are prepared to spend a large amount of their income on a sport which actively preserves our landscape and believe, genuinely and correctly, that hunting is the most effective method of conserving foxes. They also form a vital role in maintaining our rural communities both in economic and social terms. Of course they have selfish reasons for doing so; they derive great pleasure out of hunting and so what? Few of us act purely out of a sense of philanthropy. The ethics of the hunting debate are between themselves and their conscience. What matters is that hunting is one of the few effective forces that work to preserve the British countryside and which is privately funded. Make sure that your MP realises that.

Barney White-Spunner is Hunting Correspondent for The Field.

The Right to Hunt

Roger Scruton

It is a principle of modern democracy that minorities have rights, regardless of majority opinion, and that majority opinion does not make law. A democracy in which minorities are not protected, argued John Stuart Mill, is really a "tyranny of the majority". In such a tyranny social and religious practices which the majority find disagreeable will be outlawed; people whose tastes, looks or ethnic origins are offensive to majority opinion will be treated as second-class citizens; minorities might even be exterminated or driven into exile at popular request. And all this in the name of democracy.

Britain is not like that; and we should be thankful for it. Our country owes its tranquility to the fact that its citizens enjoy rights which have been fought for over many centuries, in Parliament and the courts. These rights form the background to our social life, and Parliament has traditionally regarded itself as their protector against every form of tyranny. To John Stuart Mill and his contemporaries, it would have been inconceivable that Parliament should frame laws forbidding people from pursuing their long-established customs, or destroying the natural forms of our society. It was assumed that the business of Parliament was to protect such spontaneous associations, which stem directly from our constitutional freedoms, and which form the stuff of our national life. At the same time, Parliament is sovereign, and could, if it chose, ban anything: football; education; the Christian religion. It is only the innate common sense and moderation of the British people that makes it unlikely that it would vote for such a Parliament.

Of course, Parliament must sometimes ban things; for society has to be protected against destructive acts. But the principles hitherto followed by our legislators have been liberal. Every act is permitted, unless forbidden by law; and the law forbids only what is harmful to others, or to the fabric of society.

It goes without saying that the moves to outlaw hunting with hounds go against this Parliamentary tradition. The intention is to use Parliament to abolish a long-established right, and to prevent people from doing something which harms no-one. Moreover, the campaign against hunting has expressly tried to set majority opinion against a minority, and to obliterate a spontaneous way of life for no other reason than to satisfy the feelings of those who condemn it. Thanks to the League Against Cruel Sports, proposals to ban foxhunting are therefore backed up by campaigns of vilification, in which the sport and those involved in it are portrayed as sub-human and ripe for extinction.

Posters and pamphlets put out by the League are similar, in one respect, to those used by Goebbels, in his successful campaign to persuade ordinary Germans that their Jewish neighbours belong to another species. The white stock and hunting cap have replaced the hooked nose and yarmulka; but the purpose of the poster contrasting 'beauty' (the fox) and the 'beast' (a florid Huntsman) is the same – namely, to stir up hatred for a human type. By this means many British people are being persuaded that a way of life which they do not understand should be outlawed.

If this should happen, it would create a dangerous precedent. Not only will other country sports follow hunting to extinction: any activity, any association, any way of life that displeases someone with the power, leisure and misanthropic zeal required to mount a campaign against it, will be the target of oppressive legislation. Horse-racing and boxing have already been singled out by single-issue fanatics; but who knows which gathering, custom or tradition will be safe, once Parliament has assumed the right to destroy a peaceful form of life merely because an opinion poll comes down against it?

Some opponents of hunting are aware of this, and try to persuade us that the argument is really about morality, not freedom. Hunting, they tell us, involves pleasure in the suffering of an animal – and to take pleasure in suffering is immoral. The League Against Cruel Sports therefore likens foxhunting to bear-baiting: if it is right to ban the one, we should ban the other too. The right to pursue our interests does not automatically extend to immoral acts.

Saboteurs

The argument is scarcely persuasive, however. Comparisons are easier to make than fine distinctions; yet it is the awareness of distinctions that show the moral conscience at work. Manslaughter can easily be compared to murder; there is a real similarity between rape and seduction; between beating a man and standing by while he is beaten; between starving someone to death and spending on oneself the money that could save a stranger from starvation. When it comes to moral judgement, however, it is the differences between these actions that are important. It may require a certain finesse to distinguish an innocent action from the crime that it superficially resembles: consider all the many ways in which a man may place his hand on a woman's knee.

The point of propaganda campaigns of the kind engaged in by the League Against Cruel Sports is to blind people to moral distinctions, to induce an attitude of unthinking hostility, a sentimental fervour of emotion in which the voice of conscience can no longer be clearly heard. Consider for a moment the relevant distinctions between foxhunting and bear-baiting: the fox is hunted as a way of culling him, while the bear is tormented for the torment's sake; the fox is hunted in his natural environment, where he has the advantage and is free from the terror that is the lot of a captive animal, while the bear is cornered in a world that is not his own. Most important of all is the distinction between the state of mind of the sportsman, and that of the ring-side sadist. Those who hunt the fox take no pleasure in his sufferings, and would cease to hunt if they were persuaded that these sufferings could really be compared to those of a tormented bear.

Moreover, there is all the difference in the world between taking pleasure in suffering, and taking pleasure in an activity that involves suffering, as an unwanted side-effect. Every time you throw a log on the fire, your pleasure is bought at the cost of a thousand lives, each extinguished in agony, as woodlice and spiders succumb to the flames. Every time you eat meat, or feed meat to your pets, you experience a pleasure that has been bought through suffering. But you take no pleasure in the suffering, and elect to regard it as an unavoidable part of a complex good.

Hunting too is such a complex good. The pleasure of hunting stems from pursuit, risk-taking, and the love of the countryside; from the delight in watching hounds as they track their quarry, in seeing nature as it is rather than as the sentimentalists imagine it, in being led across the country by an animal who knows if far better than you. Pleasure comes, too, through company and cooperation, and through being astride an animal whose joy surpasses in its simplicity and innocence anything that a human could directly experience. The pleasure of hunting is a pleasure not in death, but in life.

Of course, the opponents of hunting will not be moved by such an argument, since without the experience to which I am referring, they cannot see the force of it – any more than a tone-deaf person can hear the force of music. They will scoff at the suggestion that this moment of brave companionship between horse, hound and human, is a complex moral good which outweighs the fox's brief and unavoidable suffering – unavoidable, since it would occur in the absence of hunting, though in more lingering ways. Not every conscience, therefore, will be satisfied by that moral argument; good people, prompted by the best of motives, may be seriously convinced that hunting is immoral. Does it follow that hunting should be banned? Surely not – not even if a majority are opposed to it on moral grounds. For it is also a principle of democratic government that, while the law may intervene to prevent immorality, it should not do so when there is substantial moral disagreement. Many people disapprove of ritual slaughter, on account of the suffering involved – and they may be the majority. But it does not follow that this practice, so central to the religious life of Jews and Muslims, should be banned. Others strongly disapprove of the cruel habit of keeping dogs pent up in city dwellings. But by what right could we outlaw a custom on which so many people depend for their peace of mind?

More pertinent still is the case of abortion. Many people think, for good reasons, that abortion is a sin – far greater than any cruelty perpetrated on a dumb animal. A substantial minority, however, regards abortion as morally permissible, and also believes that a woman's right to happiness weighs more heavily in the scale of choice than a foetus's right to life. Hence many who disapprove of abortion (and here we are dealing with real moral judgement, and not the sanctimonious humbug of the League Against Cruel Sports) nevertheless concede that Parliament should not outlaw the practice that disturbs them. They recognize that toleration is the price of social harmony, since we must live at peace with people whose practices we may strongly disapprove. It is our duty to express our disapproval peacefully; but not to transcribe it into law. By what right, therefore, do the opponents of hunting seek to impose their moral views through law, when a substantial minority dissents from those views, and believes that it has reason on its side?

The example of abortion ought to remind us of what is most extraordinary in the campaign against hunting, and in the movement for 'animal rights'. Our country has entered a state of moral laxity without precedent in modern times. In the surge of violence, promiscuity, pornography, dishonesty and selfishness, the few old-fashioned decencies seem like the eccentric customs of a vanishing tribe. Everybody is aware of this; everybody suffers from it; and everybody would wish it were not so.

Yet there are no moralising campaigns, no urgent appeals to Parliament, no vilifying posters or public protests. Is it not strange that, in such a world, the fervour of moral disapproval should expend itself upon an activity like foxhunting, in which old-fashioned virtues still survive, and which causes no conceivable damage to the fabric of society? Or is this exercise of spurious indignation a mask for deeper guilt?

Professor Roger Scruton is Professor of Philosophy at Boston University, whose most recent published book is Modern Philosophy.

....

Whilst out hunting we came across one of those trappy jumps with a post and rail concealed within a hedgerow. My companion and I stood looking down from the top of the rise, he slowly filling his pipe and snorting at every fall. A horse caught his back legs and came down hard on his rider, who struggling hands waved feebly from beneath the horse's squirming form for what must have been half a minute, before ceasing to move. My companion, put his pipe in his mouth, and then withdrew it after a moment's thought to say, "He's dead I reckon", before applying his match.

Roger Scruton

The Rule of Law

Enoch Powell

Human society is about persuading.

We in Britain have built up and agreed upon a framework within which persuasion remains a voluntary process and is prevented from deteriorating into brutality. A powerful part of the framework is the rule of law: the citizen is permitted any behaviour of his choice which the law does not prohibit, and his infringement of that law, should it be infringed, is repressed and controlled by the courts and lawful authority observing a procedure which is itself regulated by law and must be respected.

The law is made by, or by permission of, Parliament alone. To say that law is made by Parliament carries two vital connotations. It is made by majority, and it is made after debate.

The requirement of majority ensures a more or less ongoing agreement between those who make the law and the public, who, at not too great an interval of past time, elected them, and thus guards against any intolerable gap opening up between the law and those who must be bound by it.

The requirement of debate is no less material. It implies that those who take the decision to legislate have been exposed – it may be, at considerable length – to disclosure and discussion of all the facts and considerations, relevant or irrelevant, which can be brought to bear upon it. When everything has been said that can be said about that necessary witches' kitchen, the Whips Office, the fact remains that the law is made as a result of persuasion. I confess personally, and not for the first time, that as a Member of the House of Commons I never once subjected myself to the discipline of sitting through a whole debate and failed at the end involuntarily to say to myself: "Well, Enoch, you've learnt something today which you were unaware of before, haven't you?"

When a change proposed in the law involves criminalising activities which are customarily and innocently engaged in by large numbers of citizens, the change ought to be covered by the authority of the electorate itself. In other words, legislation to such effect should always be government legislation, legislation for which the government in possession of a parliamentary majority take open responsibility before Parliament and before the public.

In summary, consent in our British system is secured, and only secured, by persuasion – by persuasion and not by duress. Or is the picture which I have presented already out of date? There are times when I fear that it may be and that we have lived on into an era when persuasion by intimidation is advocated and practised, tolerated and permitted. If that description is not mistaken, how has such a change come about?

Whatever happened to law and the making of law and of the debate which in a parliamentary nation precedes the making of law? Here the environment has changed – and to the the detriment of persuasion. Since Britain joined the European Union in 1972, a great part of the energy of its politicians has been expended upon telling people that they ought no longer to make through their own representatives the laws under which they have to live. The result has been to bring law itself into disrespect and to blur the distinction between what is law and what is not law. The change admittedly is not a sudden change, but an alteration which goes on progressively undermining one of the great safeguards of the private citizen. His safeguard consists in the fact that he is entitled to protection in behaving, including amusing himself, in whatever way he chooses which is not prohibited by law. No minority, however noisy or fashionable, which cannot bring Parliament to alter the law can interfere with him. When Parliament and its law-making function can be overridden by some external authority which he did not elect – as is increasingly the case today – that safeguard has ceased to exist.

There are other authorities created by Parliament for specific purposes. These sometimes chafe at the implied restriction upon their right to interfere with other activities of the citizen and are thus tempted to abuse the power which has been entrusted to them by usurping the privilege of making general law. Large numbers of such authorities are rightly entrusted with powers which involve becoming the owners of property, notably land. The courts however have recently established that this gives them no entitlement to usurp the power, even within that property, to make general law.

I have now come close to the protection of our right to engage in the field sport of our choice. It was not however accidental that I deferred so long to make the connection. I want to bring home that by upholding the right to our traditional form of persuasion, in other words, by upholding the rule of law, the foxhunter is sustaining something which is of value to millions who never heard a view holloa. We are only a small section of the huge majority of British public who possess a vested interest in the right to live under the rule of law, to do what the law requires and abstain from what the law forbids but otherwise to behave themselves in their own way according to their own lights.

In resisting the concerted attack of a small minority upon our freedom (subject to the existing law of property and other law) to hunt foxes with hounds, we are one part of a larger conflict which is being waged today, and our cause is the cause of a great majority of our fellow citizens. Numerically, those who follow hounds on horseback are and always will be a relatively small number. Even those who follow hounds on foot, by bicycle or by car or who take pleasure in knowing that rural England still has room for that traditional pursuit are perhaps no more than a sizeable minority. Nevertheless, the right which in upholding for ourselves we uphold for others is the right of a majority. Indeed, it is an interest of all. We ought not to be dismayed when we discover that in an age when the rule of law is under constant threat in Britain it has fallen to us to repel one of the more insidious attacks which are being made upon it.

Never let the foxhunter fall into the error of supposing himself unrepresentative. In the 1990s he has become the representative and the defender of a truly national cause.

Taken from a speech by the Rt Hon J Enoch Powell, MBE, to the Dinner given by The Campaign for Hunting at Chilford Hall, Saffron Walden, Essex on Friday 8th April 1994.

....

"I must give you an extraordinary instance of a gentleman's knowledge of hunting: He had hired a house in a fine hunting country, with a good kennel belonging to it, in the neighbourhood of two packs of foxhounds, of which mine was one; and that he might not offend the owner of either, intended, as he said, to hunt with both. The first day that hounds hunted his country he did not appear; the second day, the hounds were no sooner at the covert-side than my friend saw an odd figure, strangely accoutred, riding up, with a spaniel following him.

"Sir," he said, "it gave me great concern not to be able to attend you when you was here before. I hope you was not offended at it; for to show you how well I am inclined to assist your hunt, you see, I have brought my little dog."

From Peter Beckford's Thoughts on Hunting, *1781*

The Labour Perspective: An alternative view

Penny Mortimer

"Does your husband hunt?", people have asked me. The very idea makes me fall about in helpless laughter. The nearest he has ever come to taking part in any kind of sport is an occasional game of cards at Christmas, which he finds so boring that he overbids dramatically in order to bring the proceedings to a premature end. But, like the other people Ann Mallalieu and I asked to support our campaign to persuade the Labour Party to "Leave Country Sports Alone" (Melvyn Bragg, Lord Donoghue, Sir Denis Forman, Jeremy Isaacs, Sam McCluskie, David Puttnam, Lord Shackleton), he believes that in a free society the choice of whether or not to take part in such properly conducted sports should be left to the individual.

Over 4 million people in this country go fishing; 250 000 follow the hunt on horses, on foot and in cars; 840 000 of us take part in shooting sports. The vast majority of these individuals are respectable, law abiding citizens. We want the Labour Party to think very seriously indeed before it promises to turn any of them into criminals.

We toyed with the idea of calling the campaign 'Socialists for Slaughter', perhaps with an answering machine message saying, "Sorry I can't take your call at the moment. I've gone out to be beastly to some poor little furry animals." But irony is not an idiom understood by the zealots trying to hijack our Party.

A Labour MP has recently called people who follow the hunt "snobs and yobs". I must admit that I have occasionally come across such types on the hunting field, but so I have too on the ski slopes, and I know there to be more than a few of them in the House of Commons. What is sad is that this MP, and many like him, have not taken the trouble to go out and meet the genuine country sports enthusiasts, those decent, hardworking men and women who follow the foot packs in the north, and the ex-miners in Wales, now sadly unemployed but whose great and often only interest in life is to follow hounds. It is more than just thoughtless for an elected representative of the 'People's Party' to abuse them in such a way. They deeply resent it and this type of talk will be of no use to the Labour Party in its quest for power.

Perhaps politicians have become too urbanised; instead of listening to their rural supporters, some have fallen hook, line and sinker for the propaganda put about by those whose knowledge of the countryside stops at Brent Cross.

We have been through this well-worked debate before. The post-war Labour government, the greatest socialist administration this country has seen, set up an inquiry under John Scott Henderson. After exhaustive investigation it concluded that controlling foxes by hunting involves less cruelty than any other practical method. Most people who have studied the issue since have come to the same conclusion.

Animal rights campaigners wish to see all fox killing banned but they know that no government or local authority will do so.

Meanwhile they concentrate on the soft target of hunting while cynically endorsing other control methods, which they know to be less humane. But it's not only hunting they have in their sights. The movement is unequivocal: it wants to abolish all country sports because it believes that it can never be right for people to make a 'game' out of killing another living creature. Such a policy inevitably puts fishing and shooting in the frame for abolition. Indeed, the League Against Cruel Sports recently stated: "The argument against shooting birds, pheasant and grouse is far easier for us than the foxhunting argument". And after those have gone, what next? John Bryant, a leading official of the League, says in his book *Fettered Kingdoms*, "I have not the slightest hesitation in saying that pet animals should be completely phased out of existence... My reason for this view is that pet animals are slaves and prisoners and I am opposed to both slavery and imprisonment of innocents." The mind boggles. Does the Labour Party need such bedfellows?

Richard Course, a Labour councillor who was instrumental in forming the League Against Cruel Sports and selling it to the Labour Party, and who has now completely changed his mind and thinks that hunting should remain, for reasons of conservation and animal welfare, is an advisor to our campaign. He says: "I ran an organization with 10 000 members. You have to assume that they were the 10 000 most anti-hunting people in Britain, but half of them were Tories and most of the rest weren't Labour Party supporters. Nothing I told them and no amount of anti-hunting promises by Labour persuaded them to change their vote. If the Party couldn't get their votes, how on earth do they think we will get the votes of the majority of the public who are far more concerned with the central election issues?... I came to realise that for the overwhelming majority of the public, hunting just isn't a voting issue – the exception being the country sports enthusiasts themselves."

Genuine country sports enthusiasts

It is clear that, although public opinion polls show that policies such as capital punishment, flogging and the abolition of "blood" sports have majority support, these are not issues that determine how unaffected individuals cast their votes. Conversely thousands of country sports enthusiasts are reluctant to vote for Labour candidates because of a perceived threat to their sports. The future of an individual's chosen sport is an issue that changes his or her vote. In short, we do not gain the animal rights vote but we lose the country sports vote. This could be crucial in any rural marginal. A motion at the last Labour Party Conference on the need to win rural voters said that if the Party had persuaded just 40 000 voters in the 26 Tory-held rural marginals to change their votes to Labour, the Conservatives would not have won their overall majority at the last election. The motion concluded: "Rural areas are therefore crucial to the election of a future Labour government."

Since we launched the campaign in February we have received scores of letters from people who write, "Thank God someone in the Labour Party is talking sense at last."; "Good luck to your campaign, perhaps I will be able to vote Labour again before I die."; "I am a natural Labour supporter but if they are going to ban hunting I can't give them my vote."; or even, "I have been a lifelong Conservative voter who is appalled at the way this country is being governed. I would like to vote Labour but am unable to do so as long as they maintain the intolerant, prostrictive streak, most particularly exemplified by their opposition to field sports."

And the policy makers in the Labour Party should also take note of what the fishermen have to say. Fishing is enjoyed by millions of people and its industry is worth £1 billion pounds per annum. Yet it too is increasingly being targeted by animal rights activists. The Campaign for the Abolition of Angling was formed in 1981. Largely run by ex-hunt saboteurs, it has stepped up its activities (including propaganda in schools and direct action against anglers) over the past year and is receiving increased media coverage. *The Observer* recently reported: "Angling has moved to the front line in the anti-bloodsports arena. The Campaign for the Abolition of Angling claims two to three sabotages take place a week." A few months ago on the BBC programme "Here and Now" we saw fishing saboteurs harassing several anglers as they sat on the bank to spend what they had obviously hoped would be a peaceful afternoon. These supposed 'animal lovers' rose out of the water in wet suits, banged dustbin lids, threw bricks into the river and broke fishermen's rods in order, they said, "to save the lives of fishes and maggots". Most fishermen have no strong feelings about hunting, but what they fear is, if hunting is banned, what are these saboteurs going to do? They're not going to pack their bags, go home and take up tiddly winks, they're going to move onto the next item on their list – namely fishing.

When Labour comes to power it must concentrate on the matters that are really important – health care, education, housing, unemployment, poverty – and set about trying to repair the damage that has been inflicted on our society by the endless years of Tory misrule. What is gained by wasting valuable time trying to pass a complicated and probably unworkable Act of Parliament to stop law abiding citizens spending their leisure hours pursuing their chosen sports? Mindless political correctness is on the march in Britain. We want to stop this particular issue from being loaded on the bandwagon. The misleading propaganda machine of the wealthy animal rights movement has been rolling on unchallenged for too long. We are attempting to redress the balance.

The first government to abolish foxhunting was Nazi Germany in the 1930s (Hitler thought it was cruel). The first political party in Britain to promise abolition was the National Front in the 1970s. The country sports saboteurs are not for the most part members of the Labour Party; in fact, it is believed that they are closely linked with the extreme right wing and fascist movements in Britain. With such precedents the policy makers in the Labour Party should think very carefully about whether an attack on traditional sports, certain to alienate hundreds of thousands of country voters, would help it to win the next general election.

The Party is damaged when it is seen to be associated with an extremist movement, some of whose members use violence to promote its cause. As Denis Healey said, it is "single issue politics of the worst kind, a policy that we need like a hole in the head." For the animal activists the abolition of hunting would be a symbolic and vitally important first step, a watershed. They would have demonstrated their power and set our political agenda. We would have opened ourselves up to a full scale onslaught on more popular sports. Yet we would not actually have saved a single fox.

Penny Mortimer is a member of The Labour Party and a founder of the Leave Country Sports Alone Campaign. She is married to the author and journalist John Mortimer.

···

"I beg your pardon, Sir, but would you mind telling me have you come far to do this?"

The fifth Earl Spencer to an enthusiastic follower who had knocked him over out hunting.

From Raymond Carr's English Fox Hunting

The European View

Yves Lecocq and Charles King

Given the amount of publicity hunting has received in several Member States of the European Union (EU), one might expect significant mention to be made of "vénerie" in EU Statute books and other international legislation. The opposite is, in fact, the case.

Community law deals with hunting (the internationally used "hold-all" term for all forms of country sports) in its "nature conservation" section. Directive 92/43/EEC "on the conservation of natural habitats and of wild fauna and flora" ("Fauna, Flora, Habitats" or "FFH" for short), the EU text dealing with wild mammals, has an Annex (schedule) listing prohibited methods – no mention is made of hunting with hounds. Regarding huntable species: Red deer *Cervus olaphus*, Fox *Vulpus vulpes*, Brown hare *Lepus europaeus* and American mink *Mustela vison* are not given any special protection status under this text; as for Blue hare *Lepus timidus*, it can also be hunted, subject to management measures such as closed seasons. The Otter *Lutra lutra*, a threatened species throughout Europe, rightly receives strict protection; "derogations" (specific exceptions) allowing hunting can, in principle, be applied by Member States in those cases where hunting will maintain or actually improve the conservation status of this species, for example through improvement of river bank habitats or water quality – in other words, where such hunting constitutes a "wise use".

The only piece of EU legislation explicitly referring to hunting with hounds is an Internal Market measure: Directive 90/677/EEC "laying down the veterinary rules for the disposal and processing of animal waste". The aim of this text, as with all Internal Market legislation, is to remove physical and technical obstacles to the free movement of people, goods and services throughout the EU. In its original wording, the text would, on health grounds, have forbidden the feeding of unprocessed farm carcasses and offal to packs of hounds. FACE (Federation of Associations for Country Sports in Europe) put the point across that this activity in no way endangers public health, and ensured the Proposal was altered. The Directive, as finally adopted, makes specific allowance "for the feeding... of recognized packs of hounds." An important clause in two ways: firstly, it is an explicit acknowledgement of hunting with hounds, the only mention of these disciplines in any Community text; secondly, the term "recognised packs" may provide a useful lever to bring any undisciplined Hunts into line.

Other international legislation does not give hunting with hounds special attention either. The 1979 Convention on the Conservation of European Wildlife and Natural Habitats, also known as the Bern

Convention (after the city where it was opened for signature), is the international "blueprint" for wildlife and habitat management; it has been ratified by virtually all the countries of Central and Western Europe, including all 12 EU Member States; it is on this Convention that the "FFH" Directive was modelled.

Appendix IV of the Bern Convention lists the prohibited means of killing; again, no mention is made of hunting with hounds. Appendix III of the Bern Convention lists "protected fauna species", which may be hunted, subject to management measures such as closed seasons: this Appendix lists, among other species, the Brown/Blue Hares *Lepus europeaus/timidus*, plus all Deer species. The other quarry species are not mentioned in any Appendix, and do not therefore qualify for any special protection.

Both at the Community and the international level, therefore, hunting with hounds is, legally speaking, permissible. Indeed, as far as direct attacks on the sport are concerned, none have been successful on the European level, but rather within the EU Member States where it is practised (eight of the twelve at present).

It would, however, be misguided to believe that this sport faces no threats at the European level. A considerable proportion of the European parliament's 567 members is active in the field of animal welfare; in this context, certain political groupings consider that hunting with hounds has no place in contemporary society.

Back in December 1984 a Belgian Green MEP, François Roelants du Vivier, tabled a Motion for a Resolution "on the banning of certain forms of hunting, particularly riding to hounds"; the text considered hunting with hounds to be "repugnant" and called upon the European Commission to propose legislation to ban the sport. Individual MEPs' Motions for Resolutions cannot, however, be adopted as such by the European Parliament; far too many are tabled for this to be practicable. Instead, they are referred to one of the EP's Committees, which may decide to draw up a Report on one or several such Motions. This Report, in turn, contains a Resolution which is tabled for adoption by Parliament. The Roelants du Vivier Motion was "buried" in a Report drawn up by Gerhard Schmid, a German Socialist, on behalf of the Environment Committee, the Resolution of which made no direct reference to hunting with hounds, concentrating instead on bullfighting and animal husbandry.

More recently, in February 1993, a Draft Report was presented in the European Parliament's Environment Committee by an Italian Green MEP, Gianfranco Amendola, "on the welfare and status of animals in the Community". Its content was as wide-ranging as its title: it called for an EU-level advisory committee and educational campaigns on animal welfare, for restrictions in the fields of animal transport and intensive rearing, and for bans on force feeding (foie gras), fur farming and "the violence and suffering inflicted on animals in the name of cultural traditions.... and sport". Realising the danger this phrase represented for fieldsports, FACE lobbied for its removal. After repeated contacts with MEPs, officials and other interest groups, the message got across: this part was removed from the Report prior to its adoption by the European Parliament in January 1994.

A focus for animal welfare issues within the European Parliament is provided by its "Animal Welfare" Intergroup. Intergroups are informal gatherings of MEPs belonging to several political groups (=parties) but sharing a common interest; informal equivalents of Standing Committees, therefore. The monthly meetings of this Intergroup in Strasbourg are attended by MEPs and observers from animal rights associations, and coordinated by the influential Eurogroup for Animal Welfare, the European umbrella organisation representing such groups as the RSPCA. The Intergroup, it must be said, has not taken up a general stand against fieldsports. This does not, however, preclude the possibility of certain MEPs trying to use it as an anti-fieldsports platform or as a tool to "pick off" certain disciplines, such as hunting with hounds.

By way of counterbalancing this attitude, FACE coordinates the "Fieldsports, Fishing and Conservation" Intergroup, which it helped found in 1986. It has regular Strasbourg meetings to which scientists and conservation experts are invited. The message is clear: fieldsports are one of the principle incentives for conservation, and fully compatible with the internationally accepted doctrine of wise use of renewable resources. Several MEPs regularly attend both the "Fieldsports" and the "Animal Welfare" Intergroups.

But lobbying and PR go hand in hand: the European-level work of FACE among politicians and officials is only effective if these decision-makers get the same message from grassroots level, thanks to national campaigns educating the media, other opinion-formers and the public about the role of responsible fieldsports in rural life. The Codes of Good Hunting Practice covering beagling and foxhunting, *Hunting – the Facts*, this *Baily's Hunting Companion* and other initiatives by the Campaign for Hunting provide essential back-up for lobbying at national and European level. It is upon the efficiency of these actions and the will of all involved to show discipline, responsibility and openness to interested outsiders that the long term future of hunting with hounds depends.

Dr Yves Lecocq is Secretary General of FACE and Charles King is the organisation's Political Affairs Officer.

The French View

Pierre Bocquillon

Man is a predator but he lacks the speed, stamina and finely developed senses of wild animals. Since his birth, he has made up for his deficiencies in four ways:

- In grouping together
- In equipping himself with machines and weapons
- In using the instincts of the dog
- In using the horse for speed and domesticating it.

Hunting with hounds either on foot or horseback, remains, however, much as it was 1000 years ago. It is a tradition of France, as our literature, painting, sculpture and even our architecture bear witness. It is a valued part of French heritage which has won the admiration of people the world over. It is a school of learning and of endurance which has become codified by centuries of practice.

Hunting is about hunting a free animal in free terrain with a free pack of hounds; there are no obstacles to trap the quarry and this freedom is one of the best safeguards for it. What other type of control can best assure the future of our wild animals? In hunting the quarry is either killed or gets away – it is never wounded. A pack can never kill more than one animal during a hunt and even our largest hunts do not hunt more than twice a week. Each year approximately 3500 are taken by hounds on about 10 000 hunting days.

It should be known that it is largely due to the good management practices of the hunting community and to their financial efforts that our wildlife is safeguarded. It is right that this community should harvest a small proportion of the fruit of their effort engaged in a pleasurable activity that does not upset the balance of nature. Moreover, what could possibly replace hunting? Once a surfeit of animals has started to damage trees or crops, would you have them poisoned? Or pay people to hunt professionally? Or do we just accept the disappearance of our wildlife?

Hunting is a legal and effective method of taking game and controlling vermin. Hunts themselves insist on the strictest discipline and have a long established respect for tradition and the ways of the countryside. Yet despite this adherence to tradition, hunting has needed to adjust itself to modern times and the authorities have accomplished this well; a number of directives have been issued in recent years and hunts are now, with one or two exceptions, constituted as non-profit making sporting associations open to everyone. Each member contributes a subscription (to cover costs) which is fixed at a general meeting. Hunts continue to be the traditional and accessible entertainment of thousands of country people whose opportunities for entertainment during the winter are rare. Those who ride are becoming more numerous and more members of riding clubs are taking advantage of the exceptional opportunity that hunting offers for riding outdoors, especially outside the show and event seasons.

The essential element of hunting is the hound. The role of the human is subsidiary. The breeds of hounds constituting the French packs are unique in the world and the pride of the French canine community. These hounds are sweet natured, even tempered and very friendly to man. Hunts provide employment and benefit the economy of the region. If hunting was to disappear, more than 1000 specialist workers would be condemned to unemployment. 15 000 hounds and 6500 horses would disappear from the soil of France. What a sweet victory that would be for certain so called animal rights and anti-hunting groups! It would be the end of our great breeds of hounds. No organisation could take on responsibility for them and they would have lost their reason to exist. This would be an irredeemable sentence and would be a terrible crime perpetrated by man against domestic species, bringing no benefit to wild species.

The advantages of hunting are renowned. It is sporting: you have to be a good horseman, capable of riding across country or, for beaglers, you have to be fit yourself. It is a difficult skill: the statistics prove that you must have the instinct and the knowledge of your hound, the horse and the wild animals. You must know your countryside and your way around it. It is in sympathy with the countryside: it is not destructive of our heritage. It is a community activity and fulfils both a social and economic function. It is a wonderful spectacle and produces great music from the horns. It is natural by definition and no product from the industrial era is used. It is regulated, codified and the rules are respected more than in any other sport. Lastly, it is living.

There are actually more hunts now than before 1914. These hunts welcome many young people – more than they've ever had. These are not the signs of an ageing social entity that has failed to adapt but, on the contrary, a modern organisation full of life. This is why it is being questioned by people who have nothing to do with hunting and who have taken a negative position without taking the trouble to acquaint themselves with the facts. Could one justify the disappearance of one of the flowers of France, based on erroneous information and partisan argument?

Pierre Bocquillon is Le Délégué Général de L'Association Française des Equipages de Vénerie.

The Tradition of Hunting

Jane Ridley

Criticising hunting is a popular winter sport of the sedentary urban classes. It last peaked in February 1992, when the Labour MP Kevin McNamara introduced a private member's bill to ban hunting with hounds. The bill was defeated, and there are encouraging signs that the argument is going hunting's way. But the attitude of the Labour Party remains uncertain; advertisements for the League Against Cruel Sports featuring brutal red-coated huntsmen still stare down from London hoardings, and each November TV and radio chatshows engage in the seasonal sport of foxhunter-bashing.

At one extreme are people who criticise hunting because they believe that all killing is wrong. I have no quarrel with them. They have the virtue of consistency. They are vegetarian, drink tea and coffee without milk, wear rubber shoes. Let them worry, though, about rats, highly intelligent mammals which suffer agonies from poisoning by Warfarin. Let them campaign against factory farming and fur coats. Let them not waste their energies on foxhunting, which is a mere pimple in their catalogue of man's alleged wrongdoings towards animals.

Most people who oppose hunting are neither vegans nor hunt saboteurs. They are sedentary urbanites, armchair antis, and they 'know', often without ever having seen a hunt, that hunting is 'wrong'. What are their arguments?

In the first place, they say that hunting is unnecessary. According to them, it is an inefficient form of fox control. If foxes do need controlling, which many antis dispute, they could be better controlled by other means such as shooting, say the antis. Second, there is the moral argument. Hunting is morally wrong, claim the antis, because people derive entertainment from needless cruelty to an animal. Why not switch to drag hunting, they ask, which would preserve the fun without the cruelty? The third of the antis' arguments is about class. Foxhunters are perceived as red-coated fools on horseback – the upper classes baying for blood.

The easiest argument to nail is the one about class. Red coats and top hats are the sport's public image, but they are most in evidence in the smart packs of the Midlands. Like any other sport, hunting has its richer elements, and the smart packs of the shires are hunting's equivalent to Wimbledon. For most foxhunters the reality is very different. Where I hunt on the Scottish Borders the only two red coats in a field of up to 50 are the Master and whip. The Fell packs in the Lake District hunt on foot, shepherds and farmers in battered hobnail boots; the only red to be seen is the Huntsman's faded waistcoat.

There are good historical reasons for this social diversity. When organised foxhunting first emerged around 200 years ago, it was unique among field sports because the prey was vermin. Under the Game Laws, only the owners of land were entitled to hunt game. Foxes were a pest, not protected by the Game Laws; and this meant that hunting was, in a very real sense, open to all. Virtually anyone could join the hunt.

Unlike the older sport of hare hunting, the new foxhunting was fast. To participate you needed a horse, which by no means everyone could afford. But, as G M Trevelyan wrote, "although the democratic and pedestrian element formed a smaller part of the field in foxhunting, the "hunt", with its red or blue coats, its hounds and horn, caught the imagination of all classes in the countryside; spirited foxhunting songs were shouted as loudly and joyously on the ale bench as round the dining table of the manor." Hunting was (and is) socially inclusive. By contrast with the rich man's sport of battue or driven shooting, which evolved around the same time, hunting linked all classes in the countryside. It became a social institution. It generated its own traditions and rituals, its own rich art and literature (what other sport can boast such writers as Surtees and Trollope, Sassoon or Somerville and Ross?), even its own language.

Foxhunting was forced to become socially inclusive by its very nature. For a peculiar feature of the new sport was that it involved riding, often at speed, over land belonging to many different owners. It depended upon farmers' consent. Marxist historians would have us believe that landowners bullied and intimidated their tenant farmers into putting up with the hunt. Search the dusty volumes of Victorian hunt histories, however, and you will find barely a trace of anti-hunt feeling among farmers. Only during the crippling agricultural depression of 1878-96 did farmers register a protest. Generally, farmers supported the hunt; and they did so because they wanted to. This was not a simple matter of relying on the hunt to control their foxes. It was also a matter of the pervasiveness of the hunt as a social institution within the local community. Even if they did not themselves hunt, farmers or their men were involved with the hunt – with the mysterious, nocturnal world of earth-stoppers and terrier men, with horse breeding and puppy-walking, and, after the 1880s, with hound shows and horse shows and hunt dinners.

Hunting depended upon the consent and involvement of all classes in the rural community. It still does today. To describe hunting as an upper-class sport is entirely to misunderstand its nature and its history. Hunting could never have survived, let alone flourished as it does today, had it been confined to the upper classes and the rich.

What of the argument that hunting is unnecessary/inefficient as a method of fox control? At this point in the conversation, the armchair anti assumes an air of smug scientific certainty. Foxes, says he/she, do not need to be controlled. Their numbers are limited by food supply and habitat, not hunting. The abolition of hunting, says the anti, would make little, if any, difference to fox numbers. Foxes, it is claimed, are not a pest, they do not kill lambs; and if foxes have to be controlled, shooting is more humane than hunting.

The so-called 'scientific' part of the case is, in fact, extremely vague. The figures of fox populations, numbers killed etc are based on guesstimates of the crudest kind. Very little scientific work has actually been done on foxes. Scientists are no less biased, often more, than anyone else, and their research is by no means impartial. Take the study of Alan Clarke's Eribol estate (1987-90) which purported to show that when fox control was abandoned, fox numbers did not increase and nor did fox predation on lambs. This was published by the League Against Cruel Sports as scientific proof of their argument that without hunting control would not be necessary. In fact, it proved nothing of the sort. In claiming that fox numbers did not increase, the Eribol report failed to allow, for example, for foxes wandering off the Eribol estate onto neighbouring estates where some were killed.

Antis assert that it is illogical of foxhunters to claim both that hunting controls foxes and that it preserves them at the same time. Either the fox is a menace, or it is a species in danger, they say: you cannot have it both ways. Nature, however, does not obey these rules of logic; and the truth about hunting is that it both preserves and controls the fox.

Historically, hunting can claim responsibility for preserving the species. Scientists believe that the reason why mammals such as the polecat and marten became extinct in the last century was because they were wiped out by keepers, while foxes survived because of the hunt. There is plenty of evidence of a shortage of foxes in the early nineteenth century. Hunts bought foxes at Leadenhall market, and earth-stoppers sat up all night guarding precious fox litters against thieves. But the most effective form of preservation was social. Vulpicide – the killing of foxes – was taboo in the Victorian countryside. When the great Victorian Master Thomas Assheton Smith dropped his newspaper at breakfast one morning with an exclamation of horror, his wife asked in alarm, "What has happened?", "Happened?", groaned Assheton Smith. "Why, by Jove! a dog fox has been burned to death in a barn!"

Foxes, however, are also pests. In hilly areas – in Wales, the Scottish Borders or the Lake District – foxes do take lambs, and hunting is the only viable form of control; a point conceded by the Labour Party in the 1992 general election when it excepted the Lake District from its proposed ban on hunting.

Admit that the fox is a pest – and not only sheep farmers but hen farmers, pig farmers and gamekeepers will tell you so – and you are faced with the question of how best to control them. Shooting is among the most cruel forms of fox control because of the difficulty of making a clean kill; a lingering death in a snare is little better, and gassing and poisoning of foxes has already been made illegal on grounds of cruelty. We have to face the fact that hunting is the cleanest form of killing and the most humane. Concern for the welfare of the fox led Richard Course to resign as director of the League Against Cruel Sports in 1991. He explained his decision in *Horse and Hound* (30 January 1992): "When I became fully and objectively appraised of all the facts, and conversant with all related arguments, it was impossible to avoid the conclusion that the "prosecution" – or the anti-hunt case – would not advance "fox welfare", and consequently it could not be justified."

Refute the class argument, expose the scientific argument as meretricious, and the anti is left with his last and probably most deeply-held conviction: the moral argument. It is wrong, says he, to derive entertainment from needless cruelty. Why not go drag hunting instead?

Drag hunting, as every foxhunter knows, could never be a substitute for the real thing. Someone (a man) speaking in the debate on the McNamara bill described drag hunting as 'like kissing one's sister'. There are practical problems too. Persuading 30 or 40 farmers to tolerate the drag riding helter-skelter over their land would not be easy. Drag hunting would really be what foxhunting is so often wrongly accused of being – an artificial sport for the idle rich.

To the argument about needless cruelty, the foxhunter's instinct is to reply: I do not hunt in order to see foxes killed, that is the least enjoyable part of the hunt. It is true that foxhunters are not sadists. They do not derive pleasure from cruelty. But this does not really answer the moral point. Like it or not, hunting depends on pursuing foxes.

The moral argument for hunting must be made on broad philosophic grounds. It is a matter of rights, an issue of civil liberty. Given that hunting kills foxes humanely, and given that hunting does no harm to other people, no one has the right to pass laws prohibiting it. You may hate hunting; but that is a personal prejudice, and you have no right to impose that view upon other people in legislation.

To which the anti's response goes something like this: surely in the twenty-first century, such barbaric practices cannot be allowed to continue? Banning hunting is a mark of the progress of civilisation.

This brings us right to the heart of the matter. The progress of humanity is, alas, an illusion. Can the anti honestly look himself in the eye and applaud the progress of civilisation in the century of the holocaust and the atom bomb, of Bosnia and James Bulger? The human race has not got better. But what has changed in the twentieth century is man's attitude towards animals. At the root of anti-hunting feeling is a belief in the innocence and purity of animals. Sentimental but deeply held, it is a belief imprinted in childhood by countless animal stories, from the wartime film of *Bambi* (1942) or the *Animals of Farthing Wood* on the TV screens of today's children. It is Bambi and the like who are the real enemies of hunting today.

Jane Ridley is Senior Lecturer in Modern History at The University of Buckingham.

....

The most extraordinary thing I have ever jumped was a bed. It was one of those wonderful old Victorian brass beds, all knobs and bugles, and judging by its size it must have been intended for a family at least.

It was performing a useful function as a gate in the North Tipperary country; the head and foot were tied together to form one half, whilst the base made up the other. My mother, who followed me over it, liked it so much that she went back at the end of the day and bought it off the farmer. With a minimum of repair it was soon back serving its original function and very comfortable it was; I slept in it for 15 years!

Barney White-Spunner

Hunting and Equestrian Sports:
A Vital Link

Richard Meade

I remember well my first visit to Badminton; I was ten years old and it was the first ever Badminton Horse Trials.

The cross-country day was bright and sunny, and there was only a handful of people walking around the course. It was an inspiring sight to see high quality horses galloping round the park, jumping those enormous fences. Until that time, my only experience of cross-country riding was in the hunting field, and in those days there was not much jumping in Lady Curre's country. But I loved the excitement of hunting and the challenge of being there on my pony at the end.

At Badminton I saw a sport that capitalised on the cross-country element of hunting and that early visit inspired me to take up the sport of eventing. To this day I have found that hunting can play a very important part in the training of an event horse and rider.

Qualifying a hunter chaser

In the early days of my eventing career, I hunted my eventing horses as a matter of routine. I found it gave them a will to go across country. It appealed to their herd instinct, galloping with others as well as the added incentive of galloping with hounds. It was fun and exciting. A horse that lacks courage in cold blood can become much more confident and courageous when following a pack of hounds.

Two years before the Montreal Olympic Games I was asked to ride a thoroughbred horse called Jacob Jones. He was quite talented but lacked courage and was suspicious of ditches.

I discovered this to my cost when I took him to Colombier in Switzerland for his second three-day event and our first competition together. Half-way around the cross-country course, at the bottom of a hill, there was a large log over the deep ditch of a fast-flowing mountain brook. Jacob came to a grinding halt and I knew I had no chance of getting him over it. After the second attempt, we retired.

He was a tall horse that I believe had been rushed in his early training and had never had to look at his fences at novice level. When faced with an international course and fences that more than filled the eye, he suddenly showed his greenness and lack of confidence. I had been told that he had hunted twice and had behaved very badly. However, I believed that it was essential for him to gain some hunting experience if he was to reach the top.

First, I gave him a day's drag-hunting, which only revved him up to the point where he was almost unrideable. That was clearly a mistake. It was proper hunting that was needed, with quiet moments to allow a horse to settle and learn to concentrate, as well as exciting ones for galloping and jumping.

I was living in London at the time and so had to travel some distance to hunt. I decided on the Berkeley as the most suitable country for Jacob. Everyone had told me that the Berkeley ditches are large and numerous and, if a horse could jump them, it would be able to jump anything. I arranged to keep Jacob there until Christmas and based him with the Prout family, Ros having been in the British team with me at the European Championships in Kiev two years before.

Jacob and I had a wonderful half-season. It was a friendly country and the "Marsh", which flanks the Severn Estuary, certainly has some formidable ditches or "rhines". If there wasn't a ditch towards, there was certainly one on the far side of the big, black fences.

It was perfect for Jacob. With a good pack of hounds in front, an excellent field master, who knew the country backwards, and a thrusting field, the scene was ideally set for getting a horse going. The ground was very light, so even when horses were splashing through the mud, they did not find it too holding.

By Christmas Jacob had gained enormous confidence and everything seemed to be going well when, on the last day, he sprang a curb. However he was only off for a few weeks and the following summer won the

Bramham Three-day event and, the next year, went on to be fourth at Badminton and at the Olympic Games in Montreal.

As I said earlier Jacob Jones was not a particularly courageous horse and even after his hunting with the Berkeley I had to ride him strongly at ditches. But I have no doubt that, if he had not hunted, he would never have jumped a clear round in Montreal.

In 1971, ten months before the Munich Olympic Games, I was offered Major Derek Allhusen's promising, home-bred seven year old Laurieston to ride. I rode him in two events that autumn and, after he deposited me on the ground at one straightforward obstacle, I was convinced that, if we were to get to the Olympic Games, we needed to do some serious hunting together.

Laurieston had never hunted before and, as he was an impetuous horse, his owner wondered whether hunting would hot him up too much. However, he kindly agreed to let me give it a try and I had half a season with the Meynell. The first few days were fairly hairy, and by the third day, Laurieston had become very excitable. I remember a senior lady of the field saying, "I don't know how you think you are going to ride that horse in the Olympics. Personally I'd rather drive the wrong way up the motorway than hunt that horse!" However, Laurieston gradually settled down and by the sixth day he was looking at what he was doing and jumping with much more care.

The experience of hunting gives one the opportunity to know when the horse is tiring and what to do to help him when he is getting tired. A horse needs to make much more effort when he tires and the hunting field is an excellent training ground for this. Certainly the hunting Laurieston and I had together was invaluable; the days in the Meynell hills were as educational as those in the vale.

Laurieston was a completely different horse from Jacob Jones. He had masses of talent, a mischievous character and the heart of a lion. The hunting field provided the challenge he needed, and the experience without which, I am sure, we would never have got to the Olympic Games in Munich the following summer and certainly would not have won the Gold Medal.

In 1968, six thousand feet up in the mountains of Mexico, the cross-country of the Olympic three-day event was hit by the usual afternoon rainstorm. The only difference was that on this particular day four and a half inches of rain fell in an hour and a quarter. I was riding Mary Gordon-Watson's brilliant nine year old horse Cornishman V and the rain started while we were on the roads and tracks, half an hour before we were due to start phase D – the cross-country phase.

Cornishman was a last minute ride for me, and I had only jumped one cross-country fence on him before leaving Britain. In Mexico the training fences provided for us were, in our opinion, unjumpable, so all the schooling had to be done over show jumps during the ten days we were able to work the horses before the competition started.

The rain was coming down so hard that I seriously wondered if a horse could see the fences well enough to jump them. We had peaks to our hats; the horses had no such protection. Certainly in their natural state they would not gallop around in such conditions, but merely search out a sheltered spot and turn their backs to the rain.

As it turned out, Cornishman gave me the most memorable ride of my life and we hunted our way around the course, jumping the fences in the most economical way.

After the cross-country when the British team were in the lead, several of our supporters said that the weather played into our hands and that the British knew how to ride in those conditions because of our experience in the hunting field. Certainly Cornishman, as a good hunter, knew what he was doing and coped admirably.

Richard Meade competing on Kilcashel at Badminton

Nowadays, the sport of eventing has developed so much that, it may be thought, there are enough events in this country for horses and riders to learn enough about cross-country merely by schooling and competing in the sport. However those who believe this are missing an important trick; the hunting field can provide a fifth leg for the horse, and a sixth sense for the rider.

The influence of hunting on equestrian sports is not confined to eventing. Many of our top National Hunt jockeys start in the hunting field and progress through point-to-pointing and hunter chasing to a professional career in racing. Many top show jumpers hunt or have hunted. Point-to-pointing has its roots in hunting and the infrastructure of point-to-point races is provided by hunts. In fact most equestrian events in the countryside rely largely on hunts to supply the expertise and the volunteers to enable them to function.

Hunting can be proud of the part it plays in the organisation of equestrian events and in the development of competition horses and riders of international calibre.

Richard Meade was a member of the British Three-day Event Team for 21 years and won 13 Olympic, World and European medals.

....

A hunting parson was rebuked by his bishop. "But, my lord, I saw that you were at a state ball the other night."

"Perhaps I was," said the prelate, "but I can assure you I was never in the same room as the dancing."

"And I can assure you, my lord, I am never in the same field as the hounds."

From Raymond Carr's English Fox Hunting

An African View

Sousa Jamba

Of the many things about British life that intrigued me as a child in Africa, none seemed more thoroughly mysterious than foxhunting. The strange costumes, the extreme social complexities, the slaughter of a wild animal, all added up to a ritual so extraordinary and arcane that it might have been dreamt up by one of our wilder tribes.

I was born in Angola but grew up in Zambia, where hunting was illegal. When I arrived in Britain in 1986, foxhunting was as alien to me as it is to most urban Britons. I imagined aristocratic hunters wearing blood-red outfits and expressions of relish as a fox was ripped to shreds before their eyes. But as I made inroads into society, my opinion began to be challenged. People who knew about hunting said I had a simplistic view of the sport – and it was a sport, not just an upper-class rite of passage. Foxes, I was told, were no more than vermin whose numbers had to be kept down to preserve the ecological balance of the country. And anyway, the point of the hunt was not the killing of the fox, but the exhilaration of riding, the fresh air and exercise. I was clearly in the grip of a prejudice rooted in ignorance: why didn't I spend a day hunting with a pack, someone suggested, to sort out the reality from the myth?

There were no horses to speak of in Angola, and I had never ridden in my life. But the Hyde Park Stables in Bathurst Mews do a crash course in riding for prospective foxhunters, and I decided to enroll. I made up my mind I would do whatever it took to be admitted to one of the inner sanctums of British social life.

The first hurdle, before learning to ride, was to learn to be properly dressed. Hunting, apparently, was more than simply getting on a horse and charging after a fox. Like so much about life in this country, it was important to be seen to wear the correct uniform. I went along to a clothes hire shop for people who want to mingle with society. Disappointingly it seemed that only hunt Masters were allowed to wear the famous scarlet jacket, a 'fancy dress' I had seen in films and was looking forward to wearing. As a first-timer, I had to settle for the 'ratcatcher' uniform – a greenish tweed jacket, white shirt, red waistcoat, white jodhpurs and black rubber boots.

On my first day at the Hyde Park Stables, afraid of being under-dressed, I turned up in all my new hunting finery. Surely everybody else would be resplendent in perfect riding gear? In the event I was severely over-dressed – apart from a few women in jodhpurs and carrying whips, most of my fellow students wore jeans and riding boots.

I had always thought riding was easy. You just sat there and made sure you didn't fall off. On my first day at the stables I learned you had to sit properly in the saddle and support your body with your feet in the stirrups, keeping the reins short to control the horse. It was difficult not to feel insecure as I took my first tentative paces along the leafy rides of the park. I was warned that horses can tell whether their rider lacks confidence and will try to take advantage. So it was hardly a surprise when my horse strayed from the path and began nibbling flowers.

A horse will move in three basic gears: the trot, canter and gallop. Even the slowest of these, the trot, I found a nightmare. As the horse shunted gently along, I was supposed to push myself up and down in the saddle by pressing down with my feet in the stirrups. I seemed to get it all wrong. My rhythm was a disaster. My slow progress even began to worry some of the instructors, who wondered aloud whether I'd ever make it to the hunt. One of them shouted at me that if I couldn't even get the trotting right then I'd never be able to ride properly, let alone ride to hounds in pursuit of a fox. Try as I might, I couldn't get the technique. I was told pointedly that there was such a thing as the natural rider who could gallop and jump like a professional after a couple of lessons. This made me feel deeply inadequate, but by now I was determined to become the first Angolan novelist ever to ride in a ratcatcher's suit in an English hunt.

As the course went on I became obsessed with horses, I even dreamt about them. I read *Horse and Hound* with interest and enthusiasm. I knew I would never be a great horseman, but began to feel I could at least become a competent rider, once this temporary blip was overcome.

Having at last perfected my trotting, I moved on to the canter. We were told to ride in a circle round the instructor, who held a rope attached to our horses. The idea was to get the horse to canter by kicking the legs. Whips were of course forbidden. Whenever it was my turn to canter I had to bend over the horse's mane to hold onto it. I couldn't get this right either, especially when I had to ride with my feet outside the stirrups, apparently to get me used to sitting firm in the saddle.

In time I got the hang of that too. Sometimes, when the staff weren't looking, I even galloped a little. My confidence soared. I often found myself on an unpredictable horse which bolted off on its own or swerved suddenly while cantering if it saw something as harmless as a piece of wood on the ground. Despite this, and to my amazement, I managed to stay in the saddle. I began to wonder whether I was not, after all, a natural rider.

I learned to jump, as I would have to if I was to glide effortlessly over hedges and streams with the other huntsmen. At first the horse wouldn't jump, but stopped in front of the obstacle and refused to move. Then there was the time I fell off in front of a crowd of spectators in Hyde Park. Some of them giggled at my misfortune. "Get up, get back on the horse, and make him jump", barked the instructor. There were further disasters to come. One afternoon my horse bolted suddenly, swerved and threw me off into the air. I landed on my feet, but sprained my leg slightly in the fall. Whatever confidence I had mustered deflated at once. But I climbed back on, rode the horse as hard as I could, and felt better. From then on, I made a habit of asking other riders how many times they had fallen off, and the higher the number the better I felt.

The hunt was to meet on a Saturday afternoon at Linley Hall, in deepest Shropshire near the Welsh border. As I waited outside the house for the rest of the United Pack I was as nervous as a child on his first day at school. I knew that hunting in open countryside was more strenuous than anything I'd experienced on the manicured lawns of Hyde Park. How long would I manage to stay in the saddle? There was also the question of dress. I was worried about my rubber riding boots, which seemed tacky and inappropriate alongside the leather ones the rest of the pack would surely be sporting when they arrived. There was so much about hunting I was still unsure about. The little I had heard of its strange customs astounded me: hounds never barked, someone had said they spoke. It was supposed to be good luck to doff one's cap to a donkey. At the end of the hunt the Master blows his horn; on the way home, if he comes across a fox, he should doff his cap to the animal and say "Goodnight, Charlie!" I imagined hundreds of other such arcane rules which I would transgress without even being aware of them.

Rory Knight Bruce, the young Joint Master and editor of Londoner's Diary on the *Evening Standard* had found me a horse called Rosalynd. "She is what we call an armchair: she will do everything you want", he said. Rory is justifiably proud of being a hunt Master, as generations of Knight Bruces have been before him. He told me with a satisfied smile that in certain circumstances, for instance if the Queen were to show up at Linley Hall and want to meet local dignitaries, a hunt Master takes precedence over an MP.

More horsemen were gathering on the gravel drive of Linley Hall, the country seat of the More family "one of the four great Shropshire families" said Rory, "who have lived there since the Tudors."

One of my fears, moreover, seemed to have come true: everyone was dressed in black jackets and white jodhpurs and my green 'ratcatcher' jacket seemed quite out of place. I admired Rodney Ellis, Rory's fellow hunt Master, in his fine scarlet jacket, and his wife Georgia; who wore a blue version of the same thing, as is traditional for women Masters. Rory introduced me to Lady More, who assured me the 'ratcatcher' outfit was perfectly proper, indeed her late husband used to wear it too.

Glasses of sherry and port and plates of cocktail sausages were being handed round by the More family and their servants. Soon the horsemen would be joined by the foot and car followers. The foot followers looked like a rural version of trainspotters, in anoraks and flat caps, but supported the United Pack with a passion only equalled by that of football fans. The car followers were more high-tech, and had walkie-talkies to keep each other informed of the exact position of the foxes and the pack. I was hoping to see some hunt saboteurs, but that was unlikely. 'Sabs' tend to concentrate in universities, and Birmingham University, the nearest, was just too far away for convenient protest.

Rory made a little speech in praise of Lady More, blew a horn and we set off with the hounds through a wintry landscape of hills and dense forests. We trotted along for a while and gathered to a halt next to a hill. There was complete silence. Without warning the pack all raced to the top of the hill and down the other side, the horses excited and cantering. For all my arduous training in Hyde Park, I had no idea how to ride down a steep slope. In my nervousness I gripped Rosalynd's mane but seemed to be slipping off, until two women, who must have noticed that I was beginning to panic, kindly came alongside and told me to sit back in the saddle and press down in the stirrups to support myself.

Successfully reaching the bottom of the hill, I hardly had time to feel relieved before the entire pack roared off again. The pace was relentless. Shortly we came to the first jump. A woman in front of me fell off her horse as she tried to jump and fell into a pool of mud. I was sure I would be next, but my instructor's voice rang in my head as I sailed over the fence and, miraculously, I stayed on.

We were galloping over fields, past streams and woodlands, with the clean country air in our faces. It was true what they'd said: hunting had little to do with foxes. Hunters, similarly, seemed to have little in common with the bloodthirsty barbarians their opponents made them out to be. Socially they were not just upper-class toffs; there were a number of local farmers in the pack, as well as ordinary people who were simply there because they loved the sport. I rode alongside a computer programmer from Salford and a girl called Charlotte, who was curious about Africa and begged me to say a few words in my native language, Umbundu, from Central Angola. True, the Masters up in front of us were anxious to find the fox, and by the end of the day they had caught three. But the rest of us had no interest in the killings and were hardly aware that they had happened. There was no 'blooding', when novice hunters have their faces smeared with fox blood; thankfully, this is a practice that is fast losing favour. The main attractions for most of the pack were the lush unspoiled countryside and the fortifying swigs of gin – dispensed from flasks attached to some of the horseman's saddles.

At one point I lost sight of the pack and found myself trotting through Shropshire villages with Alison and Ana Henly, two black girls whose stepfather, a social worker in Birmingham, has a cottage in the country. The sight of three black people in full hunting gear must have caused some surprise, to judge by the straining of necks at net-curtained windows as we went by.

By the time the hunt got back to Linley Hall I had been in the saddle for six hours. I'd cantered over rough ground, jumped over fences and streams and galloped across fields, all without coming unstuck. My brief experience of hunting had shown me that the sport – and I see now that it is a sport – is far from being as senseless as I'd imagined. Despite the anxieties, I enjoyed most of the time I spent charging through the hills and farms of Shropshire. But there was a price to be paid: as soon as I stepped off the horse it was as though I'd been beaten black and blue. Every muscle in my body was sore and I could hardly walk. I went straight to bed but couldn't rest, since several of my friends who knew about the hunting expedition rang to find out whether I'd returned in one piece.

Foxhunting is not for the faint-hearted, I told those curious callers. But neither is it for people with closed minds or those with cast-iron prejudices.

This piece is an extract from an article which first appeared in The Sunday Telegraph *and is reproduced with their kind permission. Sousa Jamba, a novelist from Angola, lives and writes in London.*

. . . .

A gentleman, seeing his hounds at fault, rode up to a man at plough and with great eagerness asked him if he had seen the fox.

"The fox, sir?"

"Yes, d--n you, the fox – did you never see a fox?"

"Pray, sir, if I may be so bold, what sort of a looking creature may he be? Has he short ears and a long tail?"

"Yes."

"Why then, I can assure you, sir, I have seen no such thing."

From Peter Beckford's Thoughts on Hunting, *1781*

A Year in the Life of a Hunt: A Master's View

Rory Knight Bruce

There is, above the small market town of Bishop's Castle on the Welsh Borders of Shropshire, a farm run by three brothers called Bloor. It is the sort of arrangement made famous in Bruce Chatwin's *On The Black Hill*. They seldom travel even the three miles to the town, and why should they. Always I would see them on my farm visits, to let them know when we were coming hunting, and would stand in their kitchen drinking tea. On one occasion, what I took to be the elder brother said to me: "You come and see us so often, they must pay you a lot to do your job".

The truth of course is that, with the exception of one or two hunts, the masters are not paid a penny. Indeed it can cost them anything from £5000 to £30 000 a year to carry out their duties which involve nurturing a hunting country with more care than a swaddling child.

For many of the mounted subscribers and foot followers the season ends with the last "Blow for Home" in March, and does not mean much to them until cub-hunting starts in late August. The true picture is, as every Master or person closely involved with a hunt knows, a hunt is like a living thing, whose heart beats all year round.

The United Pack in Shropshire, with which I have been associated for the past four seasons, is no different from many of the two day a week packs across both this country and Ireland. There are many events through the summer to keep hunt supporters happy and hunt treasurers from wondering if they will ever again be able to face the bank manager.

But the lifeblood of any hunt is its kennels, and this must be seen to be working on all cylinders from the day the season ends. Foremost is early morning hound exercise, and many of our followers have enjoyed the vicarious pleasures of the hunt bicycle (I think I still hold the record for getting our's to go one yard and ten yards on two successive days). It is a lovely time to learn about hounds, their characters, and their penchant for Bill Sykes's pheasants as we pedal through the lanes of his estate, and such like.

Next on our calendar is the Sibdon Castle Pony and Terrier Show where people come from miles around to show their hunters, compete in show jumping and parade their favourite pet of fur and flashing teeth in the terrier ring. There is nothing likely to cause more anguish than judging the children's fancy dress, from which I have mercifully retired. Parents, ponies and their charges, dress up as characters from the Wizard of Oz to Kermit the Frog (I suppose one day one will come as a Nintendo Game

Boy). It draws a fantastic crowd. Even the ponies' eyes plead for a rosette after such efforts. Last year, to avoid the wrath of disappointed children, I think I awarded eight first prizes. It is a delight to see children thrilled to receive nothing more material than a tail bandage or plastic curry comb.

Rory Knight Bruce, former Master of the United Pack

Then in June comes the Puppy Show, a time of pride and anguish for the puppy walkers, and moment of rightful feasting as groaning tressel tables are filled to brimming with home-made cakes donated by supporters. The kennels look clean, with wood creosoted, lodges painted out and lawns mown. For this reason, and out of respect for the hard work which hunt staff put in all year round, I think puppy shows should always be held in kennels, rather than at the grand mansion of some worthy potentate.

The puppies, fresh from their baths, carry with them the hopes of their walkers. In an ideal world, the sun would shine, and there would be prizes for all. This year, I judged the Essex foxhounds, as junior to Jack Batterbee, Huntsman of the West Street Tickham in the wettest weather imaginable. Every time I went to mark my card, volumes of rainwater tipped off my bowler hat, making it unreadable and sodden. But still 200 supporters came. "We'd be out hunting in this weather after all," said Joint Master Pat Harrington.

For many years I have avoided giving so much as a dinner party (more out of ineptitude rather than meanness, I would like to think), so it certainly surprised my friends when I volunteered to revive the United Pack's summer hunt ball. There have now been three, and it looks like becoming a fixture. It is so easy and a certain fundraiser that I wish all hunts had one. The crucial element, from my experience, is a little uncertainty to create a friendly atmosphere.

The first year we had it, the fridge broke down just as 150 thirsty guests were awaiting their free glass of wine cup. Never mind I thought, serve it anyway. I can still laugh as I see Erskine Guinness, former Master of the Tedworth, take one sip, splutter like Captain Haddock, and hurl the contents on to the lawn. I suppose they don't have anything like warm wine cup in Hampshire.

A hunt ball should never stand on ceremony, be too smart, nor extol the virtues (which should be already known) of its Masters. Rather it is a time for those who hunt to get their friends along to see that really we are quite a nice bunch. Nor should there be endless raffles or exhortations for money. A good live band and a lively bar staff should do the trick. Last year we didn't finish until 6.00 am, so I was able to have the satisfaction of arriving early for hound exercise for once.

Another popular hunting activity is the inter-hunt quiz, a good fundraiser and usually organised by those essential enthusiasts, the hunt supporters. My one outing, however, shall be my last, I would recommend to all would be competitors: never take on a beagle pack. They seem to field teams stuffed with brain boxes. I was completely stumped. The questions reminded me of the discomfiture of taking maths O-level. "What is the list price of an Isuzu trooper diesel?", "How many acres in a hectare?", I failed the lot. If only they had asked me to sing the second verse of "I've Got a Brand New Combine Harvester".

These however, are the activities which a Master must attend, and a happy hunt is one which has a full calendar of events, each, hopefully organised by a handful of different people. Hot-pot suppers, fun rides, children's meets, skittles evenings (the United Pack, without me in their team, are rather champion at this) are all to be supported and enjoyed. A highlight of our year is also a carol service, hosted by Mr and Mrs Jock Beesley, in the small church of Bettws-y-Crwyn in the Welsh hills. It is always packed, and the natural melodies of the congregation make one happy to believe that God approves the Christian spirit in which hunting is performed.

But crucial to a Master's happiness and satisfaction must be the running of his country, the providing of a cheerful and efficient collection service for fallen stock and, in my view, a personal visit to all farmers, keepers and landowners over whose ground one is to hunt. On these occasions, I have heard more historical anecdotes and rural tales than could be believed. Most are joyful and illuminating. Some, such as collecting or putting down a favourite pony or cow, must be treated with gentle compassion.

Then there are those people, still a minority, who may not see hunting as a way of life. I have always maintained that such people deserve extra attention, and we all have a duty to make ourselves known to them, and respect their views. This sometimes takes special energy. On one occasion, when I was hunting the hounds on foot, a smallholder started shooting at them. Going to apologise to a man with a loaded twelve bore is not the best of feelings. It is a credit to the United Pack hounds that they caught their fox as we spoke.

Such things are not a problem to a Master. They are part of the terrain he takes on with his duties. Only then can everything come together for the Opening Meet and the great celebration of nature be fully enjoyed. And, although, contrary to the impression of the Bloor family, one is not paid, one is repaid in a thousand different ways: foremost to hope to have the trust of hounds, fellow hunters and the community. And if, on the odd occasion, they are all happy, then a Master feels like a million dollars.

Rory Knight Bruce is a journalist. He has recently retired as Master of the United Pack.

Some years ago Hounds completed a hot dry cub-hunting morning by killing a fox they had been hunting for some time in the middle of Langley Wood, Ashdon – a covert of about 75 acres. All Hounds were on and we set off home. Counting the Hounds out of covert we were one short and we went back to look for the missing one. There we found a bitch, Pigeon, burying the remains of the corpse with great care, a paw from one side, then a pawful of dead leaves from the other, more dead leaves over the tail end and then a nose worth over the head, the whole being given a final pat and last inspection. She was then ready to come home.

Edmund Vestey

How a Country is Organised

Alastair Jackson

I can sympathise with the celebrated after dinner speaker who told our Hunt Supporters Club that he had once been married to a 'Joint Mistress' of Foxhounds. He would get home in the evening to find a note: "Gone to see farmers about hunting tomorrow – supper in the fridge." The following day there would be another note: "Gone to see farmers to thank them for today – eggs in the hen house!" Hunting three days a week, that took care of every day except Sunday!

My own wife is now a Joint Master of Foxhounds, running a three day a week country, but after only three seasons we are somehow still married! The autumn hunting period is actually probably the hardest work, as the Cattistock hunt five and sometimes six days a week from mid-August to November – and every morning an early start. I am also certain that in the six years since I gave up the job, a Master's work has increased considerably. The countryside and farming are under increasing pressure and the list of people that need to be consulted before a day's hunting gets longer and longer.

Alastair Jackson with the Cattistock hounds

However, although the Mastership is the central cog in the running of a hunting country, Masters are only elected on a year to year basis and are answerable to the Hunt Committee. If they are not giving satisfaction in the country, it will not be long before they are replaced. A modern hunting country is organised on very much the same lines as a business – with a Chairman, a Board of Directors (the Hunt Committee) and Managing Director (the Master). The roles of the characters who make up the hierarchy of any Hunt will obviously differ, but the emphasis has changed enormously over the last 20 or 30 years. In the past, the day to day work of a Master was far less onerous, although many Masters subsidised the finances of the Hunt in a much greater proportion to the total income than they could possibly to be expected to today. The Hunt Chairman, who would almost certainly have been a local dignitary of considerable standing, was only expected to preside over the odd 'no nonsense' meeting and thank the Master for what he had done.

The pressures of running a Hunt nowadays, inevitably resulting in a quicker turnover of Masters, have now made the Hunt Chairman's role far more demanding. He should still be a man of authority and tact, but it is now equally as important that he has a business head on his shoulders. The income raised by a Hunt Committee from both subscriptions and caps and other events such as the point-to-point, dances, auctions etc, go to make up the "guarantee" offered to the Mastership. This is rarely enough to cover the Masters' costs of wages, horses, vehicles, forage etc and the negotiations between Masters and Committees on this subject in order to reach agreement for the following season can be needle affairs.

There are many weird and wonderful computations as to what the Committee are responsible for and what the Masters should pay for and some Hunts have taken over all the financial responsibilities themselves, leaving the Masters with the sole job of organising the days' hunting. In this case they are technically referred to as 'Acting Masters', although by the time they have mounted themselves and put in the time necessary to run the country, their costs can still be considerable.

The Hunt Committee itself should be made up of subscribers, landowners and farmers, who in more up to date Hunts will serve a fixed term on the Committee. However, it is almost more common to find vast and unwieldy Committees, whose members are on for life and most probably have not hunted for years. "I can't think what the Masters want all this money for," is usually the cry; "It was never like this in Lord Shorthorn's day!" It needs a Chairman with authority and skill to get any business through these Committees!

The Hunt Secretary is responsible for the collection of subscriptions and caps and good secretaries are worth their weight in gold. You would be amazed at the lengths some people will go to in order not to pay their full subscription and it is up to the Secretary to decide who are the genuine cases and who are 'trying it on'. In some of the grander hunting countries the Secretary is expected to undertake further duties, such as organising fencing and liaising with farmers. In these cases he will work on a more professional basis, but this is the exception rather than the rule.

Hunt Supporters' Clubs are of course a vital part of the organisation of most Hunts nowadays. Representing the 'grass roots' support and certainly the car followers, they run all manner of money raising functions and create an enormous amount of goodwill in the country. They are usually very independently minded when it comes to spending their money, preferring to buy something tangible, such as a vehicle, rather than putting their hard earned profits into the 'bottomless pit'.

The success of a Hunt depends on the sport that it shows and, however good the Huntsman and hounds, if the organisation of the country is not right, it will be to no avail. Thus the role of the Master is vital. It is well recognised that continuity is the key to success and therefore, in order to spread the load of responsibilities, Joint Masterships are usually the order of the day. In some cases these Masters may each be responsible for organising a different part of the country, in another case one Master may run the stables or the kennels, or Masters may be in the position of being able to generously subsidise another 'working Master', while not having the time to do the job themselves.

The running of the kennels is dealt with on page 87, but the amount of time that this will involve a Master very much depends on the staff. Most kennel staff are keen and dedicated and visiting the kennels should be a pleasure for a Master. The stables are often a different matter. Looking after Hunt horses means long hours, with some very early starts and late nights as well after hunting. All the stable staff usually see are beautifully turned out horses leaving in the morning, coming back tired and filthy at night. They do not get the fun of watching their charges perform, as they would do in racing or with competition horses. Coupled with the fact that many Hunts lay off their stable staff in the summer, the turnover of Hunt grooms tends to be high.

The stables usually involve the major part of a Hunt's budget and the horses are probably the largest capital asset. It is therefore vital that this department is run very efficiently indeed. Employing new staff is time consuming, as is training them, so a permanent Stud Groom or Head Girl is worth anything to a Hunt establishment. I will say straight away that, having always run the stables for me when I was a Master, my wife now has one of the very best Head Girls possible, which releases more of her own time for the part of her job that she cannot delegate – liaising with the farmers.

"But what do you do all summer?" is the question usually put to Masters of Hounds by the uninitiated. They presumably think that horses and hounds can be conveniently mothballed to be produced magically in time for the Opening Meet. This is certainly the view of some Committee members, who seem convinced that the guarantee is being spent on the 'Costa del Sol'.

In fact as soon as the last day's hunting is over, a plan for covert laying and fencing must be made. Those coverts that are getting thin and are suitable for laying must be earmarked and the necessary permission sought and agreed. This job, like hedgelaying, must be completed before the sap starts rising in late April or May. The maintainance of good fox holding coverts is one of the most important factors in a successful hunting country. Then there is no time to be lost in getting on with fencing jobs. This might involve the maintenance or erection of new jumping places, the building of bridges or putting in gates. In an arable country it is often difficult for the fencing vehicle to get about once the corn is growing, but in a grass country it is usually possible to sneak in between cuts of silage and hay.

However, organising all these jobs will mean contact between farmers and the Master, and probably visiting the site as well. It goes without saying that during a Master's first summer, all farmers and landowners will have to be visited, along with shooting tenants, keepers and all manner of other parties involved in the country – from badger groups to war games enthusiasts. The numbers involved could well run to some eight hundred visits. Some Masters like to see their farmers on a market day, but I was always strongly warned against this. The important farmers will be too busy conducting their business to discuss hunting and the rogues will corner you in the bar! There is also the real danger that seeing a semi-familiar face away from his own farm, you will fail to recognise someone and cause great offence.

The list of meets start to take shape in mid-summer as the shooting dates become available, and the autumn hunting dates must be arranged to fit in with the November meets, leaving each area quiet for at least four weeks after that first visit. Each farmer's requirements also have to be taken into consideration when arranging the meets and the requests for lawn meets can be a nightmare – "But you MUST meet here at half-term when little Frederick is at home!" Warning cards then have to be sent by the Master – some Cattistock meets involve sixty or seventy – and the Field Master, the Huntsman and the earth-stoppers must be briefed as to the draw and the possible problems in good time before each day's hunting. Equally, a choice of horses will have to be made and a plan for meeting second horses.

Having got this far, some Masters like to restrict any further visiting of farmers until the end of the day, but my wife, like many others, insists that she cannot be confident on a hunting day unless she has seen the main farmers the day before. She is also much happier not to be Field Master so that she can deal with any problems as they arise during the day. After hunting there will be reports from the damage stewards, probably some fences to be mended, and further visiting of farmers before returning home to face the telephone.

Believe it or not, after a good day it can all seem worthwhile!

Alastair Jackson is a former Master of the West Percy, the South Dorset, the Grafton and the Cattistock, where his wife is now a Joint Master. He is Area Public Relations Officer for the BFSS in the South of England.

....

I was hunting the South Dorset in their vale country near Sherborne in the early seventies and hounds were running near Boys Hill (which is actually just in the Blackmore and Sparkford Vale country!) We had all the Woodhouse family out from the Portman, including John, who was then a Joint Master and an exceptionally bold Field Master in their Wednesday country. One of the popular family of brewers from Blandford, John was no lightweight, but was always beautifully mounted on enormous quality heavyweights found by his wife Susie and which often came from Dr Tom Connors in Leicestershire.

Hounds had crossed a deep brook bounded by a straggling thorn hedge and were streaming on towards Middlemarsh. The brook was considered unjumpable at this spot and, as an impecunious young Master, I was not known for the quality of my horseflesh. I therefore crept through a gap in the hedge down into the brook and waded along looking for a suitable spot to climb out again. However, as my horse leapt out of the stream, I was caught in a branch and left ignominiously dangling over the water as my horse galloped on after hounds.

At this juncture I heard the unmistakeable voice of John Woodhouse as he roared at his son Mark, "Gallop at it boy and we'll get over!" With a thunder of hooves and a crash over my head the Master of the Portman landed all clear and galloped on without a backward look. His son, with his horse, landed in the brook beside me, knocking me off my precarious perch into the water alongside them.

Alastair Jackson

Field Mastering

Johnny Shaw

"Let it be understood that I am speaking about foxhunting, and let the young beginner always remember that in hunting the fox a pack of hounds is needed. The Huntsman, with his servants, and all the scarlet-coated horsemen in the field, can do nothing towards the end for which they are assembled without the hounds. He who as yet knows nothing will imagine that I am laughing at him in saying this, but after a while, he will know how frequently men seem to forget that a fox cannot be hunted without hounds. A fox is seen to break from the covert, and men ride after it; the first man, probably being some cunning sinner, who would fain get off alone if it were possible, and steal a march upon the field. But in this case one knave makes many fools; and men will rush, and ride along the track of the game, as though they could hunt it, will destroy the scent before the hounds are on to it, – following in their ignorance, the footsteps of the cunning sinner. Let me beg my young friend not to be found among this odious crowd of marplots."

Hunting Sketches by Anthony Trollope

This extract from Trollope must rate as one of the soundest passages of advice to a novice foxhunter that has ever been written. I would suspect that it will ring in the ears of many a Huntsman and Field Master up and down the country, who may think that their followers would benefit from having it read out at every meet of hounds. "The cunning sinner" is the bane of every Field Master's life, who can ruin a promising hunt almost before it has begun, or can cause many hours of post-hunting diplomacy for the Masters.

A start point for any article about the Field Master would be an attempt to define the role. As in all things to do with hunting this is not as simple as it first appears. Conditions and circumstances vary from place to place, and thus so does the job. Having followed many and led a few, I would venture the following job description: "The Field Master is there to enhance his field's enjoyment of hunting by keeping them in touch with the pack, whilst at the same time curbing their natural tendency to over ride hounds."

That description is the job at its most basic and only covers the role on a hunting day. So what is needed by the incumbent Field Master? Some would answer: "A loud voice and a good jumping horse should see you right enough." There are occasions when these are useful aids, however they remain only that and our Field Master needs much more besides.

The first thing our man needs is "The Knowledge". In just the same way that a London taxi driver needs to know the streets of his city and how to navigate them in the quickest fashion, so our Field Master needs to know his country. However, this is just the start, throughout his journey he needs to be aware of whose farm he is on and whose he is approaching, and where – for whatever reason – his cohort is unwelcome. This knowledge will cover every aspect of crossing the country successfully, including the location of such things as bridges, gates, paths, and most importantly in the upland areas where the bottomless mire can be found and thus avoided! All this information is supported by his experience of hunting in the country concerned, he is thus able, after due regard to the weather – and in particular the wind – to place his field where they will have a reasonable chance of observing proceedings and then getting away on a well found fox.

How? Thankfully in this modern world hunting, remains an area of life which is free, and even an avenue of escape, from technology. Preparation is the key, and experience of the country is near vital. My qualification stems from having been propelled into the job in a country of which I had no previous experience. Thankfully the field were very long suffering as well as being very knowledgeable foxhunters, and with their help I avoided making too much of a fool of myself.

So, to the preparation; autumn hunting is a very important time for a Field Master. It is a period when he can reacquaint himself with the country and see the results of autumn cultivations as they are taking place. He will be able to get a feel as to the density of the fox population as well as noting their consequent dispersion as it takes place. All this information will be very useful after the Opening Meet. It is also a time to get the maps out and give them a glance over. Many will scoff at this suggestion but maps hold a fascination for me and I find the large scale Ordnance Survey maps an invaluable aid, however well I think I know the country!

Another useful exercise is to keep a hunting diary. This process forces me to review the day as I write it up and as a result remember where I went wrong! In doing this I have to remember place names and where we managed to get through, over or by, whose land we were on, and the influence of the elements of hounds' performance.

Autumn hunting is a fairly relaxed time for our Field Master, on the whole, his charges are dedicated to their sport and they are few in number so keeping them up to their work is pretty easy. Thus lulled into a false sense of security, the Opening Meet arrives. Where there were twenty quiet enthusiasts, there are now up to a hundred thrusters on fresh horses, who can't have seen each other since the final day of last season, judging by the noise they make! The Huntsman's nerves are strung tighter than any bow at Agincourt and sitting in between these two forces is our Field Master. It is not a job for the faint hearted!

When I started to Field Master my father gave me three pieces of advice:

- "Foxes usually run down wind except in gale force wind."
- "You can only control your field from the front."
- "If you want to stop your field, hold them up in a defile such as a gate."

With this sound advice ringing in my ears I set off from the Opening Meet and we duly found a fox. This gentleman had different ideas, and promptly set his mask into the teeth of a near westerly gale and ran up into the Cheviots. Nevertheless I was still leading from the front, until I turned base over apex in a bog. Having recovered my horse and some degree of composure, hounds checked and at this point the last bit of advice went out of the window, there was no handy gate, there wasn't even a fence to put one in, only miles of rolling white grass!

Despite that experience, I find that his advice holds true most of the time. At the first draw of the day I will generally keep the field up wind of our Huntsman and the hounds, but at the same time be able to see down wind. In a country with large woods and deep dales I will ride on the down wind side of these features. This presents two problems from one source – the field. There must be a law of hunting that amusing anecdotes begun at the meet reach their conclusion when the field arrives at the first covert. As the Field Master strains every sinew to hear hounds, the gossip reaches a crescendo. This noise is a distraction to hounds, so the field have to be kept at a suitable distance; however the Field Master is then hard pressed to hear what is happening. One solution would be to turn round, stand up in your stirrups and deliver a stunning blast to the field shocking them into a subdued silence. Yet we are all out hunting for fun in whatever form it may take, so that is probably not the best approach. I get round this by moving away from the field to where I can hear, so when you see your Field Master standing away from the mass with his mouth open he is not being anti-social, he is trying to hear.

Once hounds have found there is another tricky moment for our man; he has to judge the quality of the scent which will very much govern how close he can safely ride to hounds. I say this is a tricky moment because whilst he is judging the moment when hounds are settled to their work the field are generally getting overexcited and the flanks are thrusting ahead. Once settled, we are away and from then on it should be plain sailing. The Field Master must give a bold lead after hounds; once his courage fails he has as good as lost his field. He must have a minimum of 180 degrees of vision with the occasional glance in his wake. When hounds check he must have the authority to hold his field so they do not interfere with hounds, and his brain is in overdrive considering the country over which he is passing.

So there we are, simple really isn't it! Field Masters on a hunting day do have a fair bit on their minds. So the next time yours is a little bit short with you, consider what he or she is trying to achieve for you. After hunting hounds it is the most challenging role in the whole cast of characters on a hunting day.

Finally, I would enter a plea on behalf of all Field Masters in the country, if you want to recount the one about the Englishman, Scotsman and the Irishman, or how little Daisy did at the Wet Willowthorp Show on Bunneykins, please do it at a respectful distance from the Field Master – he will be listening to hounds.

Johnny Shaw lives and farms in North Yorkshire where he is Field Master of the Sinnington on Saturdays. Previously he lived in Northumberland where he was Field Master of the West Percy.

....

The Master and Huntsman of the Cottesmore in the middle of a good run, had to stop to open a gate. One of the field who could not stop in time cannoned into the back of the Master's horse. He opened his mouth, turned round, saw it was my wife, bit his tongue and asked, "Annie, how's your knee?"

Edmund Vestey

Your First Day Out

Peter Rogers

How to be a good follower and a good visitor

"Hounds Please." With a toot on the horn the Huntsman leads his hounds through the followers, mounted and on foot, towards the road. The Master follows, the rest of the field closing in behind. You are heading for the first draw.

I am assuming that so far, so good. You arrived with sufficient time to unbox at a reasonable distance from the meet and hack on without arriving at the trot or in a muck sweat. You will have taken the trouble to ensure that your turnout is complimentary to the hunt. If you are in any doubt, look at the Huntsman. He will be immaculate despite being out probably four or five days a week. The rules of dress are well documented, so there is no need to emulate a young man I once saw visiting Leicestershire who, presumably worried about his sartorial impact in the Shires, came out in a black morning-coat. Cleanliness and comfort are more important than elegance at this stage.

First day out

Ideally you will have introduced yourself to the Field Master. Some Field Masters move around at the meet and are easily approached. Others remain with the Huntsman discussing hunt business and will not thank you for interrupting them. If you miss him at the meet, make an effort to have a word sometime during the morning and thank him for letting you come out. In addition to the Field Master there will almost certainly be other Joint Masters. With no specific task to engage their attention they can sometimes be beady about new faces so should be treated with caution. Try to get them pointed out to you at the meet. The same goes for wives, or perhaps I should say spouses, of the Masters. They are also worth humouring. At the start of the day most get quickly involved in hunt gossip, but some have an inflated idea of their position in the hierarchy. A deferential acknowledgement is unlikely to go amiss. Certainly, before moving off you are advised to know who they are. You can then make appropriate noises, or at any rate avoid criticizing the Master, when you find yourself upsides or queuing for a hunt jump.

More importantly from a practical point of view is the Secretary. Your first task on arrival at the meet should be to make yourself known to him or her. You may have arranged the day by telephone, but courtesy dictates that you now show yourself at the earliest opportunity to enable them to connect names with faces. The Secretary may be paid or unpaid. Apart from the fact they more or less control entry to the hunt, they are usually the best informed about the practicalities of the day. In my experience they are usually friendly, helpful enthusiasts, but do not attempt to gossip until after the first draw as their attention will be fully occupied.

As the field head off down the road, take care. Some people can be extraordinarily dim about controlling their horses. They will stop without warning right in front of you for no better reason than to talk to a friend on foot. If you knock into them it will be seen as your fault. Doubly so if you are a visitor! A gossiping spinster who runs into the back of your horse despite you tying a red ribbon to its tail to denote a kicker, will also blame you, thereby deflecting the displeasure of others upset by the ruction.

The first covert will be an opportunity to check your girth and have another look at the field. At this stage I should continue identifying those already mentioned with whom you should make your mark. Local land-owners and farmers are also worth discovering if only to show them your appreciation should the occasion arise during the course of the day. There will be time for social and amorous talent-spotting later.

Once away you should feel happier, not only because a hunt is about to begin, but also because the whole field will be united in a common cause.

Do not forget to keep your eye on the Field Master. Obviously he controls events, and by watching him you can anticipate the speed and direction of the advance. If it is your first day out with this particular pack, I would caution you, however experienced, against taking any line other than his. Nowadays with certain landowners holding strong views, you can do nothing but harm by jumping into a banned field. There may anyway be local factors dictating his line of which you cannot possibly be aware. Having said that, this guidance is more applicable to hunting over farmland. It may be easier to take your own line on moors or downland, but I would still advise caution to the newcomer. At all costs avoid getting ahead of the Master – as great a sin as overtaking the colonel at the head of a cavalry charge.

If the country has a lot of hunt-jumps, gaps, gates etc which necessitate queuing, normal good manners should prevail. You may be surprised though at how some of the most demure-looking women crash and barge their way to the front of the queue apparently forgetful of manners acquired during an expensive public school education. At this stage I should curb your first inclination although persistent offenders should not be accommodated indefinitely – even if they do own half the country!

There is another phenomenon of which to be aware, namely the type of person who panics as they near the head of the queue. Most horses only need a couple of strides for the average hunt-jump, but these people delay and dither trying to settle their horse for a perfect approach from the length of a cricket pitch. Stuck behind them you can see the field disappearing out of sight. It is best to note the offenders and take whatever steps necessary to be ahead of them at the next queue.

Gates can also be a nuisance. Fine if there is some kind soul on foot to deal with it, but if not, you will lose a lot of points if you allow a gate to swing shut behind you. I recommend going to some lengths to hold on to an open gate until the next person can take over even if it does slow your progress. If you need to make up points or if hounds are not running, you can do yourself a lot of good by dismounting and holding open a tricky gate for everyone else. It is always much appreciated, but do make sure you are noticed!

There is a butcher in Newmarket famous throughout the East of England for his sausages. My old friend Humphrey Mews used to tell the story of a friend of his who bought a famous hunting mansion in a well-known country. He decided to host a large hunt breakfast for all the swells before his lawn meet. He took great care with the guest list, and also the breakfast. When both where nearly complete he bumped into a well-known peer who has hunted in that part of the world all his life. Hoping to add him to the list of good and great attending the bunfight the squire started to explain his plan. His Lordship, a tall, senior-looking gentleman renowned for his dry wit, seemed unexcited by the prospect. In order to tempt him further the squire enthused,

"All the Masters are coming, and I've asked the Hetheringtons, the Blenkinsopps, Sir Aubrey Belvedere, oh and the sausages will be coming up from Newmarket."

The peer looked thoughtful.

"I know most of the people you've mentioned," he said, "but I don't think I've ever met the sausages from Newmarket."

Arguably the most important person in the hunting field, and certainly the hardest worked, is the Huntsman. Anything you can do to help him like holding his horse, opening gates etc, is useful, although the opportunity may not often present itself. Conversely you must take special care not to hinder him. The biggest sin would be to tread on a hound. Whenever you are near hounds, make sure your horse can see them. If, for example, the pack turn round in a confined space, get out of the way and turn your horse so that it is facing them. Watch out when you pass the hound box. Beware of jumping near a lost hound in case it suddenly changes direction and runs under your feet. If you see a hound in difficulty, do not think twice about dismounting and giving it a hand.

Please keep your wits about you. One often sees a hard-worked whipper-in returning to the fray from the back of the field, being hampered at every turn by people ranged across the road and verge, talking themselves stupid and barring his way. Even the cry of "Whip, please" produces no reaction until the third time of asking and by then he has had to break his rhythm or even stop. On a Leicestershire Saturday with 200 people out it is not always easy to know exactly where hounds are. But even so just a little attention can make such a difference. One day with the Belvoir, when not much was happening, I was having an interesting discussion with a visitor who had recently returned from South America. I can distinctly remember the topic was venereal disease. After some time I looked round to see what was happening and then interrupted him in full flow.

"Where are hounds?"

Miffed at being interrupted he gave the immortal reply,

"I don't think that is at all relevant, is it?"

Some people develop a head of steam about hunting terminology. This can be a bit of a minefield although I do not believe nowadays it is taken as seriously as it used to be. There are certain technical venery terms which must be known in order to talk about the subject. For example, field, covert, draw, line, etc. The hardy perennials about red or pink coats, stocks or ties, will go on forever. As in so many walks of life, the expert can say what he likes and get away with it, although the novice does so at his peril. I have more than once, for example, heard famous hunting men refer to hounds as dogs. I would not recommend such to a visitor on his first day out, although personally I think excitement about such trivia shows something of a small mind.

I was once in a stand at Windsor Horse Show. Sitting in front of me was a 'county' type older woman with an attractive, teenage grand-daughter. For some reason which I cannot now remember, a horseman rode round the ring dressed as Davy Crockett.

"Look Grandma, that man's got a fox's tail on his hat," exclaimed the excited little nymph.

"Yes," replied Grandma, "but in this part of the world we call it a brush." Rather lovely for the Thames valley I thought.

It is surprisingly easy to get lost out hunting. It may be that at the end of day you have a long hack back to the box and no-one else is going the same way. More likely you will lose a shoe or have some other mishap and again find yourself returning to your box alone. The first precaution is to make absolutely certain, probably by writing it down, of the name of the village where you met. Then at least you can seek directions. It also helps to spend five minutes looking at a map before you start in order to get some idea of the layout of main features. Better still is to carry a hunting map in your coat flap. My aforementioned friend of South American venereal disease fame went one better. He carried a portable telephone. At the end of day, he hacked to the nearest pub, summoned his box, and awaited its arrival in the warmth of the bar.

In conclusion I would say that common sense and good manners dictate how to survive one's first day out hunting. The hunt is in effect a small private club. Not only is it essential to thank those responsible for allowing you to join, but also your appreciation and enjoyment should be made known to landowners, farmers etc all of whom have contributed to it. Most hunts are relatively tight-knit groups of country people so you will be unlikely to go down well if you are pushy or flash. Conversely, if you follow the spirit of the above, you will undoubtedly receive a great welcome and find a friendly fun-loving bunch to add to the thrill of the chase. If you are anything like me your first day will be the start of some of the happiest of your life.

Good hunting – Oh, and do not forget to say goodnight to the Master before you head for your box.

Colonel Peter Rogers is The Lieutenant Colonel Commanding Household Cavalry. He has hunted for 25 years with many different packs.

....

"You 'air dresser on the chestnut horse," he roars during a check, to a gentleman with a very big ginger moustache, "pray 'old 'ard."

"Hair dresser," replies the gentleman, turning round in a fury, "I'm an officer in the ninety-first regiment."

"Then you hossifer in the ninety-first regiment wot looks like an 'air dresser, 'old 'ard!"

R S Surtees, Handley Cross

....

An ignorant visitor to the Blackmore Vale was trampling around at a check well out on some very tender winter corn.

I said, "Do you know you are destroying someone's bread and butter?" He replied, "I am so sorry Master – let me give you my sandwiches!"

Biddy Wingfield Digby

Car Following

Max Stewart

Following hounds on foot is traditional but cars are controversial. Anyone who owns a pre-War copy of *Baily's Hunting Directory* will recognise such delightful phrases as "Motors are not objected to at the meets, but it is preferred that they should not follow hounds" (Duke of Beaufort's – 1936-7). They would never get away with it these days. However, if you follow by car, do use some common sense and have consideration for other road users. If you block a gateway when you leave your car, you may incur the anger of the Master, a farmer, or a local resident (and if it is a special meet – Christmas or New Year perhaps – they might be one and the same person, in which case adjourning immediately to the nearest pub for a very stiff drink might be a sensible option if someone can drive you home). Lastly, if you have a 4WD vehicle, you don't need to prove it can plough deep ruts in a recently-sown field. We believe you. Get out – the walk will do you good. The Hunt's fencing- and terriermen may have the farmer's permission to drive a Land Rover through the field but you haven't.

A cavalcade of horses can do an amazing amount of damage to a field particularly a soggy one. For someone on horseback, going around the perimeter is not a matter of follow-my-leader but consideration for the landowner. Would you want the cavalry in full flight through your garden? No? Well farmers generally don't either, and ignoring this can result in an unsolicited lecture on pithy Middle English epigrams. Walking, particularly over dry unseeded land, may well be acceptable, but if in doubt, don't. Gates are an exception: whether or not you opened it, do shut it unless its owner obviously intended it to be tied back. If you are the sort who likes to curry favour – and even if you're not – please help the mounted field (and the Hunt staff in particular) with a spot of gate duty: manipulating a gate when on horseback is harder than it looks (and it usually looks pretty awkward...). The resulting kind word or two should be reward enough; a great personage might even nod benignly; you are being useful instead of just someone who doesn't pay a sub.

What to wear? This is where you have a big advantage over the mounted fraternity. You can – and probably will – wear an anorak, gumboots or walking boots and just about anything else you like, however shabby. Those on horseback usually stick to arcane conventions which are enforced by the Masters more or less strictly depending upon the time of year and prestige of the Hunt. On foot, you can rest in the knowledge that at the end of the day you can go home, scrape the worst of it off your wellies and pour yourself something large and rewarding, content that had you been on a horse, you would now be giving it and its tack and your clothes a good scrub. Stretch riding breeches are easy, but the proper cord or twill article needs lots of elbow grease. And leather boots need washing and waxing – if you can get them off in the first place (which is sometimes no mean feat when they are wet – your companion's rear end, strong hands and patience are needed). Foot followers can rest assured that no Hunt busybody will monitor their boots for 'brown for cubbing and black for hunting', with or without tops.

Hedges are placed there by nature or the farmer to keep stock in – or out. They are also the highlight of a 'quick thing' on horseback. Hunt jumps are usually pretty safe but you never know quite where you are with a hedge, particularly in autumn when the country is still 'blind' and ditches are invisible. On foot, you have the greatest advantage over the mounted rabble – you can go (gingerly) over wire and through gaps denied to horses. Foot followers quickly find out that going through a gap in a prickly hedge is best done rear-end first. Your bottom can shrug off the odd thorn but your eyes cannot. Beware. But beware also of damaging the hedge. Making a permanent hole to creep through will not endear you to the owner of the hedge. Carrying a stick can be useful for scrambling over ditches or avoiding emasculation on barbed wire, but unless you are an amateur shepherd or pole vaulter, anything over eight feet is a poseur's affectation. And hunt saboteurs like nothing better than someone else with a purported weapon: "...he tried to hit me with his stick, Your Worships, so I defended myself...". Don't get trapped like this.

Standing on one spot for too long can have its perils too. Several years ago I once stood in the centre of a ride – a very muddy and deeply rutted ride – which wends its way through the middle of the largest of the Cottesmore Tuesday-country woodlands. Sensible souls, and those in shoes, had called a halt at the entrance to the ride. The rain was falling in buckets and I was becoming suitably sodden when, after around fifteen minutes, a fox crossed into the undergrowth to my left. I turned to look and fell face down into the mud while glued to the spot. This was the highlight of an otherwise rotten afternoon to all the onlookers. Moral: lift feet occasionally and check for quicksand.

Centres of both foxhunting and farming such as Melton Mowbray are used to muddy apparitions, both in hunting dress and otherwise, going shopping towards the end of a Belvoir Wednesday or Cottesmore Tuesday. A couple of years ago in the lowering afternoon of an atrociously wet February day, I was standing in a queue in Melton's nationally-known pork pie shop immediately in front of an immaculately dressed blue-rinsed lady of a certain age who was very clearly not a local. There was a scraping of muddy boots at the door and in walked someone whose black coat and breeches had probably been pristine at 11.00 am but were now a quite instructive swatch of muddy shades. He was certainly muddier than my own encounter with the floor of Owston Wood. The lady looked aghast, clearly expecting the shop staff to turf him out as an undesirable. To their credit, none of them turned a hair. When she became discomfited enough to expostulate "…isn't anyone going to do something…" Mr Mud smiled wanly at her and remarked sadly in a stage whisper "Blasted Quorn Friday…".

Saboteurs – 'antis' – are (along with hidden barbed wire and increased subscriptions) the biggest bane of a foxhunter's life. The mounted field have a sporting chance of getting out of the way but the foot follower often has to face the inevitable abuse – and worse. Having spent three years as a hunt Liaison Officer – a buffer between the Hunt, the police and the antis – I know that the policeman's lot is not an easy one. Whatever their personal beliefs, most try to stick to the rules. And these rules are not black and white as the lay public think but a variable shade of grey influenced by the latest Magistrates Courts' convictions and on what they throw out. Whatever the Good Book says, it takes superhuman stoicism to turn the other cheek when the first one has had someone's spittle rubbed in with a pickaxe handle. Occasions like that apart, simply ignoring antis or pretending they are human after all is, in the long run, more productive than fighting a battle: this is, after all, what they want. Nothing peeves an anti more than ignoring his or her presence or – more radically – treating antis as potential if naive supporters. Remember that, at the time of writing at least (although this may change with impending legislation), trespass is – with certain exceptions such as on railways – not a criminal offence: 'Trespassers will be Prosecuted' is usually a hollow threat.

Visitors who know nothing of hunting should be welcomed but may test the patience of Job. One – after watching hounds rummage around in woodland for an hour or so with no apparent result – asked one of our more famous post-war amateur huntsmen "Is this serious or are you just practising" to be met with the considered response "I have been practising for the last 25 damn years and I haven't got it right yet!"

Those brought up via a Pony Club used to be given strict instructions on what to do when they saw a fox: count to ten – or was it twenty – slowly, take a deep breath, and then holloa (a loud drawn-out wail) with hat raised high for as long as one breath would last. Then wait a few moments and holloa again. You may – depending on which Pony Club you were drilled in – have been told to canter to the edge of the field to pinpoint the fox's direction before holloaing. Those on foot may be asked to do something similar. You may be asked to go 'on point' at the margin of a wood, or to keep your eyes skinned on a ride. If you see a fox cross within the wood or emerge for a quick sniff at the world and sneak back again, don't holloa: the Huntsman will think a fox has broken out and is off for pastures new. But do let the Huntsman know with a 'tally ho over' or 'tally ho back' respectively. And if – when on point – you see a fox breaking cover some distance away, again don't holloa or hounds may come towards you but shout 'hike holler' (just like that – try it...) and point with your cap if you have one, hopefully in the direction of someone better placed who is holloaing. If several foxes are afoot, beware of holloaing the wrong one. If hounds are busy hunting one fox, the last thing they want is to be lured on to another one, especially by you. And be sure it is a fox. A friend who is now a Joint Master of mink-hounds in the East Midlands once told me of his great moment of shame when he holloaed one of the great Shires packs on to a fox, only to immediately realise it wasn't one... "...Sorry Sir – I've just holloaed you onto a cat..." had the rejoinder "...ah well, it will do to be going on with...". (Yes RSPCA – hounds were dissuaded...)

There are two magic times of the day: the very early cubbing mornings in early September and mid-afternoons in January. There is something very special about being in the middle of nowhere with the dawn chorus well underway and the sunrise raising mist off the dew-drenched golden-white stubble. Gumboots are definitely needed. But within an hour or so, anyone on foot will wish that they had left their anorak at home. Incidentally, cubbing days are perhaps the best occasions to get close (but not too close) to hounds and to watch them work for a sustained period in woodland. Those fit and on foot should be able to stay the course without difficulty. Afternoons in January have a different appeal. Scent is a strange thing and 'experts' frequently disagree. But there is a combination of light, weather and time of day which – when it occurs – can provide something to be treasured for your old age: a pleasant morning – perhaps overcast to keep the ground warm, with the sky clearing at about 2.00 pm; the westering and then setting sun giving way to a clear sky which goes purple and then leaden-violet with the start of an evening frost. If hounds find then, they might conceivably run until Domesday and you will have something to tell your grandchildren. Should hounds be in woodland, stay with them and keep very still. With most of the field and foot followers away to an early tea, the silence is almost tangible, the feeling of being at one with whatever wildlife is around is palpable, and the expectation of hounds finding a fox keeps nerves taut and ears pricked.

Hounds speaking then have an unearthly wild and resonant quality from the dawn of the world.

But for something even more eerie, how about hunting by moonlight? Some years ago, as the day drew to a close, as the frost returned to crisp the grass, and as the last few mounted folk wended their way back to their boxes, I trudged back to my car and started scraping the mud off my boots ready for home. Night was falling but a full moon was shedding its usual weird ghostly-white images and long shadows over the fields. I was getting into my car when something in the air – a faint spine-tingling wail – stopped me dead in my tracks. It got closer, and soon revealed itself as seventeen-and-a-half couple of hounds in full cry hunting by moonlight up the old railway track into Uppingham followed by Brian Fanshawe hunting alone. A few incidents like that live on in one's mental archives for a very long time. John Peel would have approved.

Finally, on most days – but almost certainly on Saturdays – Badges Will Be Worn. Wearers will range from the all-around-my-hat variety, perhaps worn in memory of Steeleye Span or some great train-spotter, to hardened footsloggers whose tatty Barbour lapel will sport the one badge of their Supporters' Club. Keener ones will perhaps wear the tie as well. Approach them, join the Club (and the BFSS, and the National Hunting Club), and do something for it. Hunt Supporters' Clubs, like just about every other voluntary organisation bar those which seem to exist mainly for the benefit of We-who-Lunch ladies, are run by a handful of people who often wonder just why the rest of the idle membership cannot pitch in and help occasionally. And if you really draw the short straw, you might eventually rise to the dizzy heights of Secretary!

Max Stewart is Secretary of the Cottesmore Hunt Supporters' Club. He wishes it to be known that his views are personal!

With Boot and Stick: A Week Following on Foot

John Howard Jones

"Blow me tight! but I never sees a chap trudging along the turnpike with a thick stick in his hand and a pipe in his mouth, but I says to myself, there goes a chap well mounted for harriers!"

Mr Jorrock's Sporting Lector, *Handley Cross*. R S Surtees

Mr Jorrock's may have been somewhat derogatory about hunting on foot but that probably had something to do with his girth! Surtees was of course talking about hunting in the last century. Today, tens of thousands of people follow the hounds on foot – foxhounds, beagles, basset hounds, harriers and mink hounds – all have their loyal foot followers. The lack of a horse is absolutely no bar to the enjoyment of hunting in the very varied terrain over which hounds hunt their various quarry in the British countryside. Any reasonably fit person with a modicum of country sense should have no difficulty in keeping in touch with the hounds – even in the so called "galloping" countries. The only equipment necessary is a pair of strong, comfortable boots and perhaps Mr J's proverbial stout stick.

In the 1930s Lionel Edwards sketched the Aldridge brothers crossing Leicestershire together, Denis on his horse "Granite" and brother Travers on "Shank's Pony", the latter clearing the fences with the aid of a short vaulting pole. Nowadays, clearing wire fences is a problem – it is difficult to decide between stooping underneath and tearing one's pullover or striding over and ripping one's trousers.

In fact, let us look at the practicalities of following hounds on foot. This may come about by choice or necessity (the mounted follower's horse may be, for one reason or another "off games"). Or there was never the desire or means to have a horse in the first place. You may have read what to wear in the previous chapter but your choice of where to go must be dictated by that all important element – the weather. That can sometimes be assessed by looking at the weekly weather forecast. The foot followers planning should certainly take the regional weather predictions into account.

Anyone with a choice would be foolish to set out for the Cumbrian Fells or the Border countries if there is a forecast of "heavy snow on high ground". Better to set one's sights lower geographically and go down to the relative shelter of the ancient hunting grounds in the New Forest where the hounds sound marvellous in the deep woodland but can also be seen out on the large, open heath land stretches.

Dartmoor, Exmoor and Bodmin Moor pose problems as access roads to get a good start are sparse or non-existent. The flatter countries of East Anglia are not the best place to follow foxhounds but are fun for the hare hunter with plenty of packs of harriers, beagles and bassets to jog after.

High Leicestershire with its rolling grassland provides good fun and good viewing for those who follow in Travers Aldridge's foot-steps. Indeed, a well-known first class professional county cricket umpire keeps fit this way, jogging after the Quorn.

But, weather permitting, it is the hill packs in Wales and the North that the foot foxhunter should visit to feel in the right element. The Snowdon area of North Wales boasts a number of hunts who hunt the hill foxes on foot in very rugged terrain. In the somewhat less harsh country in mid-Wales, where there are hundreds of square miles of totally unspoilt and well tracked moorlands, some of the fox hunts operate a 'mixed' regime – some days following hounds on horses, some days on foot.

In the Lakeland Fells, the keen sportsman can hunt on foot six days a week; indeed he is spoilt for choice. On popular days in good viewing country hundreds of followers can be seen crossing the hills in the hope that they will see the hounds in action. But it can be a frustrating hike sometimes. Paradoxically, the better the scent and the faster the hounds run, the less of it is seen by the followers. Having had a good view of 'the find', the hounds can be gone "o'er top" in minutes, and if the hunt is good and straight, that can be the last seen of the hounds for hours on end. But, of course, that is the glorious uncertainty of foxhunting.

Foot followers take to the high ground

Now, what about a perfect week's hunting? Let us assume that the weather is set fair, the boots are ready and the stick polished. Perhaps a small item to help would be a magic carpet (a helicopter is too noisy) to get between the meets. To give variety, there is a lot of intervening land to be crossed between hunt countries. Up to Wales for a day with the David Davies in the hills south of Newtown. Next day we go higher and drop silently into the the "hidden" valley of Martindale to hunt over the aptly named High Street with the Ullswater fox hounds. Then our silent conveyance whisks us south for a day's beagling on the Cotswolds with the fast and furious Dummer beagles. Next day to flatter country to see the Easton Harriers hunt the hare under the big skies of East Anglia. Shaking the Suffolk clay off our boots, our carpet lands us near Great Dalby for Friday in High Leicestershire with the Quorn. All grass, but surprisingly steep hills and very fast hounds.

So, after such a strenuous and magical week, with, of course, ideal scenting and top of the ground walking, we might end on a less strenuous note for a day with Huckworthy Basset Hounds in Dorset.

Thus, we have covered a lot of beautiful country in England and Wales (there are no beagles in Scotland) and followed three different breeds of fox hounds and three sorts of hounds who hunt the hare. All accomplished with only a bit of imagination.

John Howard Jones farms in Buckinghamshire and hunts on a horse with the Bicester as well as many other hunts on foot.

Fundraising and Hunt Entertainment

Sophia Peel

Fundraising has always been a part of hunting and the most realistic form of action nowadays is to form a fundraising committee. Some are born to sit upon committees, some achieve a seat, and some have positions thrust upon them, frequently at gun point. You will need an equal mix of intellect, commitment over-and-above-the-call-of-duty, and professional cunning with opportunism. I should also mention the material benefits of comfortable drawing rooms and malt whisky, not to mention a chairman with those qualities required to command a submarine during battle. Subcommittees can be hard to keep track of – like those Russian dolls that come apart revealing ever diminishing wooden ladies.

The first item on the agenda should be the Hunt Ball. This is an excellent activity for extracting monies from foreign sources. Tickets tend to be bought eagerly by people from the neighbouring metropolis, less eagerly by the Hunt officials, and scarcely ever by the subscribers. Fire regulations and recessions have deprived us of the joys of dancing the night away in the ballrooms of great houses. Nowadays we have to fall back on good parking facilities and a well-known address; an imposing sweep of gravel and large lawn must suffice for a marquee or a good hotel that isn't so new as to show up the stains and patches on your Hunt Servants' No 1 rigg as they take the tickets.

Decorating a marquee can bring out some considerable talent, and I have danced in the past among some very lovely effects. The music is, of necessity, loud. But as long as your elderly guests have paid for their tickets, you won't miss them if they leave before the fun. Let the young struggle out, at 3 am in the pouring rain, to wade across the mud in their satin sling-backs, and Barbours on their heads.

The point-to-point is the other mainstay of fundraising. If you have found a suitable course, one might think you had not a care in the world, but on the contrary, your problems have only just begun. There are two types of point-to-point. There is the one attended by a select, knowledgeable group of tweed-clad persons, shod in strong shoes with sticks in their hands. The female of this species can be seen head down, occupied with hampers, at the back of the Bentley or aged Landrover. The binoculars will be largely from the two world wars. The Fields will be small, and the horses will be ridden by the third or fourth generation of those standing about giving free advice. These do not make money.

The other has large crowds, bare knuckle fighting in the beer tent, mass cleaning up operations, harrowing and re-seeding. These make lots of money. One could be considered fortunate in organising the latter, but God help any naive committee who attempts either event without first consulting their Elders, Wisers and Betters.

There are other fundraising activities which immeasurably grace and benefit the countryside, as for example, the Gymkhana. For this you will need string, good weather, kind judges, strong men, patient women, dogs, ponies, megaphone wiring (up to six miles) and a car park attendant who can spot the difference between the noble patron of the Showground and Lady, and very tiresome parents from the neighbouring pony club branch. You also need a great many rosettes; you do not need any mothers. This activity seldom makes either money or friends, although the English countryside would be a poorer place by far without the Gymkhana.

Then, there is the team chase. This is very fast and very dangerous, and will be enjoyed immeasurably by all the people who stayed to the end of your Hunt Ball. Do not put the posts too close together.

Another activity that can be very profitable is the Race Night. This is also an excellent form of entertainment. It involves a lot of medium-sized tables in a grand drawing-room or a village hall. You will need a quantity of generous, gambling, drinking, competitive folk and an auctioneer who has sold sheep or horses in that neighbourhood for most of his life. He will know exactly how to set cousin against cousin, and son against father-in-law to the best advantage. This is not a safe place for the faint hearted.

Next we have the Hunt Open Day and Terrier Racing. This is often held at the kennels. All the early afternoon activities, like terrier showing, coconut shying, cake stalls, three-legged races, etc are as nought compared with the Terrier Racing. The competitors in this event are vengeful, hate-filled and devious; they circumnavigate, ride-off, levy blows-beneath-the-belt, kill and maim, but seldom pause to pillage or rape. In the event of a terrier surviving to cross the finishing line, the subsequent finishers will be held aloft adhering to the person of the victor.
  This event makes a little money, but more importantly, life-long friends, and some enduring enemies.

Fun rides can also be just that – great fun – although not necessarily very profitable. Many of us who own only a modest garden or a highly polished pony paddock or two are grateful and eager to ride across someone else's well-upholstered pasture. In the spring, summer and autumn of England's green and pleasant, the sun is bound to shine for two or three days, when to saddle up the favoured horse, throw a few children in the plate, and trek off into the reasonably wild blue yonder can only be a pleasure, given of course the comfort and reassurance of flags, stewards and numbered, hand-crafted fence-ware.

The Auction of Promises is seriously good fun; you will need a very big room and an auctioneer holding a reliable and fully operational microphone. He need not necessarily be the same one who set his neighbours against each other at your race night. He will still be in Stoke Mandeville. But he must be a silver-tongued persuasive type who could "sell the Queen a packet of Daz" to quote my Joint Master who has some experience in these matters. You also need the services of a gifted barman who will be invaluable in helping to broach the defences of the rich and cautious. Then you must call on the cunning and innovative qualities in your committee and subscribers.

Some there are who can be persuaded to part with a Munnings or an Edwards, but most of us are still hoping to inherit. Others can promise the more solid joys of life, and every one has something he can give away without causing unrest in the bosom of his heirs. The promise of a week's house sitting (Bantams included), the portrait of a favoured terrier, a field of hay, a day's hunting, shooting or fishing.

I once knew a man who owned the most unreliable hunter in the country. He offered the loan of this animal with the price of a day's hunting tied to its bridle. No one in the country ventured a single bid, but a chap from up country congratulated himself on his luck in buying the horse for the day, for a tenner.

Later that season, on a crack day, across some stern fly fences, the chap from up country was seen, briefly, to advantage giving the Huntsman a lead over the first couple of fences. They say he left the owner to negotiate with a farmer for the loan of a tractor and some rope to assist in the reclamation of the horse, from the bottom of the third fence. James Uppe-Country Esq walked back to the nearest country public house regretting his ill spent tenner.

Some surprising skills and accomplishments can appear on the surface of otherwise calm and unruffled waters. A man who hunted locally, riding across country, all 18 stone of him, with hands like country hams, offered to play the flute at an evening recital. A friend of mine who had been bumped and bored all season by his clumsy horsemanship and uncouth manners, bought his promise, more out of disbelief and curiosity than anything else. His flute playing turned out to be so exquisite and divine, that she allowed him to trample all over her during the season, so long as he promised to play his flute in her garden again next summer.

I once spent, in my excitement, £50 on a dozen jars of home-made marmalade. At over £4 a jar, I scraped every last globule off my husband's plate rim at breakfast for the entire season.

The Hunt Pantomime. This event needs a whole committee "even unto itself". Don't mess with this unless you can claim at least seven generations back, either to W Shakespeare Esq, or through Knights Gielgud, Olivier or Richardson.

Be careful about promising to either take off your clothes, sing, dance, or try to be funny. Don't attempt to stage this event too often. Your theatre staff may well go "nappy" on you, and lie down from exhaustion, or from the drying-up of the well-springs of creativity. Sometimes the leading actors die of old age. It is often a close run thing between the Hunt horses and the stars of the panto stage, as to whether you can get them through another season.

It is inappropriate to blister the legs of aged players and, of course, the dust out of the costume cupboards tends to make them thick in the wind. But a good, topically amusing pantomime, where you can see your friends at a disadvantage is always a merry evening.

Lastly, the Hunter Trials. These are usually conducted, annually, over the same fixed course, as these are expensive and artistically demanding to build. The farmers and landowners over whose land these courses are constructed are to be prized above pearls. Creatively designed fences are difficult for true hunters as these competent and purposeful animals are not keen on wasting time jumping fences which they can gallop around with no more than a minimum of clever footwork.

As with all field events, the committee must bear in mind two points. Car parking and lavatories. All else will follow. Do also alert the police, as you will probably be creating a traffic jam considerably more effectively than a failed set of traffic lights at 5 pm on a Friday in the Edgware Road.

I could mention many more witty and interesting events. But I hasten to add that unless you have a stern team of, more often than not, ladies who can smile and joke in war-time Blitz conditions, all the most cunning plans of mice and men will come to nought.

The subscriber who finds time at weekends to join in and lend a hand might be surprised by moments of the greatest fun!

Sophia Peel has raised money for the Old Surrey and Burstow hunt; she is now Joint Master of the North Cotswold with her husband.

Foxes and Pheasants

Edmund Vestey

"The great mania for Game, and the useless quality of it with which we find most coverts glutted, is a great misfortune to Foxhunting". So wrote Colonel John Cook, Master of the Thurlow from 1800-1804, in his book *Observations on Foxhunting*.

Many foxhunters today tend to think the difficulties between the fox and the pheasant are something comparatively new, but those words were written nearly 200 years ago. Colonel Cook left the Thurlow after four seasons due to a "scarcity of foxes and subscriptions", a sentiment reiterated by Squire Osbaldeston when he left the country after one season some 20 years later.

Edmund Vestey, Master and Huntsman of the Thurlow

As a Master and Huntsman of the Thurlow Country today, I like to think we have come quite a long way since then. Changes in the methods of rearing pheasants have led to changes in the attitude of most gamekeepers. There can be few shoots where the rearing field, adorned with coops occupied by hens or bantams bringing up their broods of pheasant chicks, still survives. The rearing field required constant supervision and woe betide any kestrel, owl, sparrow hawk, stoat or fox who came anywhere near. Because the odd rogue could cause mayhem, the general policy was blanket extermination to avoid any risk.

With the introduction of the game farm, the incubator, the brooder, and the release pen, almost fool-proof protection is now available and has removed the excuse or the need for such practices. Equally the cost of staff has probably rendered them impossible for most shoots.

As a boy I spent quite a lot of time in the rearing field. I had my first day's shooting and shot my first pheasant before I had my first day's hunting, though I have to admit it was in a strong wind, with two high pheasants sailing down the line of guns and my 0.410 brought down the bird several feet behind the one I aimed at. I was lucky enough to spend many happy hours with first class keepers who had learned their craft between the wars, who were wonderful naturalists and who knew so much more about the law of the country and its ways than many of the experts who expound on the subject today.

I can only write from my own experience in my own hunting country, but I suspect rural Suffolk is not very different from most countries where a lot of serious shooting takes place and Hounds have to work in with it. I have been a Master here since 1967, have been closely involved with the fortunes of the Hounds since the end of the Second World War, and have been lucky enough to enjoy the greatest fun both in the shooting and the hunting field here for nearly 50 years.

During that time I have gradually come to a number of conclusions. The first is that so much of the perceived difficulty of having plenty of foxes for Hounds to hunt in a largely shooting country is the fear of what might happen, rather than what does. Few Masters sleep much the night before the Opening Meet and therefore they appreciate more than most the apprehensions and fears of owners of shoots and their keepers in the run up to a big day. All the potential horrors of what may go wrong fill their dreams and become nightmares, but how many of those nightmares ever happen?

To avoid conflict it is vital to have close cooperation and understanding between Masters and the owners of the land over which they have the privilege to hunt. In no other way can there be a proper understanding of the needs and predicaments of both. Equally, Masters need to have similar contact with the keepers. So much damage has been done by regarding keepers as enemies rather than making them friends, but friends are only made when there is an understanding and a meeting of minds.

With the declared aim of the League Against Cruel Sports to see the end of all country sports – hunting, shooting, and fishing – it is crucial that those friendships are made and an appropriate understanding of each other's position established.

But many of the perceived nightmares do seem to me to be unwarranted. There was a time when quite a number of the bigger shoots did not welcome Hounds until February when the shooting was over. Then there might be a couple of weeks until they were barred again, for fear they would upset the catching up of hens for the laying pen. Two weeks made a very short season for Hounds and when they went to those sorts of places the Huntsman's job was not made easier by the amount of carrion, and often winged birds, to distract Hounds.

There was a fear that a visit from the Hounds would put every pheasant over the boundary to their neighbour's benefit, and the season's shooting would be ruined. I am sure the fear of disturbance by Hounds is unfounded, provided birds are fed at regular times each day. They are shrewd enough to know when and where breakfast or tea are on offer, but they will start to lose faith if time and place leave them disappointed.

However, I seem to have jumped a step and left the rearing field too soon. Modern methods of buying-in day old chicks, rearing them in one of the many excellent varieties of brooders, with the grass run netted in against predators from the air, and an electric fence to protect the birds from ground predation, have eased the keeper's life enormously and enabled one keeper to bring up far more birds than the old fashioned rearing field allowed. Now the risks are different. The birds may be too hot or cold. There may be a thunderstorm and the field could be flooded. They may start to feather-pick, and there are remedies for that, but at least they should be safe from predators.

Then comes the day when the young birds are ready to be put out into the woods into the release pens. Everyone seems to have their own idea about the ideal pen, but the one common essential is an adequate electric fence round the perimeter. I have found keepers who maintain an electric fence does not work, and when I have looked at the single slack strand I have not been surprised but two, or better still three, strands, eight inches apart with the bottom strand eight inches off the ground, are a pretty effective defence against any fox.

First light, however, can still be a dangerous time, whether it be a soldier waiting for a dawn attack or a young pheasant starting to feel his spurs and venturing beyond the bounds of safety, only to meet a fox whose nightly prowl has not satisfied his stomach. So despite all the available precautions any prudent keeper will take a look round in the early hours to see that all is well, but surely that effort is worthwhile. It is a far lesser demand than that shouldered by his predecessors, and will do much to maintain a happy liaison with his local pack, and ensure the safety of his birds.

Whether one is hunting or shooting it is, or should be, the quality of the sport that matters, beyond anything else. Of course, a pack of Hounds is not performing as it should unless it can claim a respectable tally at the end of the season but it is the way they catch their foxes that matters. Equally, the way the birds fly and are presented ought to be more important than the number on the card at the end of a day's shooting. Persuading reared pheasants early in the season that on this day they are expected to fly as fast and as high as possible instead of being given breakfast can sometimes be a difficulty, especially on a warm, still, sunny morning.

More and more of our shooting friends now ask Hounds to come during cub-hunting, which gives the birds a stir and reminds them that they possess wings, and they are settled again for tea, if indeed they are not already in their usual place waiting for lunch. That is all very well, but one has to remember that cub-hunting is the schoolroom for the young Hounds. It is the time when they should be learning that their hunting instincts, bred into them for centuries, must be applied only to the fox. It is then that they start to learn about the infinite wiles of the fox and the multitude of ruses he has up his sleeve to evade capture. But they cannot do that if there are no foxes present.

So if the local pack of Hounds is going to help to produce better sport with the pheasants, it is implicit that the keepers must have left the foxes alone so that the young Hounds in turn can learn their craft. By doing so, the bond between the two sports is strengthened, the shooting is improved and the litters will be broken up, culled and dispersed.

Far too little recognition is given to the part that Hounds play, especially during cub-hunting in the autumn in the dispersal of foxes. By the time the cub-hunting season starts the young foxes are virtually fully grown, ready to look after their own futures, but still living as a closely knit family. If this happens to be near a pheasant pen, the dawn raid may be quite a worry. But if they have been chased around by Hounds and one or two have been caught, the rest will find other quieter quarters and spread themselves out, finding other sources of food to keep them happy.

But there is one further point I must make. The Masters of Foxhounds

Association, of which I have the great honour and privilege of being Chairman, works to a strict set of rules. The first and most important states "Foxhunting as a sport is the hunting of the fox in his wild and natural state with a pack of Hounds". No keeper can be absolutely sure which way his birds are going to fly, as the wind may do something unexpected or for some other unforeseen reason they may go the wrong way. Even more so there is no predicting what the fox may do when Hounds find him.

From time to time one hears of someone complaining that a pack of Hounds in full cry behind their fox is out of control, when in fact they are doing exactly what they have been bred and trained to do. When they run fast and outdistance the horses and the fox takes an unexpected route, they may land up where the Master wished they were not, and on those rare occasions one can only wish for a little understanding all round. In my family, my wife was the first member to be persuaded to take a pack of Hounds. On a day when I was shooting at home and Hounds were meeting several miles away, before the fourth drive I thought I heard Hounds, and then a very grubby fox ran through the line of guns, followed two or three minutes later by the Hounds, and then a bit later by the Huntsman, my wife and the field. When all that was over the beaters set to, the proceedings recommenced and we had the best drive of the day.

So may I return more or less to where I started. Long may the two sports of hunting and shooting continue to flourish in harmony with each other. With mutual respect for both sports by all those involved I am convinced there is no need for conflict, that the two can, should and will continue to work well together, and between us all we shall put paid to the arrogant, ignorant and malevolent gang who would like to put a stop to everything we all enjoy.

Edmund Vestey is Joint Master and Huntsman of the Thurlow and Chairman of the MFHA.

A Year in the Kennels

Adrian Dangar

Traditionally the hunting year begins on May 1st when most packs have long since finished hunting and the hunt staff are able to take their well earned holidays. The kennels are run by a Kennel Huntsman who lives on the premises and is appointed by the Master. It is his job to administer the kennels, care for the hounds and either whip-in or act as professional Huntsman on hunting days. There is normally another man to assist him in this task whose job description might range from kennelman, terrierman to second whipper-in and often a combination of all three. The larger hunts, and those hunting more than twice a week will need more staff, some four day a week packs employing up to five men in the kennels.

Although the start of autumn hunting is four months distant, May is the time of year when many kennel huntsmen like to begin exercising their charges on bicycles; not the two or three hour marathons of late summer but a steady early morning meander each day down quiet country roads. This helps to relieve boredom and fighting in the kennels, and keeps the hounds' nails worn and pads hard for the season ahead.

Tom Normington exercising the Grafton hounds

By now most of the puppies, born ideally between January and March, will have been placed at happy homes for the summer joining the families of local hunting folk and farmers. For the next six or eight months they grow up fast in an atmosphere that exposes them to far more than the routine of kennel life could ever offer; the conscientious Kennel Huntsman will spend many evenings driving out to these walks delivering flesh and keeping tabs on the progress of what will be the following year's young entry.

The highlight of the kennel year is undoubtedly the puppy show when young hounds, actually about 18 months old, are shown first in couples then collectively before two judges, normally adjacent Masters or hound breeders of distinction from afar. Each hunt has its own tried and tested formula for the day and most like to hold their puppy show between the months of June and August. The common denominator is that the kennels must look at their magnificent best; preparations start almost as soon as hunting has finished in the spring and include hours of steam cleaning, days of gardening and weeks of painting. Often a marquee is erected in the kennel grounds and once the judging has finished puppy walkers, farmers and friends of the hunt are entertained first to a huge tea and later to more substantial refreshments.

The annual puppy show, with the attendant noise and crowds, will have been a great test for any young hound and you can be quite certain that those puppies coming into the ring happy and confident will not only have been the beneficiaries of good walks but also the product of countless hours of practice and care in the previous few months leading up to the big day. The best of the young entry, and indeed the older, may well be shown at one of the big regional hound shows during the summer and many hunts have the commendable policy of always supporting their nearest big show together with one or two further afield depending on the quality of hounds that their kennel can produce.

As the summer ticks slowly on the length and duration of early morning exercise will gradually increase so that by the end of July the pack will be leaving the kennels at 6.30 or 7.00 am and returning two or three hours later before the day becomes unbearably hot. Often the route, which must be kept as varied as possible, includes visits to farms and villages together with offers of breakfast and liquid refreshment. The timing of hound exercise and the transition from bicycles to horses inevitably depends upon the individual country; some moorland packs can begin hunting in early August but the majority of Hunts must wait until the harvest has been cleared before a start is possible. Most huntsmen like to have the benefit of at least a month's exercising from the back of a horse as this later stage of exercise opens up stubble fields, moorland and farmland over which hounds can gain vital confidence and experience.

Just as a racehorse can only be brought to peak fitness by an outing to the racecourse so also a pack of hounds require a few mornings hunting to perfect hundreds of miles of summer exercise. Packs that during the season proper hunt twice a week may go out three or four mornings a week throughout September and October whilst a four day a week outfit might find itself hunting every day except Sundays. This is the busiest period of the year for hunt staff and with the daily routine on a September morning starting at around 4.30 am, a time requiring great reserves of stamina and energy.

Feeding a pack of hounds (most kennels using raw flesh) so that all carry the same amount of condition is a complex and skilful task during the summer and, to maintain high standards during the periods of intensive hunting, requires much thought and attention to detail. Thankfully there are enough people hunting who appreciate this art and for a Kennel Huntsman to be complimented on how well his hounds look is welcome praise indeed. Not all kennels feed raw flesh exclusively, some preferring to cook meat whilst others favour the inclusion of cereal-based porridges to which extra ingredients such as cod liver oil, salt and sulphur can be added from time to time. When available a little greenery can be introduced to the hounds' diet. One Kennel Huntsman of my acquaintance religiously feeds a nettle stew every year at the beginning of May. There is a famous story of Sir Peter Farquhar showing American visitors around the Meynell Kennels in the 1930s, who, when introduced to the Hunt staff, took the opportunity of discussing feeding policy; the Kennel Huntsman's comments as to the dubious benefits of watercress which Sir Peter was very fond of feeding when set against the inconvenience of collecting it prompted the Master to remark that his hounds would be fed poached eggs if he so required. This amusing incident so impressed the visitors that they commissioned the sporting artist F A Stewart to paint a picture depicting a Kennel Huntsman coming into the feed room after hunting with a tray of steaming eggs; the original complete with suitable caption, now hangs in the home of Sir Peter's son, Captain Ian Farquhar.

Watercress apart, the subject of feeding hounds has caused Masters and hunt committees no small degree of anguish in recent years. Up until 1990 the small payment made for collection of offal and those carcasses picked up from farms but not used for feed was a welcome perk and in some cases contributed towards the cost of collection. With the advent of BSE, the companies dealing with offal disposal began to charge for their removal service, initially at a reasonable level but later increasing sufficiently to cause many hunts to reconsider whether the traditional system of collecting fallen stock from farms, skinning the carcass at the kennels and feeding the product to hounds, could still be economically viable. Most have now evolved ways of solving the economics and indeed charges have levelled out to more affordable levels. For a two-man kennels the great bulk of each working day not spent in the hunting field is taken up by driving out to local farms and collecting dead sheep, cattle and horses. Very often the purpose of the visit is to humanely destroy sick or injured livestock. This is a service much appreciated by the farming community and as our sport depends on its goodwill, one that will probably be available for as long as the laws and regulations allow.

Back at the kennels the preparation of carcasses, to the uninitiated a dirty and difficult job, can be performed with remarkable alacrity by an experienced man at the end of a sharp knife. Visitors to kennels in the spring and autumn, the busiest time of year in the fallen stock department, are astonished how quickly a pile of woolly sheep can be transformed to a neat row of carcasses hanging in the flesh house.

A predominantly flesh diet means that hounds should be treated for worms several times during the course of the year, ideally a different medication for each occasion so that no immunity to any one treatment is allowed to build up.

With the start of hunting come the inevitable injuries to hounds and many hours will be spent attempting to keep individuals on the road. At the Sinnington in North Yorkshire, where a morning's autumn hunting can consist of two hours inside a dense thorn covert, every pad of every hound is later inspected. The thorns extracted would be enough to cover a saucer. Other countries cite thistle seeds and wire fences as the source of their problems.

As November draws ever closer many of the long suffering puppy walkers will be realising that their twelve week old bundles of innocence have now turned into destructive monsters. Once hound puppies begin to travel further afield than the boundaries of their own farm most walkers will be telephoning the kennels and organising their return, only a few have the facilities to keep them throughout the winter. These new recruits to the pack will have to wait until the following September before they have the chance to hunt, and often take some weeks to settle into kennel life. Most kennels accommodate the puppies separately from the main pack through the winter although they will be exercised with their elders shortly after arrival. For the first few weeks each puppy is coupled to an elder hound, chosen for his strength and placid temperament, and thus learns the important lessons of discipline before being allowed to exercise unattached.

It is always quite a relief to reach the first week in November by which time valuable information as to the supply of foxes, state of the country and ability of the young hounds will have been gleaned from the many early mornings and kennel life settles down into a well ordered routine through the winter months. In addition to the everyday kennel chores, most hunt staff these days are required to assist with some earth-stopping and maintenance of the country, jobs for which some of the better off establishments engage a full-time employee but for which the smaller hunts rely heavily on amateur help and the kennel staff. Such tasks range from the mending of broken fences and creation of hunt jumps, through to ride cutting in August and covert laying, so important in the creation of a warm habitat for foxes, during the months of February and March.

During the winter it is unusual for sport not to be interrupted at all by hard weather and although we all pray for an open time over the Christmas period, a break of a week or so in the New Year, greeted with dismay by the subscribers, often allows hounds, horses and staff to catch their breath and provide a welcome mid-season break. Mid-winter is also the time when important decisions as to the breeding policy of the kennels must be taken. In order to have puppies out at walk by May bitches need to be put to, or mated, in January or February. Not all bitches come into season at such favourable times, however, and this is reflected in the number of late litters that all kennels have at times to contend with. Decisions as to breeding are normally taken by the Masters, almost always so if he also hunts the hounds, and his choice of doghound often involves a time consuming visit to kennels situated at the other end of the country. For the Kennel Huntsman of a fashionable pack whose doghounds are much in demand this often means accommodating other hunt's bitches for two or three weeks as well as the tricky task of ensuring that each visiting bitch gets covered twice at the optimum time by the chosen dog.

Bitches give birth about nine weeks after conception and once they begin to struggle whilst out hunting it is time they were left behind and put on the easy list. Some two or three weeks before she is due the expectant mother will be accommodated separately in a whelping lodge by night and given the run of the kennel premises by day. Once the puppies have been born they must be kept warm at all times with the aid of a heat lamp and, when a few days old, the dew claws should be removed together with any weak or unhealthy whelps. The weaning process is accomplished together with routine worming, injections and tattooing before at twelve weeks old, and as fat as dumplings, the youngsters are ready to go out to walk and with their departure in May another hunting year begins.

There is one important event in the calendar, falling in mid-winter that I have deliberately left until last and I refer, of course, to the Boxing Day Meet. To produce a pack of hounds and horses for this occasion means that Christmas is spent very much as any other normal working day and it is traditionally the time when all those who hunt should show their appreciation for the very hard work put into stables, kennels and the hunting field by the hunt staff. A career in the hunt service is not so much a job but more a way of life in which the word overtime has no place. The hunting world has for long been fortunate in attracting men and women of the highest calibre in which the virtues of loyalty, dedication and honesty play key roles. Remember this at Christmas time, together with the long, cold hours in the field and kennels spent in the provision of your sport.

Adrian Dangar is Master and Huntsman of the Sinnington.

The London Hunt was out one cold November day. It was beginning to snow, but the scent was good. The fox ran to a large swollen river, and crossed it. The hounds also swam across the river, so the Huntsman gave his horse to the whipper-in, and he too swam across the river. It was too deep for the field to cross, so they huddled together on the river bank, and tried to keep warm. Eventually the fox went to ground, and the Huntsman returned with his hounds, and they all swam back again.

When the Huntsman got the water out of his boots, and remounted his horse, the Master asked why he had crossed the river. The Huntsman replied that he had to do it in order to be with his hounds. Then the Master said, "Well we'd better go back to the kennels, so you can get some warm, dry clothes on", at which the Huntsman drew himself up and said indignantly, "I'm a Huntsman, Madam, not a hairdresser!", and they went on hunting.

Bill Bermingham

A Huntsman's Day

Sidney Bailey

Not one day is the same as the next. However, a regular routine for the hounds is important. When walking them out in the morning before hunting I look them over and check that none are lame. I make a note in my book if any are. I think about where the meet is, the type of country and any of the problems we are likely to encounter during the day. Therefore, the pack selection is important. We have two packs in the VWH country, a mixed pack who hunt on Mondays and Thursdays and the bitches who go on Wednesday and Saturdays.

"Drawing" or selecting the hounds from one of the lodges into the draw yard, which is done after we have walked out, is critically important. I try to pick the ones that I think will be best for the day. You do not want a lot of young hounds if you are likely to come across a lot of riot or if the weather is very rough or windy. All of this is done after I get up and see what the weather is like. I also list all of the hounds which go out, so I know exactly who has gone out.

During cubhunting I will take a pack of around 24 $^1/_2$ couple, of which no more than five couple will be puppies. After the opening meet I take out a pack of 18 $^1/_2$ - 19 $^1/_2$ couples, including the young hounds.

The evening before hunting I speak with the Master in charge the following day and discuss where we can go. Sometimes there are changes and we talk about these when we unbox. I like to unbox away from the meet to give the hounds and horses a chance to settle and empty themselves before we start.

While at the meet I like to talk to either the keepers or our terriermen to find out if they know where any fox is living or where we are likely to find.

During the day's hunting I concentrate on watching the hounds, thinking where they are going to check next, wondering where they will check next and why and what I will do about it, whose land we are on, whose land we are heading towards, and where the next problem areas are to which I should send my whipper-in, such as railway lines and main roads.

These are the thoughts going through my mind constantly. Watching the hounds work and assessing them is a continual, absorbing process, which enables me to select the best working hounds from which to breed.

Hunting the hounds is a great job, but you need a lot of help, and luck. A good whipper-in is most important as you want to know if hounds are all on when you leave covert – if not he will have to go back and fetch them.

After a day's hunting I look at the hounds hacking back to the box to see if any of them are lame. These have to be seen to after they have been fed and put to bed on a good clean bed of fresh straw.

The day does not end then. There is still valeting to do and preparing clothes for the next day. After a few phone calls to discuss the day with various people, I am ready for a good drink and an evening meal! I then like to get my legs up and I am no bother to anyone.

I have hunted the VWH hounds for 28 consecutive seasons and made a lot of friends but the best of them all are the hounds.

Sidney Bailey is Huntsman of the VWH.

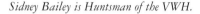

Women never look so well as when one comes in wet and dirty from hunting.

R S Surtees from Mr Sponge's Sporting Tour

How to Breed a Pack of Hounds

Ronnie Wallace

Ronnie Wallace, Master and Huntsman of the Exmoor

Very few people have the good fortune to breed a pack of hounds and only a handful of the blessed enjoy the opportunity to develop a pack over a lifetime. Hound breeding is not an area in which the ordinary hunting person gets involved and although many will be quick to comment on the qualities or, more normally the deficiencies, of a particular hound there are but very few of us who can honestly say that they understand either the factors that lead a Master to decide upon a certain breeding policy or the mechanics of implementing it. That is not a criticism in itself; heaven knows where we would be if all the subscribers to a hunt were asked to have an input to breeding their kennel! The ungainly camel is alleged to have been bred by a committee and we would probably end up with hounds that did not look dissimilar! However, we should all be aware of the thought process through which our Masters must go so that we appreciate just what a difficult and scientific job breeding a pack of hounds can be.

The first step our Master must take is to acquire a split pedigree book. These are volumes of blank family trees, divided in the middle, so that doghounds pedigrees may be entered on the top set of half pages and the bitches on the bottom. They go back five generations, or six if you count the hound in question itself, and enable one to compare the breeding of any of your doghounds against any of your bitches at a glance. It is not much use walking into W H Smith and asking for a Split Pedigree Book; you are more likely to end up before the Race Relations Council than to acquire what you are looking for but they are obtainable from specialist suppliers.

The second step is to get hold of The Foxhound Kennel Stud Book, which is published annually via the Masters of Foxhounds Association and can be obtained from Anthony Hart. Ideally you would acquire a complete set. The first volume covers the years 1800-1844 and it has been published ever since; some volumes cover a single year whilst others encompass two or three together. Sets do sometimes come available second-hand but they are rare and our Master is as likely to have to consult a friend's as to be able to buy their own. However, it is an essential tool for a Master as it records the breeding of every hound bred in a recognised kennel and thus enables you to trace the breeding of your hounds back for generations.

The third step is to consult someone who knows what they are talking about. Some countries are lucky enough to have resident experts who know a pack intimately; others will be less fortunate and may have to seek advice from a knowledgeable hound breeder outside their own country. Talk over your plans and find out how people have set about similar problems. Next, work out the female tail lines in your own kennel. What do we mean by a female tail line? We mean the lines that go back from dam to dam to dam etc within your own kennel. These lines are going to be crucial to your breeding. Observe those hounds closely out hunting and, if you are satisfied with their performance, then breed from them. Try hard not to lose these precious lines; they are really the core of your pack and dictate its individuality. It maybe that you have only got one line and you may have to try to obtain one or two more. This can be difficult to do and will require hours of detective work. Do not be too quick to draft (give to another pack) hounds that are key to a pack's established breeding policy unless they do not hunt well and you intend to remain in office in your particular country long enough to breed some more effective replacements. It is arrogant to be too hasty to condemn the breeding plans of your predecessors, especially if they moved on before they brought them to fruition.

The next step is to look at other packs of hounds and to see which ones you admire for their type or hunting reputation. Ask permission to visit their kennels and look at them carefully and, if possible, have a day's hunting with them. Once you are satisfied that you have made the right choice, ask their respective Master whether you may use one or more of his doghounds. It is very rare for a Master to refuse and there is, of course, no stud fee but it is politic and correct to make a present to their Huntsman. By using high quality doghounds you will upgrade the quality of your own pack. This is the most important ingredient of developing a pack and you must be careful not to use a chance bred stallion hound from a pack whose reputation is not established just on the off chance. Stick to kennels of quality – as yours is fast becoming!

A few more detailed points; first, proliferation of the same hound back in the pedigree of a proposed mating is an advantage but be careful not to proliferate with poor hounds several generations back just because it happens to be convenient. Bad points have a nasty habit of re-appearing and they are likely still to breed out soft hunting lines. Avoid mating hounds of the same tail male line. Generally, I consider tail male and tail female the greatest influence in pedigrees.

Much discussion has gone about showing hounds over the generations. By all means try to breed for show type conformation and levelness but remember that your hound's primary job is to catch foxes so do not neglect working qualities. The old adage of "'ansome is as 'ansome does" generally applies but judging on the flags does, of course, reflect these vital working qualities.

Next consider the question of outcrossing. There are various other types of foxhound kennel to which you can turn; apart from the Welsh there are Fell hounds, the West Country Harrier, the American hound and possibly, the many types of French hound. Before you think about outcrossing, work out, in military parlance, what your aim is. Do you want more voice? Do you want better scenting ability? Make sure you are not just following a fashion or out crossing for its own sake. Never forget the advantage of the old English hound if you have the modern type. Use any outcross sparingly and try to integrate it into your breeding rather than let it take over. A sure way to upset even the most reticent of the old subscribers is if they see a pack of white coated hounds at the Opening Meet when they've had the traditional type since 1800, especially if the newcomers do not catch local foxes.

Involve your Huntsman or Kennel Huntsman fully in your breeding plans. He has as active an interest and as deep a professional interest as you do and he may remain to continue your policies when you cannot resist that tempting offer of a four day a week grass country that materialises the following May! Look after your puppy walkers; they are a vital part of any Master's kennel management. Acquire good ones and cherish them. Good walks make hounds and there is a world of difference between a really good walk and a place which takes puppies to get them out of the kennels. Puppy walkers are all too often the unsung heroes of a hunt and many will do extra worming etc that you or your Huntsman just do not have the time to do. Should you be subsequently showing their puppy at a hound show then make sure that you invite them.

Greatwood, Champion Dog Foxhound at Peterborough 1994

Really successful hound breeders have "green fingers"; they seem to know instinctively which bitches to use and they get it right but, as with gardeners, if you do not have the knack, you can still get a long way by following the rules. Whether you are lucky or not you will find that breeding your hounds is one of the most rewarding aspects of hunting and one that will give you the most lasting pleasure.

Ronnie Wallace has been Master and Huntsman of the Eton College Beagles, the Ludlow, the Cotswold and the Heythrop. He is now in his 18th season as Master and Huntsman of the Exmoor.

....

"I am sending a couple of bitches to such and such a dog."

"Oh, really?" replied his friend. "Do you know anything about his work?"

"No," was the reply, "d--n his work; but he will just correct the little weakness of my bitches below their knees."

From Fairfax Blakeborough's Hunting Reminiscences *as reproduced in Raymond Carr's* English Fox Hunting

Puppy Walking

Charlotte Campbell

In one of my favourite childhood books, Beatrix Potter's *Jemima Puddle Duck*, there is a charming picture of two hound puppies escorting Jemima home in tears, after her ordeal with the foxy whiskered gentleman. They are moving back to the farm in a stately and decorous procession, the very models of virtue and sobriety, and although I have since discovered that hound puppies actually possess none of these admirable qualities I have been charmed by them ever since.

Walking hound puppies is a relatively easy pastime. All they require are large amounts of food, love and to join in your every day life as much as possible.

If you are tempted to try, your Huntsman will come out to see if you are a suitable "walk". I qualify as I have a large, luxurious and empty bull pen, no near neighbours and I hate gardening.

The telephone call announcing their arrival usually comes out of the blue, any time between April and October. The Huntsman rings and unless you have an excuse at the ready, they arrive a few hours later, in the back of the kennel van; feeling very homesick and bringing with them a card with their names, breeding and ear numbers on. Also enough flesh to keep them going, usually a joint slightly larger than themselves.

I always have a couple of puppies, and more years than not an extra half comes too. It always amazes me how quickly they settle to their new life and how every generation of puppies hide their favourite toys – tail bandages, woof boots and dandy brushes – in the same place around the farm and garden, and make the muck heap the centre of their lives for the whole of their stay.

The puppies must be allowed as much freedom as is sensibly possible. One is not doing one's job if the puppies spend their entire day in their run, however large and luxurious.

My nerves and everyone else's are strained during the harvest. When grain carting is at its height, the boys race back and forth to the dryer. Engines and stereos are at full blast. The puppies then loiter round the stables, where you get accustomed to averting your eyes as they sit under the horses' back legs and swing on their tails. Or toboggan off the muck heap, landing with a sickening thud on the concrete before continuing across the yard apparently unscathed. Hound puppies are extremely resilient.

One of the great pleasures of walking puppies is going out around the farm with them, accompanied by a motley procession of the family and resident dogs, and later when the hunters come in we ride. Until the puppies get the hang of it, the secret – I find – is to keep going with one's own dogs. Don't look back, they always catch up, I only really worry when they are older and get too far in front.

On these walks we meet various hazards that the puppies will have to contend with in later life: sheep, pheasants, water, walls and noisy machinery. Pilgrim, now a model hound in his fifth season, had to be carried past the dryer in his early days and took longer than any puppy to negotiate successfully a dry stone wall.

The hunt staff will come out regularly both to inject the puppies and keep you supplied with raw flesh. They will also do the worming for you.

There are, of course, drawbacks to walking hound puppies. Being a gardener is one. Hound puppies are single-minded and ruthless gardeners. My neighbours' gardens are show pieces. Mine resembles a lay-by only very recently vacated by so-called New Age Travellers, and it always seems pointless to tidy up. It is only a matter of months before more of their relations return (the puppies' that is).

During the summer months one is asked to view this year's entry, safely returned to the kennels the previous autumn, hopefully unscathed, and with the sadness at parting faintly tinged with relief. These are very select and enjoyable occasions, which serve the sensible purpose of getting the puppies accustomed to being shown off and for us walkers to see how our charges have grown on, also to assess their chances in the puppy show several weeks hence.

Puppy show day is always looked forward to, particularly if one's puppies haven't fallen by the wayside or been deemed really too ugly to appear at all. We are given a delicious tea, a spoon for every puppy walked bearing his or her name and year on it and we are thanked profusely by all the Joint Masters. Some years there might be the bonus of one's puppy winning a prize – our hunt gives extremely lavish ones.

Dressing for the puppy show can be difficult, but one should not be put off by the vagaries of the weather. It is a big day in the hunt calendar and the hunt staff will have spent days cleaning and manicuring the kennels and camouflaging the flesh house to impress the visiting judges. So it behoves you to do the same. If when you are seated for the judging, surrounded by floral prints and bowler hats, it pours, the guests sensibly just add a layer or two of old macs.

Of course things do get a little competitive among the walkers – rather in the nature of school sports day. The failure of one's beautiful but shy puppy to shine during judging is apt to be blamed on, say, the imposing girth of the dark suited judges, but on the whole we are fairly sporting.

The final accolade for puppy walkers, I imagine, is to be seen attending the puppy show in their dotage and helped into the ring by an alarmingly young looking mastership, and to be presented with a serious piece of silver or a picture, and applauded for dutifully walking puppies for 50 plus years. During life, ambitions are realised or cast aside but perhaps this is one I should cherish.

Charlotte Campbell lives on a farm in Gloucestershire and walks puppies for the Heythrop.

How to Judge Foxhounds

Martin Scott

One of the aims of holding a puppy show is to thank those stalwarts of the hunt, the puppy walkers, for their valuable contribution to the hunt. Hound shows, on the other hand, allow comparisons to be made with other packs, thus enabling the Huntsman to improve and maintain a level pack.

Charlie Watts shows the Cattistock puppies

Conformation of the hound is not the main ingredient in selection of prospective sires and dams, **work** is the primary consideration, with pedigree of the family counting above looks. However, a well made hound is likely to go the fastest and furthest for the longest, and this must be the breeder's aim. Therefore, judges will be looking for attributes to sustain this aim.

At these shows one often hears the judges' decision disagreed with by those on the outside. In most cases, judging from inside the ring gives one a chance to see things which cannot be viewed from outside; however, those who judge from outside the ring often think they know best!

As a rule, the judges are looking for a pack animal which has pace and stamina. Ideally we want a level pack that are all similar so that they can be seen as a handkerchief when hunting, rather than spread out like a washing line.

To enable the hound to move effortlessly, it must be well balanced and be able to move correctly. If it has quality so much the better. A hound can look balanced when stationary but is unbalanced when it moves, thus I emphasise the importance of *balance* and *movement*.

Duke of Beaufort's Daystar

Other points the judges will be looking for include whether the front half equates with the back half and if the weight is evenly distributed on to all four legs; if the legs and feet are all taking an even amount of pressure, you will have even wear and tear but if you have the wrong pressure part of the 'tyre' will wear out quicker.

The position of the shoulder and the hound's pace points are discussed in many different ways. Fundamentally, if a hound can move freely with a good long stride, it will be faster and be able to turn better than a short striding hound.

The length of the stride is governed largely by the position of the shoulder, the length of the humerus bone and the length of the leg. If the shoulder is well laid back, and the humerus bone and foreleg can go forward in a straight line, the stride will be longer than a hound which has a straight shoulder. The longer the humerus bone (point of shoulder to elbow) the better the stride and likewise with the foreleg. A round arm or crooked action is bound to produce a short striding hound, as well as wearing down the outside toes.

A good depth of chest rather than a barrel shape is needed to provide room for heart and lungs; the barrel shape pushes out the shoulders and therefore restricts the length of the stride.

A muscular back, good strong loins and powerful hind legs and second thighs, not only propel the hound but enable it to keep going. A chopped-off back will be a weakness.

Exmoor Raindrop, Champion bitch at Peterborough Royal Foxhound Show, 1993

The hind leg needs to have the hock well let down, but able to pass the forelegs when galloping. 'Cow' or 'Sickle' hocks do not provide this power.

It is not always easy to see hounds which have bad feet from outside the ring, especially if the judging is on grass. Apart from toes wearing unevenly, which will not help with longevity, feet and toes are important. Toes which are down (at the knuckle) are a blemish which will not be tolerated at a hound show (with the exception of the stallion hound or brood bitch class) and toes too close together or too far apart are not desirable, as they cause lameness. A hound which knuckles over at the knee will not last, and similarly you do not want hounds to be too exaggeratedly 'back at the knee!'.

Neither does one want a snipey head nor a swine chopped mouth, whose teeth are overshot or undershot. They are less likely to feed well, and they pass this bad characteristic on and should not be bred from. A head with a good eye and, if a doghound, a masculine head is needed.

As the object is to breed a pack of hounds to one's liking and not the foxes, curly sterns are unattractive but do not slow down a hound at all. However, we do not want to breed a pack of pugs!

Quality in a hound is something which is just that little bit extra and it is hard to define. Maybe it is similar to something us mortals may see in someone of the opposite sex.

People often ask what or how one marks a hound. I usually give a tick for a hound I like and a minus and the reason why for one I do not like. This enables one to inform an irate puppy walker quite truthfully why you preferred their neighbour's beast to theirs!

Hound judging is great fun, and provides the time in the summer for foxhunters to get together when they can discuss the important things in life in an entertaining way. Never forget that although you may have your opinion, the judge's decision is final – well, maybe till the next time!

Martin Scott was Master of the Tiverton 1969-1977 and of the VWH 1977-1983. He is a regular judge at hound shows and puppy shows.

There are many amusing stories concerning that wonderful hunt servant, George Gillson, who had many stories told about him and his wit and humour.

One day at a hound show, someone made a remark that such and such a hound was "Chance Bred" ie although it may have been good looking, it was a pure fluke. A rather unattractive Master of the time who had an equally unattractive wife but rather a pretty daughter asked George what he meant by "Chance Bred".

"Well," said George, "there's you Sir and there's Madam, and then there's that pretty daughter of yours, now she's Chance Bred!"

Martin Scott

Earth-stopping and Terriers

Brian Fanshawe

The position of the terrierman will vary hugely from hunt to hunt depending on the affluence of each particular organisation. The smaller hunts frequently rely on volunteers who may only operate on certain days or in certain areas of the country, whilst the larger hunts may well employ a full time professional. However, all terriermen who act on any hunting day have to be registered with the Masters of Foxhounds Association and be holders of a valid firearms certificate in order that they can kill a fox humanely. Every terrierman on the register is issued with an extract from the MFHA rules and instructions by his Master. Disregard of these rules renders the terrierman liable to being struck off the register and hence out of a hunt job.

In the public eye terrier work is the most misportrayed facet of foxhunting. Our opponents like to claim that digging is a major part of most hunting days – nothing could be further from the truth.

In many hunting countries the digging out of a fox is a necessary and essential part of the overall management of the fox population – some hunts may never dig at all. The sole reason for digging is to kill a specific fox – in no way is it any part of the day's sport. Of course, it has to be recognised that the killing of any wild animal is an emotive subject.

Bill Langridge and Ron Kemp at work with terriers

Hunting has always been a very open and public sport with many hunts being followed by hundreds of enthusiastic spectators. Whilst it may be true to say that some of the dismounted followers would be more than willing to help at a dig, any dig is most effectively carried out by the terrierman with one, or at the most, two helpers.

It is always the decision of the Master in charge as to whether to dig or not. His decision will be based on the requirement of the farmer, his own knowledge of the local fox population and the practicalities of being able to implement the dig successfully and within a short space of time. Generally, it is advisable for the terrierman to be left in peace and quiet to work with his dog – terriers, like all working dogs, dislike noise and interference from strangers, which is probably also true of most terriermen.

The true advantage of having a full time man is that he should work closely in the planning and the organisation of the hunting days. He should be the informant to the Master/Huntsman as to where foxes are lying, the basis of which is to discover in the summer where cubs have been born. Physically walking the country, eyes down, and talking to locals will further his fox knowledge. The terrierman may well organise all the earth-stopping – finding local people to help. He will want to know exactly what each earth-stopper does so that every known earth is either stopped or put to. Some earth-stoppers may be willing to do a night stop but are unavailable to check the earths in the morning, others, maybe, can't or won't go out at night but are willing to do some checking in the morning or even unstopping after hunting. Good coordination is paramount in improving sport. The most important part of the terrierman's work is to have the local fox population above ground and available on the hunting day. Reliable information provides both the Huntsman and his hounds with confidence – which is a major key to success. Blessed is the Huntsman who has a good terrierman.

A further luxury of a professional terrierman is to have someone physically available to implement the conservation and maintenance work of the hunting country – the planting of new coverts, covert laying and making the perimeter fences stock proof, ride cutting, hedge laying, gate hanging and the repair and building of hunt jumps and bridges. Of course, no one person can do all this single-handed but with an enthusiastic lead from the Masters, the terrierman can provide the base to engender help from others within the hunt.

Just as the captain of the cricket XI requires good batsmen, good bowlers and a reliable wicket keeper, every Master requires good kennel staff, good grooms and a reliable terrierman. Nothing beats teamwork.

Brian Fanshawe, a former Master and Huntsman of the Cotswold, the North Cotswold, the Warwickshire, the County Galway and the Cottesmore, is Director of the Campaign for Hunting.

Galway 1969

Libby Fanshawe amateur 1st whip awaiting back hounds catching up. "Get on you fat old bitch – get over that wall."

Large troublesome lady jumps wall. Field cheers.

North Cotswold 1977

Brian Fanshawe, Huntsman, to Libby Fanshawe, Field Master,
"Send six people on to Larkwood."
Six people go on.

Brian Fanshawe, "I don't want that bloody lot."

Libby Fanshawe, "Nor do I."

Brian Fanshawe

Hunting Dress: What to Wear

Taken from Foxhunting
by The 10th Duke of Beaufort

Fashion is not very rife in the hunting field – tradition seems to be the thing – though in the early days at Peterborough I understand that the huntsmen wore long tops and their coats came down to their ankles. Caps were worn as a regular thing until the Marquess of Waterford broke his neck in 1859 when wearing one, and then people took to silk hats, and to bowler hats when they became fashionable towards the end of Queen Victoria's reign. That people were swayed by strange things is indicated by the fact that they gave up wearing black velvet because Mrs Manning, the notorious murderess, was hanged in a black velvet gown in 1849!

The 10ᵗʰ Duke of Beaufort leading hounds from a meet at Badminton House in 1960, with Kennel Huntsman Bert Pateman (left)

It is not known for certain why the red coat became *de rigueur*, though my own green derives from the colours of the family livery, as does the Berkeley yellow.

The two buttons at the back of the Huntsman's coat serve as a reminder of the sword belt, and the buttons below were for the looping up of the garment when the lanes were muddy and foul.

The cut of a red coat is important. It should have a fairly long opening at the neck with two buttons and a hook and eye where the third button should come, well-rounded points in front and not be straight cut like a hunt servant's. The back should be lined with flannel and it should have two side pockets with flaps set at an angle on the skirts. Make sure that the back is really well lined, as that is where the cold strikes hardest. On the way home you will find that newspaper is a wonderfully simple way of restoring heat to the body.

White breeches should be worn with a red coat, either made of cotton or cavalry twill which, although more difficult to clean, is the more durable material. Nowadays there are new materials on the market which are extemely serviceable in that not only are they very easy to clean, but they fit of their own accord, stretching to mould the contours of the body. These "stretch breeches" have been adopted by most of the younger people who hunt.

The waistcoat may be of yellow or checked material, although some people elect to wear a white one. Again it should be well lined for the same reasons as for the coat, and the pockets should be made with flaps to prevent your loose change flying out.

Boots should be of black leather, though nowadays there are excellent rubber ones on the market which for reasons of economy and because they are so easy to clean, have been adopted by very many people. I personally am of the opinion that although they certainly have their merits, they are not nearly as safe as leather, as they do not offer anything like the same protection to the legs. Also it is often necessary to use irons a size or two smaller than normal because rubber boots are narrow and the soles tend to slip when they get wet. Boots should have light tops, though here again brown ones have been adopted by many people because they are easier to clean. The boot garters would be white if white breeches are being worn. Their tongues should go outwards and they should fix between the third and fourth buttons of the breeches. For some reason three buttons should be shown for leggings and four for boots.

Leather boots must be thick soled, as not only will they be much warmer, but you will find them much easier to get off at the end of the day. There should be a spur rest just above the instep.

It is interesting to read that Beau Brummell (1778-1840) designed the modern hunting boot; before he entered the hunting field, pictures and caricatures showed baggy long-topped boots with broad garters coming above the knee. Brummell's boots always had white tops, and these always used to be the correct wear. He told an admiring enquirer that the wonderful polish on his boots came from using blacking mixed with peaches and champagne! Certainly many people used white of egg to get a lustre on their boots which made them look like patent leather.

Beau Brummell, although not noted for being a wise man, was however wise enough to say that the best-dressed man in the hunting field was the man whose dress attracted least notice.

On the question of spurs, a lot of people think that they are a necessary part of hunting wear, but it all depends on how they are to be used and also on the horse you are riding. So do not let yourself be influenced too much by others, do what you yourself think right.

Black coats should be cut on the same line as red ones, with black or black-engraved hunt buttons, but the breeches should be buff or yellow. If you wear white breeches with a dark or dark-grey coat, you should wear light coloured tops. With other breeches the tops should be of patent leather, and a silk hat should be worn.

It is entirely a matter of personal choice whether you choose a cut-a-way or swallow-tailed coat in either colour.

The following story I am assured is true. Two sportsmen once went to hunt in Ireland with the Meath, where there are so many banks and ditches of such proportions that men known as 'wreckers' stand on top waiting to collect half-crowns for rescue work. Both these hunters were beautifully turned out, and would have graced Beau Brummell's company. Their hats gleamed, their coats looked as if they had been painted on them like those of toy soldiers, their leathers looked as if they had just come from the tailor's, and you could have seen to shave in the shine of their boots – and to crown it all, both of them wore exquisite bunches of Parma violets in their buttonholes. Sad to say, both came to grief in the same ditch.

Said Pat to Mike, "What have ye there, Mike?"

Mike said he wasn't sure, but he thought it was a "rider and his harse".

After some of the clinging mud had been scraped off, and both the sportsmen were standing on dry ground once more, Pat exclaimed:

"Begorra, Mike, it is no man at all, at all: sure, they're a couple of paycocks!"

Always bear in mind Egerton Warburton's famous poem:

> *T'aint the red coat makes the rider*
> *Leather, boots nor yet the cap.*
> *They who come their coats to show, they*
> *Better were at home in bed;*
> *What of hounds and hunting know they?*
> *Nothing else but 'go ahead';*
> *At the Kennel I could train 'em*
> *If they would but come to school,*
> *Two and two in couples chain 'em,*
> *Feed on meal, and keep 'em cool.*

Some further points

The Red Coat Dress (please, not "pink", though scarlet is acceptable)

- Headgear: A silk hat is, I think, probably the safest headgear, though I am happy for the lady members of my field to wear hunting caps. This is normally the prerogative of ex-Masters of hounds and of farmers and their wives. By and large, very many ladies nowadays wear caps when they have obtained permission from their Master of hounds to do so. The ribbons at the back should be sewn up – I know not why – as to leave them dangling is to denote that you are an official or a member of the hunt staff. A hat-guard should not be worn, as not only is it always thought to be the sign of a cad – again I do not know why – but it certainly prevents the hat from being taken off to signal which way a fox has gone.

- A plain white hunting tie, which I was brought up to call a tie and not a "stock". To me a stock is part of a gun; goods in the shop; or, my lady friends tell me, something that is used to make soup. It also, of course, denotes sheep or cows. Please make sure that you learn to tie it neatly and correctly. Most are sold nowadays with easy-to-follow instructions, but the tying soon becomes second nature. Be sure to secure the first knot with a safety pin from underneath and also pin down the ends where they do not show very securely. Nothing looks worse than a flapping tie.

- A plain, gold horizontal tie-pin should be used to secure your tie, unless you belong to a hunt that has its own pin. If worn vertically, it could run into your throat.

- A hunting waistcoat: either yellow, checked or occasionally white. This should be worn with the bottom button left unfastened, as with an ordinary waistcoat.

- A red coat.

- A pair of white breeches with a red coat.

- A pair of white garter straps with white breeches.

- A pair of top-boots, which should be black with mahogany tops. With my Hunt it is traditional to have pink tops with Blue and Buff.

- A pair of spurs, if you think them necessary. Do not be driven by convention to wear them if you do not feel your horse needs them or, indeed, if you think you would be safer without.

- A pair of gloves, which should be white, pale yellow or tan leather, wool or string. It is a wise provision to carry a spare pair under your girth in wet weather.

All the above notes also apply to a black coat, though nowadays ladies tend to wear navy-blue coats with navy-blue caps, and skin-tight yellow breeches. These latter look very smart, always providing the shape underneath is suitable! Ladies wear butcher boots, ie boots without coloured tops.

The Ratcatcher's Garb

This is the name given to dress worn before 1 November when cub-hunting, and after 1 March. Some members of staghunting packs wear it all the time, though some change into black coats for hind-hunting from November to mid-February. A silk hat is out of place and tends to look downright ridiculous in a Moorland setting and, traditionally there, no one but the Master and hunt staff wear red coats. It consists of:

- A bowler hat, or velvet cap.
- A collar and tie, or a spotted or pale-blue four-fold silk tie. A white hunting tie is permissible.
- A hunting waistcoat.
- A tweed riding-coat of suitable weight according to the weather and the time of year.
- A pair of buff breeches.
- A pair of brown field-boots or black butcher boots.
- A pair of brown or black garter-straps according to the colour of your boots.
- A pair of spurs, if you think them necessary.
- A pair of gloves.

Now let us have a check on our pockets:

- A handkerchief (take a clean white one if you are hunting with a Moorland pack, as it will show up when held to one side to denote which way the fox has gone).
- A knife with a strong cutting blade that is easy to open, and with a spike so that a hole may be made in leather to effect a running repair. Also it really can be used to take stones out of a horse's shoe!
- A leather bootlace and a piece of binder twine, which you will find useful for all sorts of things, tying up gates, repairs to saddlery, and so on.
- Disinfectant in a puffer-spray bottle.
- Tourniquet bandage dressing.

- Money (loose change – make sure you have the right denomination so that you may make an emergency telephone call – tied up in the corner of a handkerchief so that it does not jingle).
- Safety pins.
- (For ladies) – hair pins and spare hair nets.
- Keys – though I think it is wisest to leave them hidden either in or about your vehicle.
- Sustenance – do not forget that many a rib or worse has been broken by coming in contact with a steel flask.
- Your name and address with a telephone number on a card.

If you stay away, paste a comprehensive list of all the things you are going to need inside the lid of the suitcase that you habitually use. Everyone's needs vary, but the following list which does not pretend to be complete, may be found useful when compiling your own:

- Boot-hooks or pullers.
- Jockeys, if used.
- Put your own boot-jack in the back of your car or horse-box, as nobody else's is ever quite adequate, and can cause a rapid rise in blood pressure at the end of the day when your feet are maybe wet either with water or sweat, and will have swelled in any case.
- Hunting tights.
- Warm socks.
- Spare hunting ties, breeches, shirts and waistcoat just in case you are invited to stay on for a further day's hunting.
- Coat.
- Hat or cap.
- Button-stock for brass buttons on red coat, and a cleaning pad.
- Boots complete with trees

Provide yourself with two canvas boot-bags and elastic covers for your boot tops, so that brown tops will not come into contact with black boot polish.

Refreshment

Although I know there is a school of thought that reckons that a hunting day should be a day of starvation, I myself always carry some sandwiches wrapped in an easily squashed paper, so that I can shove them back into my pocket as hounds find, which they invariably do, the moment one's thoughts turn to food. I have heard it said that the ideal package of sandwiches should be capable of being opened by one numbed, gloved hand without being removed from the pocket. Again I turn to David Brock: "Hunting sandwiches differ from all other sandwiches in that they are eaten under vastly more rigorous conditions, and they should be prepared with that in view. They should be so cut, formed, and packed that they can be enjoyed even though eaten upon the back of a runaway mustang, in a hurricane of wind and cold rain, by a man who has recently broken his right wrist."

I personally tend to rely on car followers for a drink, for a saddle flask is invariably made of glass, tends to be slippery, and is generally irreplaceable. I do wish they could be made aware of the desperation they arouse in the breasts of the mounted followers as they stand by their cars downing mugfuls of coffee when conditions are icy, and lovely refreshing cool drinks when the sun is shining. I myself am generally too busy to worry about it, but I must say I am very thankful when someone comes up and offers me a short drink at the end of an arduous run and, more particularly, a cup of tea at the end of the day before our horses' heads are turned for home.

This article is reproduced by kind permission of David & Charles and the present Duke of Beaufort. It is worth noting that it was written before it was normal, and acceptable, for people to hunt in crash hats.

....

Lord Leconfield, who hunted his own hounds before the last war, was an eminent foxhunter known universally as Lordy. He hated jumping fences and had a series of hunting gates erected throughout the country. Whilst hunting his hounds, he was always accompanied by a mounted manservant whose job was to assist "Lordy" to open the multitude of gates. He was known as John the Baptist (for he followed the ways of the Lord).

One day his Lordship was drawing one of the many large woodlands (the Frith) for a fox when he wanted to have a pee. He called John to come and hold his horse for him whilst he performed this operation. Whilst in action, John saw a mounted lady riding towards them and quickly exclaimed, "My Lord, my Lord, there's a lady coming."

His Lordship's retort was, "John, if she's a lady, she won't look; but if she isn't a lady, it could not matter less."

From Raymond Carr's English Fox Hunting

How to Buy It and How to Clean It

Robin Smith Ryland

In selecting hunting kit I would never economise on a coat. A second-hand or off the peg coat can be altered but a tailor-made coat is best. Box calf boots that last two seasons or nylon breeches are good economies but a good coat has great advantages.

Having a coat made

The two buttons at the rear should rest on the pin bones and should be three quarters of an inch lower than the bottom button in the front of the coat. When seated, the seam of the coat will then rest on the join where the pelvis meets the top of the thigh, so no wind can get underneath and blow it up, leaving you with wet breeches. Low buttons at the back also means a longer back and you will achieve the correct length of skirt – just below half-way down the thigh when seated on the horse.

Gloves

Thick gloves that cover the wrists are obtainable but are difficult to remove when getting out a penknife, chocolate, etc. I recommend cheap wool gloves with plastic studs on the inside. On cold days I recommend cheap blue mittens which have long wrists and can be bought in any agricultural suppliers. These are worn underneath brown gloves.

Cleaning and general management of hunting things
Velvet caps

Hold over steaming water so that when the mud is sponged off the nap is not destroyed.

Top hats

Wipe the dirt off with water using a sponge or a small stiff brush. A good polish may be effected by using a hat pad and a silk handkerchief.

Scarlet coats

If the coat comes back quite dry and there is only superficial mud on it, it may be possible to scrape off the mud with a knife and brush it dry. In normal circumstances the coat should be thoroughly scrubbed in soft rainwater and hung up to dry away from any direct heat. It is important that in the final stages the collar, if velvet, is pinned down or it will shrink and require replacing. It is especially important to scrub off the horse sweat on the skirts.

Breeches

Wool or Bedford Cord breeches should never be put in a washing machine as even on a warm wash their life is shortened. They should be soaked overnight in a mild detergent and then gently scrubbed the next day.

Whips

These should be scrubbed clean with a brush, using warm water and a little washing-up liquid. Once dry, leather food cream should be applied to soften.

Spurs

First scrape the mud off on to a newspaper, then squeeze out a sponge in warm water and washing-up liquid and wipe clean. Put them to dry under a flat piece of lead in a warm room. When dry they will be found to be in shape which they would not be if dried in the ordinary manner. Spur straps should be cleaned on a flat board with a couple of screws in the top that the straps can be attached to in order to achieve tension while applying the polish.

Top boots

Firstly, remove all surface mud with a blunt knife and use a small, stiff brush dipped in warm water and washing-up liquid to brush the mud off the soles and out of welts. Scrub vigorously on the inside of the boot to remove all sweat but only use a sponge, squeezed out in warm water and washing-up liquid on the rest of the leather. When dry, a little dubbin should be applied with a brush where the boot creases on the ankle and this should then be boned in to keep them soft. As leather stretches it is important to have the trees built up, especially round the ankles, so that when they are inserted all the creases in the leather are ironed out. Polish should be applied and left overnight and then boned in with the shank bone of a deer or the back of a warm spoon. A second coat of polish may be applied if there is time and when finishing the boot, give a coating of the white of an egg and polish off quickly with a soft brush. Box Calf Boots do not crack but only last a few years and the leather lifts when it is scratched. If you are having a pair of wax calf boots made, it is recommended that they should be at least one and a half times bigger than your normal shoe size.

Robin Smith Ryland is Master of the Warwickshire.

The Ten Commandments of Foxhunting

Mr Young

Article I

Every man shall present himself at the place of meeting quietly, suitably clothed, and in good time. He who rides his hunter steadily thereto is better than he who uses a hack. He who drives tandem for display or who uses any manner of engine or machine, except as necessity, is an abomination.

Article II

Every man shall first salute and speak words of comfort to the Huntsman and whippers-in, knowing full well that they have hard work to perform. He shall then count the hounds and examine them with great joy, but in a quiet manner. He shall likewise cheerfully salute his friends. He that shall say the day will be a bad-scenting one, or in any manner endeavour to prophesy evil, is an abomination.

Article III

It is acceptable that those of experience shall, at all times, give explanation and encouragement by word and deed to all young persons, so that foxhunting may continue in the land from generation to generation. He who thinks he knows, when he knows not, is an abomination.

Article IV

Every man shall remember that the ground he passes over is not his own property. Whosoever uses not due care and consideration is an abomination.

Article V

He who talks loudly or who leaps unnecessarily is an abomination. He who wears an apron or mackintosh on wet days or who uses any other device for making a mountebank of himself, or who in any way causes inconvenience to any hound or hunt sevant is an abomination.

Article VI

If it be possible, let every true believer abstain from all meat and drink, save only such as is necessary to sustain life. Let the whole day be kept as a special fasting and strengthening of the mind for the chase. In the evening he shall partake of suitable meat and drink, and on the evening after a good day he shall have a special allowance.

Article VII

He who, of his own free will, goes home before the hounds do, or who is displeased with the day, or who is not fully uplifted, joyful and thankful because of the day, is an abomination.

Article VIII

Whosoever kills or takes a fox by any other means save by hunting is an abomination; his dwelling shall become desolate and his possessions a desert; may his mind be filled with bitterness and his body with pain.

Article IX

Whosoever lives a cheerful, good neighbour, striving to help and encourage his friends at all times, and who hunts on foot if he has not a horse, and by whose behaviour the Scarlet is never brought into dishonour; may he live long, and be happy and may his possessions be as the sand by the sea-shore for multitude.

Article X

And may all men, rich and poor, have equal rights and pleasures in the chase if they devoutly agree to these articles.

Taken from Foxhunting *by Mr Young which was published around the turn of the century.*

....

"I have a good reason for going. I discover many a man who will pay me fifty guineas for painting his horse who thinks ten guineas too much to pay for painting his wife."

Ben Marshall, sporting artist, explaining his reasons for visiting Newmarket. From Sparrow's Sporting Artists *as reproduced in Raymond Carr's* English Fox Hunting

Foxhunting in Scotland

John Gilmour

It may not always be realised – by Sassenachs at any rate – that there are hunting countries in Scotland that are every bit as good as anything south of the Border. Despite the fact that there are fewer packs in Scotland, compared to England, there are few bits of huntable country without a pack of hounds. And the number is growing, with three new Fell-type packs hunting the Highlands with great success.

John Gilmour, Master of the Fife

In nearly every case, it was about the middle of the eighteenth century when foxhunting began to be established in Scotland. The old sporting families established their own private packs, and it was from these packs that the present Scottish packs have arisen. In certain Scottish families there runs an inherited tradition of horsemanship and foxhunting. Such names as Jardine, Barclay, Usher, Spencer-Nairn, Dudgeon, Scott, Harker, Cunninghame and Donaldson come to mind, and, of course successive Dukes of Buccleuch. Scotland also produced some great Masters who made their mark south of the Border, Colonel Jack Anstruther Thomson and Sir David Baird, of Quorn fame, who both came from the Kingdom of Fife, to name but two.

In the past, Scottish Masters were content to remain in Scotland, which explains the fact that the peripatetic or 'carpet-bag Master' was nearly unknown, each country producing its Master from within its midst. It's probably a sign of the times, but this useful source of Masters is sadly drying up, and more are now coming in from outside, the Dumfries and the Fife still retaining the tradition of having local Masters.

The greatest changes have come in the last few decades. As in the rest of the British Isles, changes in agriculture and the greater necessity for farms to pay their way have made it more complicated for packs of hounds. Central Scotland too, has got more than its fair share of motorways and new towns. And although the spread of forestry has reduced the size of some of the Border countries, the one thing they do have is marvellous open hill and white grass to gallop over. The Buccleuch has always been the senior pack in Scotland and still maintains that position. The hounds have been maintained by successive Duke's since its formation in 1827, when the fifth Duke took over Mr Baillie's hounds. From 1787, Mr Baillie of Mellerstain, had hunted an enormous country which included the present Buccleuch, Berwickshire, Lauderdale, North Northumberland and part of the Percy. More recently, Sir Hugh Arbuthnot hunted these hounds, with Tom Smith as his Kennel Huntsman, while his brother Will hunted the Fife. Their father, Frank, who was Huntsman at the Dumfriesshire, was a direct descendant of the Smiths of Brocklesby, who had served the Earls of Yarborough since the eighteenth century. Though not as large as it once was, it is still a marvellous country to watch hounds, which indeed can be said for most of the Scottish packs.

The Lauderdale was once described to me by its Master as "God's gift to the amateur Huntsman!" It is a lovely country with stone walls, good grass and great views across the Borders.

The Berwickshire has probably suffered most from the changes in farming, but it does have good hill country to compensate. David Thomson hunted these hounds to great effect for many years, and now they have one of these peripatetic Masters coming in from the south!

Cross over to the west, and its a very different story. A much higher rainfall and lots of dairy cows mean totally different hunting conditions.

At the Eglinton, the senior Master deals with them in his own inimitable fashion! But they do have a marvellous pack of hounds, not only on the flags but in the field.

The Dumfriesshire hunt a lovely bit of country, with a unique pack of black and tan hounds, bred by the Buchanan Jardine's, with a voice that really thrills.

The Lanark and Renfrew started life as the Glasgow Hunt, when they hunted a lot of what is now the City of Glasgow. It's a wet country, great for scent and and can be difficult to get over, but they show great sport.

The Fife Foxhounds have hunted the Kingdom since about 1756. They used to hunt parts of Perthshire and Angus, but the gentlemen of Angus "fell in arrears of their subscriptions" so the privilege was withdrawn. The country is very mixed now, with lots of arable, but some good hill and woodland. Famous names abound – Tom Crane, who hunted the Duke of Wellington's hounds in the Peninsular War and then came back to hunt the Fife from 1825; John Whyte Melville, father of the hunting poet; Captain Jack Middleton, brother of 'Bay' Middleton, and many more.

Hunting a pack of hounds in Scotland is not that much different from anywhere else, but the Scottish hill fox is much bigger than his southern cousin and more difficult to catch. Apart from that, what are the pros and cons of hunting north of the Border? Without doubt, the chance to watch hounds hunt without the pressure of large fields and masses of people, wide open country to ride over and the marvellous enthusiasm of the supporters. Against that, a later start to the season as harvest up here is later, and the threat that from Christmas onwards you might lose a months hunting or more to ice and snow. Would I swap it for an English pack – never!

John Gilmour is Master of the Fife and farms in the Kingdom.

Foxhunting in the Borders and Northumberland

R W F Poole

Northumberland and the Borders cover some of the most varied and sporting hunting countries in the realm. The area stretches from the River Tyne in the south to the Tweed and the Cheviot Hills in the North. There is a great tradition of Hunting in this area. Modern times and conditions have brought their difficulties, but have not abated the passion for the chase. This area contains all sorts and conditions of hunting countries and all sorts and conditions of packs to cope with them.

In the rich farming areas to the south and east of the area, there are still some good riding countries and still some stretches of old pasture to be enjoyed, although these have greatly diminished during the last 30 years. Do not expect to "leap the thorns" much in this part of the windswept north. The jumping is mainly hunt jumps, which are plentiful, but there are still some excellent bits of stone wall country, which provide a challenging ride, especially as many of them are wired. The enclosures tend to be large and undulating and well bred horses are required.

As you go north, the land rises to the steep uplands of the Cheviots. Here is some of the wildest hunting in Britain. The hills are high (The Cheviot is 2500 feet) and steep. The country can be rough and broken with stretches of unrideable peat bog. Here, there is no jumping, just miles of open hill, where you can ride all day on heather and white grass. You can gallop a horse to a standstill in half an hour in these hills and you have to learn to "ride canny" and have a horse that is hill fit. The natives have mostly resorted to quadricycles, which do not get tired, do not go lame, will climb the steepest hills and do the shepherding as well. For those for whom hunting means hound work, the northern hills provide a wonderful grandstand for watching hounds and foxes.

In the east, this area is bounded by the mighty Kielder Forest (Europe's largest man-made forest) which requires a specialist sort of hunting. There have been other large plantings of conifers on the hills since the Second World War. Sheep walk is still disappearing under Sitka Spruce.

The Borders are not as well foxed as the south, but the foxes tend to be bigger, stronger and travel further. In recent years, there has been a sharp rise in shooting pressures. This has seriously affected some hunting countries.

Another problem in some parts is the shortage of good fox coverts. A casual glance through the area would show lots of good looking little coverts dotted about. Sadly these are mostly coniferous and for most of their life offer little serious protection for foxes, who like warm, dry, draught-free lying. Many of the once numerous whin coverts have been grubbed out in the name of progress. This means that foxes can be hard to find later in the season, when the bad weather has driven them to lie to ground.

This brings us neatly to the weather, which is a major factor of life in this area. The weather in the Borders can be harsh. The rainfall in the west of the area is high and low in the east. In a "normal" winter (whatever that is) it would be unusual if snow did not stop play at some stage. However, the Borderers are hardy people and "fit to hunt" means something quite different to what it would in, say, Sussex. The wind is a great feature of life up here. It is fortunate that the prevailing wind is westerly (although it can still lift the fillings out of your teeth) but if the wind gets in the south-east stand by to batten down your hatches.

The Border Hunt has been in the hands of two (inter-related) families for more than a 100 years: the Robsons, father and son, and the Hedleys, father and son. Michael Hedley, who now carries the horn, is a remarkable hound man and fox catcher. The hounds may be best described as "Fell Cross". They are one of the fastest packs of hounds that I have ever seen and when they really run you need nerves of steel to keep in contention. These hounds hunt some of the wildest country in England and continue north over the "Scotch fence" into Scotland as far as the Kale Water. It is a hunt of farmers and hill shepherds and makes no bones about the fact that it is there to keep the hill fox population within reasonable bounds. Hounds will kill about 200 foxes a season on average and nearly all above ground. It is not always tactful to attempt to discuss the tally with some of the other packs mentioned here.

The College Valley and North Northumberland: The College Valley was started in 1924 by Sir Alfred Goodson, Bt, and the Hon Claude Lambton to hunt outlying hill countries of the North Northumberland, the Duke of Buccleuch's and the Border. It is probably the steepest part of the Cheviot hill country. Sir Alfred became a legend in his life time, both as a Huntsman and a breeder of hounds. In 1964 he was joined by Mr Martin Letts as Joint Master and Huntsman. Mr Letts is still in command and it is fair to say that he too has become something of a legend. In 1982 the College Valley amalgamated with the North Northumberland, who had long been associated with the Joicey family. The North Northumberland was a quite different type of country which lay between the Cheviot Hills and the sea. Once mile upon mile of old pasture and fly fences, it is now mostly plough and hunt jumps. This dichotomy of country is presenting quite a challenge to Mr Letts in breeding a pack of hounds to hunt both types of country satisfactorily.

The Haydon: For 20 years the fiefdom of genial Donald Edgar, this Hunt has been in a state of flux in recent years and one can only wish the present mastership a more settled time in the future. Andrew Robb is in his third season as Huntsman and has been showing good sport – that wonderful panacea for all hunting problems. The country straddles the west end of the Tyne valley and also crosses Hadrian's Wall. This always looks a nice bit of old grass and stone wall country when I drive though it.

The Jedforest: For nearly 30 years, this was the domain of the great Mr Roly Harker, who was definitely a 'character'. The present acting Joint Master and Huntsman is Mr Wat Jeffrey who also has quite as much character as is good for him and shows fine sport as well. The Jed hounds used to be "fairish old puddings", but are now much more of a decent class of Standard Foxhound. The country lies entirely on the Scottish side of the Border and still has some nice grass country especially on the south side, where there is also some forestry. There is a lot of shooting as well.

The Milvain (Percy): In 1921 Lt-Col Milvain, who had been Joint Master of the Percy, was loaned some country by the Duke of Northumberland to form his own pack. This was a private pack and was maintained as such until 1955. Col Milvain's daughters still own the hounds. Since 1974 hounds have been hunted by the amiable Mr Anthony Barnett. Hounds tend to be of the Old English type with a smattering of Dumfriesshire blood. The bulk of the country lies on a high ridge that runs parallel with the A1 trunk road. There is still a considerable amount of old pasture interspersed with stretches of rather sour, wet, heather moorland. The fences are mostly wire and there are a large number of hunt jumps. The country is heavily shot.

Morpeth: This country has had a long association with the Cookson family (no, not the novelists) and many people will remember the redoubtable Lt-Col John Cookson about whom many stories abound. His son, Mr Michael Cookson, is now the senior Joint Master and the country has been fortunate in long and respected masterships. Ronnie Mackay has been Huntsman for many years. Hounds were of the traditional Old English type, but, in recent years, some Standard Foxhound blood has been introduced; not always an easy blend to achieve. The Morpeth has had to abandon its country east of the A1 because of increasing urbanisation. The southern end of the country has now mostly been ploughed up, but there is still some lovely old grass country in the north of the country. Shooting pressures have greatly increased in this country in recent years.

The North Tyne: The North Tyne is run by a committee. The present acting Master is Mr Richard Walton of that famous Border clan. A more cheerful and hospitable lot of foxhunters you will never find. Anthony Gaylard is the Huntsman and the hounds are Fell Cross. Your biggest problem with the North Tyne might be in finding them. Most of their country lies under the trees of Kielder Forest, where they make a great job of fox catching. Your other problem might be finding you way home again after hunting.

The late Duke of Northumberland was truly a "grand veneur". I have heard graphic descriptions of his fox sense and of how he could "walk a fox to death". Alnwick Castle was always the power house of hunting in the Borders and the Duke's death caused great sadness amongst all foxhunters. It is fortunate that the late Duke's daughter, Lady Victoria Cuthbert, has inherited her father's passion for the chase and carries on the family interest. Don Claxton, that doyen of professional huntsmen, has carried the horn since 1965. These hounds still stoutly maintain their Old English tradition. The country has shrunk somewhat from the south. The A1 runs through the middle of the country and the now electrified main line railtrack runs down the eastern flank, both of which must cause considerable headaches. The "Vale" which was once a delectable expanse of old grass and fly fences is now mostly winter corn. This is still a very sporting country, with a great tradition of hunting farmers, and is socially gilt edged.

Tynedale: Mrs Rosemary Stobart runs a tight ship and regularly keel hauls hunting malefactors. The Tynedale is run in good style and shows good sport. G Barrett took over the horn in 1993 and they say that he is making a good fist of it. Mrs Stobart is very much a disciple of the best possible Standard Foxhound bloodlines. The country, which lies to the north of the Tyne Valley, is still a good one, although much of the eastern end has gone under the plough. The western end of the country still has much grass in big enclosures with stone walls. The ladies and gentlemen of the Tynedale like to think that they go a bit and you need a horse that can gallop and jump in this country.

The West Percy has always been a happy country under the benign autocracy of the Carr-Ellison family. Sir Ralph became Master in 1950. He was subsequently joined by his wife and later on his daughter. Major John Carr-Ellison carries on the family tradition. Hounds are hunted by Mr Artie Hunter, a great dog and horse man, who has come to hunting hounds rather later in life than most, but has won much praise in his first season. The hounds are mostly Fell cross, with many treasured lines back to the best of Sir Alfred Goodson's old College Valley. They are a fine pack of hill hounds. The country is mostly open hill with a bit of "in bye" ground in the Whittingham Vale. There is a scattering of hunt jumps. Most of the hill is good sound galloping; not as wet as the Border, or as steep as the College Valley. There is considerable afforestation in the west. The West Percy has suffered more than most from increased shooting pressures.

Willy Poole was a Master of Foxhounds for 25 years but is now reduced to journalism. He lives in Northumberland, where he last held office as Master of the West Percy.

Willy Poole with the Sinnington hounds

Foxhunting in North Yorkshire

Johnny Shaw

Given a moment's thought when asked to describe the features of this part of the world, most people would mention coal mines, chemical plants and, that home of ghost stories, the North Yorkshire Moors. Not exactly a litany of the ideal conditions for the pursuit of foxhunting. How wrong they would be, and selfishly your misconception is our gain!

This area of the north east of England is very roughly bounded by a line drawn east from Flamborough Head to the Pennines, and then north to the River Tyne. From a southern perspective it is between home and Scotland and thus is generally viewed from a train or a car window as you speed – or crawl – up the A1. The area has two outstanding things going for it, firstly its country and secondly its people.

The region has a number of natural features which divide it as well as a few man-made divisions which interfere with, but do not prevent foxhunting. The Pennine boundary in the west is the natural division between Lancashire and Yorkshire. The top of the range provides some of the best grouse moors in the realm and is hunted by the Pennine foxhounds on foot. The eastern foothills and dales are sheep lands, predominately grass and stone wall country which is interesting to cross on a horse! These hills give way to The Vale of Mowbray (sometimes erroneously called York) in the south. This is rich arable land but as you move north it turns to mixed farming with more grass. The north east contains the urban conurbation of Tyne and Wear and at the mouth of the Tees, Middlesbrough and Stockton. Below this is the wild, upland area of the North Yorkshire Moors, giving hunting for no less than seven packs of hounds, two of whose countries run down to the arable Ryedale and Pickering Lyth in the south. What should be apparent from this very brief tour around the area, is the variety of country in the region and thus the variety of foxhunting available to the enthusiast.

This region is acknowledged to contain the very cradle of foxhunting. The district of moor and vale now hunted by the Bilsdale, Farndale and Sinnington Foxhounds was hunted by the Second Duke of Buckingham in the 1670s. Whatever his faults – and there seem to have been many – his hunting must be to his credit and it is recorded that he died in "the meanest house in Kirkbymoorside", of a chill caught out hunting in 1687. It is small wonder that the area now contains a people who are keen supporters of foxhunting to this day – horses and hounds are part of the very fabric of the region.

They say "You can tell a Yorkshire man – but not much." They rightly think they know a thing or two about foxhunting, and have a great abundance of high quality packs of hounds in the county. The Vale of Mowbray is hunted by four packs all of whom provide great sport and are not for the faint hearted. The West of Yore and the Bedale hunt the bulk of the vale and share the same kennels at Kirkby Fleetham. They are very friendly and hard riding countries. If you visit you can be assured of a generous welcome, but you will need a horse that jumps anything from stone walls to big ditches. The north of the vale is the home of the Zetland, sometimes referred to as the Quorn of the North; it is predominately a grass country again with a great variety of obstacles but few ditches. The west of the vale is hunted by the Hurworth, a small but sporting pack; its country covers up to the western edge of the North Yorkshire Moors. To some extent all these packs are affected by communication links, both road and rail, but they seldom interfere with hunting. The rivers which run through the countries, however, are a different story, and can give a few heart stopping moments.

In Durham to the north, apart from the Zetland, there are the Braes of Derwent and the South Durham foxhounds. The Braes country – said to be the land of the original Jorrocks – lies to the south and west of Newcastle with predominately mixed farming in the east, and woodland hunting interspersed with grass on the rising ground in the west. The South Durham country is found between the urban areas of Sunderland in the north and Middlesbrough in the south and again this is an area with mixed farming country but tending more and more to arable. Between the Tees and the Moors is the Cleveland country, which has been squeezed somewhat by urban development, but can be fun on the steep northern slopes of the moors.

In winter the North Yorkshire Moors can be one of the bleakest parts of our islands – this is especially so when a malevolent easterly gale decides to visit from the Arctic wastes of Siberia. The area is high heather moorland interspersed with dales, dissected by stiff stone wall enclosures for sheep. Some would look at this hunting, describe it as too wild and woolly and go elsewhere, which would be their loss. Old fashioned hunting is the practice of these moorland packs, and were the Duke of Buckingham to return from the grave, he would recognise it in a flash. Whilst there is little jumping – a past Huntsman of the Farndale when confronted by a wall used to dismount, clamber over, shout to his horse "howay then" and when she arrived on the other side, remount and continue – as much nerve is required to cross these moors as in high Leicestershire. As in any upland sheep farming area, foxes are a menace and these hunts provide the invaluable service of controlling them. The moorland foxes are renowned for their size and strength with consequent results. Long hunts are the norm and there are few better places to see hounds work. For all these moorland packs you need a sure footed horse which is fit and good at going both up and down hill fast. The welcome, though cautious to start with, soon becomes generous to a fault with consequent effects on head, girth and liver.

The south side of the moors is hunted by two unique packs of fox hounds – unique due to the variety of landscape which can be found in their countries. These are the Sinnington and Derwent Hunts. Their southern boundaries run through Ryedale and Pickering Lyth. This is a district of rich arable land and stock farms, well fenced and interspersed with ditches, some of which are near "arms of the sea" in size. The vale gives way to limestone riggs dissected by deep wooded dales, before a steep bluff drops down to the moor. In *Notitia Venatica*, a *Treatise on Foxhunting*, R T Vyner Esq writing in 1841 gave the following less than complimentary description of the Sinnington: "the hounds are little better than a trencher-fed pack, the country round composed of everlasting dingles, woods and precipices". The establishment has come on a bit since then but the country remains as challenging as ever. A strong fox running across the grain of the high side of either of these countries can provide the most exhilarating sport and hounds are hard to live with.

At the start I mentioned the people of the area. By this I specifically refer to the farming community. They are generous – and often long suffering – in their support of our sport. It is this support which provides the richness of variety of hunting throughout the region and we remain in their debt. This area also finds many who fill the top rank of equestrian endeavour – be it racing, eventing, show jumping or showing. In the winter they can be found in the front rank out hunting and they take some keeping up with. Come north and give it a try, you will experience a variety of emotions but I can assure you disappointment will not be one of them.

Johnny Shaw farms in the Sinnington country where he is Field Master on Saturdays.

Foxhunting in the Fells and North-West

Edmund Porter

Foxhunting in the Fells and north-west provides plenty of variation and good viewing for the hunting enthusiast. We have two mounted packs hunting in the north of the county, namely the Cumberland Foxhounds and the Cumberland Farmers Foxhounds, and in the Lake District we have six Fell packs of foxhounds who all hunt on foot amongst some of the roughest terrain in England. The six fell packs are the Blencathra, Coniston, Eskdale and Ennerdale, Melbreak, Lunesdale and Ullswater foxhounds. Officials from these six hunts make up what is known as the Central Committee of Fell Packs whose task it is to deal with any problems or complaints that may arise and also to keep in contact with the Masters of Foxhounds Association and therefore keep up to date with things on a national level.

On the fringe of these hunting countries we now have three new foot packs who hunt in the same way as the Fell foot packs and have just become affiliated to the Central Committee. These are the North Lonsdale, North Pennine and Wensleydale Foxhounds.

Hunting in the Lake District is a tradition that has been carried on for a great many years and provides a service to the farmers in the region. Mostly sheep farmers, they depend on the local hunt to keep the number of foxes to an acceptable level. In the spring time each Fell pack goes on "call out" to answer calls from farmers who are having trouble in the lambing field through foxes taking lambs.

Fell foxhunting is carried out in a totally different way to the mounted packs and can provide the followers with plenty of opportunity to view hounds at work on the Fells at close quarters. Hounds often hunt unaided for many hours once their fox has been found and only return to the meet at the end of the day or after a successful conclusion. It is an old custom in the Fells for a pack to hunt the same area for a week at a time (usually four days hunting). It then moves on to hunt the adjacent valley the following week. This custom goes back to the days when there was no transport and hounds and huntsmen would stay away on farms in each valley in the hunt district.

A great deal of the country hunted by the Fell packs is very mountainous and contains the highest peaks in England. Each pack also has a certain amount of lower lying ground where hunting can be easier, but in these areas there is now a considerable amount of afforestation which means that viewing may not be as good as on the mountains.

The weather in the Lake District can be a major factor in the planning of a day's hunting and the hills can often be shrouded in mist which may cause last minute changes to the intended draw or sometimes cancellation. Hard frosts or snow during the winter which cause the crags to become ice-bound and dangerous sometimes means that hunting has to be cancelled for a week or more.

Someone visiting a fell pack for the first time is best advised to get in touch with the local followers, most of whom view proceedings from the roadway through a good pair of binoculars. For the more energetic follower it is best to get a good vantage point on some mountain top from where you are likely to see some of the best hunting and true houndwork that can be found in the country. Then, if you have enough stamina left at the end of the day there may be a sing-song in progress at the nearest public house where you could join in the singing of hunting songs into the night.

The cost of a day's hunting to the visitor depends on the person's generosity and although he may be asked for a small subscription to the hunt there is no obligation.

The Blencathra foxhounds are probably the best known of the Fell packs, having been found in 1839 by the most famous Huntsman of all, John Peel. He lived at Caldbeck and hunted these hounds for well over 50 years. More recently they were hunted by the late, great Johnnie Richardson and are now under the control of his protégé Barry Todhunter. The country is situated at the north end of the Lake District and has some of the best hunting although a constant danger now is the A66 trunk road to West Cumbria which runs right through the middle of the country and is a great hazard to hounds.

The Coniston are kennelled at Ambleside. They hunt a varied sort of country from the mountains of Langdale and Grasmere down to the low-lying woodlands and fields of the Lythe Valley near Kendal. Through being situated in the centre of the Lake District they have to contend with the problem of tourists at certain times of the year. There have been three generations of Logans as Masters of these hounds and three generations of Chapmans as huntsmen during the hunt's history. Today the late Anthony Chapman's daughter is Joint Master. They are hunted by Stanley Mattinson.

The Eskdale and Ennerdale are the only Fell pack to be privately owned, having been founded in 1857 by that great character, Tommy Dobson. Upon his death in 1910 he bequeathed the hounds to his Huntsman, Willie Porter, grandfather of the present day Master and Huntsman Edmund Porter.

The country includes some of the roughest in Lakeland with Scafell Pike (977 metres), England's highest mountain, being within its boundary and from here we hunt back towards the west coast and the more gradual slopes on Black Combe in the south of the country.

The youngest of the Fell packs are the Lunesdale foxhounds who were founded as recently as 1932 and hunt an area of easier country to the south and east of Kendal. Although the M6 motorway now divides their area in two and has meant the loss of hunting in some regions, there is still plenty of room to see some good hunting on the moors. John Nicholson has just retired as Huntsman to these hounds after 40 years service and his place has been filled by Paul Whitehead who previously hunted the Pennine foxhounds.

Edmund Porter with his hounds

The Melbreak foxhounds have the distinction of being the oldest established pack of Fell hounds. They were founded in 1807 by a man called William Pearson who it was said kept a few hounds for the amusement of his friends and eventually called them after a local mountain.

It has the smallest country of all the Fell packs and also has to contend with the A66 trunk road running through the centre. Although some country has been lost in the west due to opencast coalmining operations there still remains some good Fell country around Loweswater and Buttermere. Previously hunted by Harry Hardisty for many years they are now under the control of his son-in-law Richard (Pritch) Bland.

The Ullswater foxhounds complete the six Fell packs and are situated on the eastern side of the Lake District. They hunt the largest area of all from the mountains of Helvellen right over towards the Pennines beyond Brough. They were formed in 1880 by that truly sporting Earl, Lord Lonsdale (or the Yellow Earl as he was known), who was also Master of the Cottesmore Hounds. He sent some hounds up to the Ullswater to help them get started. Lady Jane Benson, who is a direct descendant of Lord Lonsdale, is a present Joint Master of the Ullswater. They are hunted by Dennis Barrow who has spent a life-time hunting.

The Cumberland and Cumberland Farmers foxhounds are both mounted packs who hunt three days a week in the north of the county and whose countries are much the same, with many dairy farms restricting hunting in some areas.

The Cumberland foxhounds are kennelled at Westward and are hunted in the west of the county by Jeff Bowes who is also Joint Master and has hunted all over the world. The Cumberland Farmers foxhounds are based at Welton and hunt the area south of Carlisle as far as Caldbeck. The Wyburgh family have had connections with these hounds over a great many years and the present Joint Master and Huntsman is that great hunting man who would hunt all day and all night – Peter Wyburgh!

The three affiliated packs all hunt in the same manner as the six Fell packs and all have some good open country where there is plenty of opportunity to see hounds at work.

The North Lonsdale hunt around the Old Furness District from Ulverston in the west to Windermere Lake in the east and are the charge of Jimmy Mallett.

The North Pennine are under the guidance of that great ambassador for hunting, Michael Tones, who formed the pack only a few years ago. They hunt the area of the North Pennines, while further south we have the Wensleydale foxhounds whose present Master and Huntsman is also the founder of the pack, Maurice Bell.

Edmund Porter is Master and Huntsman of the Eskdale and Ennerdale.

Foxhunting in South Yorkshire and Lincolnshire

Nick Lane Fox

With the possible exception of the outskirts of London the hunting countries from mid-Yorkshire to Nottinghamshire have lost more good country through urbanization, road and rail construction and the move to arable farming than any other area since the war. However, this does not mean that there is not as much fun to be had here as anywhere else in the country. Sitting in the shade of the Pennines, this area is dryer than most. Even in a very wet spell (most Januarys and Februarys, just before the frost sets in) hunting can continue while foxhunters in other areas find time to check the gutters.

As the towns have grown and new roads have been built, commuters have found that they can move further into the surrounding country and this has provided quite a few 'new countrymen' as recruits to the packs of foxhounds in the area. This phenomenon has great advantages: hunt secretaries have found that the money these people bring in has been an enormous help to the cause and the late converts tend to embrace their new faith with great fervour.

After all of the talk of urbanization the Pennine provides the perfect antidote, covering the Derbyshire and Yorkshire area of the Pennines. Here foxes are hunted on foot, like the Fell packs of the Lake District, and indeed the hounds are bred along Blencathra lines. They hunt along the Pennines in the country not hunted by any other pack of foxhounds and their range is from Pateley Bridge in Yorkshire down towards the Derbyshire Peak District. As with all Fell packs, a strong pair of lungs (or a quad!) and an even stronger liver are requirements.

The York and Ainsty was formed in 1841 by some York gentlemen who borrowed the country from local packs. In 1929 the York and Ainsty split into North and South although they have been having preliminary discussions with a view to a possible amalgamation in 1995.

The York and Ainsty (North) hunt the area to the north-west of York going along the north bank of the River Nidd beyond Harrogate and up the Vale of York as far as Ripon. For the past 14 years they have been run by the redoubtable Major Roddy Bailey and his wife Ronnie, who became a Joint Master in 1980. He has managed to combine a career as a serving officer in the Green Howards with hunting hounds.

The advance of arable farming has been less kind to the York and Ainsty (South) than the North. The York and Ainsty (South)'s pure bred Old English hounds were the life's work of Mr James Bloor, longtime substantial Joint Master. Many other packs have used his bloodlines to return to a more traditional type.

The Middleton has one of the largest countries in Britain, stretching from just east of York to Bridlington (some 50 miles away) and from near Market Weighton to Gilling. In the past it has been hunted as two separate packs but now it is hunted four days a week by the gifted amateur Mr Frank Houghton Brown who took over from Col the Hon Nick Crossley in 1990 after he had hunted hounds for ten seasons. Two families have dominated the mastership – the Halifaxes and the Middletons. Their two estates, Garrowby and Birdsall, still account for much of the good country. The country divides naturally into the Vale of York and the Wolds. The Vale can be wet but is usually better enclosed, making for better jumping days and a trip up and down Garrowby Hill rivals Hose Thorns. The Wolds are mostly light arable land with some steep dales which need a fit horse to stay with hounds. This is wonderful 'hound hunting' country, with few roads or railway lines to interfere.

Formed in 1740, the Bramham is one of the older packs and has a distinctive silver button with the word 'Forward' over a fox running on moorland. The hunt servants are also distinguished by wearing buff breeches instead of white. The country runs from Otley in the west to five miles short of York in the east and from Harrogate in the north to Selby in the south. In the past the best of the country was to be found in the Vale of York and much of the ground north-west of Harrogate was loaned to the York and Ainsty (North). Now the best hunting is to be had further to the north west as arable farming has taken the vale. The Bramham was reputed to be 'the second coldest scenting country in England' but nobody is rude enough to name the worst. Hound breeding used to be based on Middleton lines with some Puckeridge blood but recently more variety has been introduced, although the emphasis has always been on nose.

Although on a map the Holderness country looks vast, in fact the country over which they can hunt is quite limited. In the past they have been generous to their neighbours, lending country around Burton Agnes to the Middleton and country east of Selby to the York and Ainsty (South). The modern North Humberside covers most of the Holderness country and the drainage ditches or dykes of this area can be fearsome to cross. Modern farming methods at least mean that the banks of the dykes are mown and they are not the hefalump traps that they used to be. Shooting is a big influence on the country before Christmas and the Masters have much planning to do to hunt Tuesdays and Saturdays. One piece of country that has come back in is Warter Priory since the big money Greek shooting syndicates have left.

The Badsworth country has five motorways (M1, A1M, M18, M62 and M180) running through it and to look at a map it is difficult to see where they could possibly hunt in the area between Barnsley and the Humber which is theirs. But hunt they do on Tuesdays and Saturdays up until 1 February and then with Thursday bye-days until the end of the season. This hunt was formed in 1720 and some would contend that its heyday was last century; there are, however, still pockets of good country and under the dynamic Joint Mastership of Mr Charlie Warde-Aldam and Mr Askew they enjoy themselves.

The Brocklesby was formed along the present lines at the beginning of the eighteenth century by the ancestors of the 8th Earl of Yarborough who is now a Joint Master. The kennels have been at Brocklesby Park ever since and because of this amazing continuity the hounds are still bred along the same lines as were first recorded in the hound lists of 1746. The country lies to the south of the Humber, extending some 45 miles south between Scunthorpe in the west and Grimsby on the coast.

Formed by an amalgamation in 1952, the Grove and Rufford's country runs south from the western end of the Humber estuary to Newark. Largely flat with lots of plough, it is nevertheless a very sporting country which enjoys tremendous support.

The recent history of the Barlow is dominated by the Mastership of Miss Elsie Wilson who held the Mastership (either solely or jointly) from 1956 to her death in 1988 when she left the hounds and her estate to the Hunt Committee. The country is centred on Chesterfield and includes parts of South Yorkshire, Derbyshire and Nottinghamshire. They have suffered from the advance of Sheffield, but still have some very nice country in the west where great sport is to be had.

The Burton and Blankney were once both part of the Old Burton, another extremely old established pack which John Monson hunted in the 1670s. They split in 1871 and the country has been the same since. They have been another victim of the march of arable farming since the Second World War, but again, still have great fun in a predominantly plough country.

Having split from the Burton some years earlier, the current Blankney country was established in 1895. It is broadly a square to the south of Lincoln with the neighbouring countries being the Burton to the north, Belvoir to the south, Grove and Rufford to the west and South Wold to the east. The country is mainly arable land and shooting is becoming more popular in the area.

If you thought that Lincolnshire was all flat, then the South Wold will be a pleasant surprise. The hills of the Lincolnshire Wolds provide a lovely hunting country along the coast for the pack which has been kennelled at Belchford since 1857.

Should you wish to escape the crowds of Leicestershire and the Meynell has become too smart for you but you like grass, walls and fly fences then the South Notts is the place for you. The north east of the country has been spoilt by farming and the M1 goes straight through the middle, but the western end in the Derbyshire hills is as good a piece of country as anywhere.

Nick Lane Fox lives in the Bramham Moor country and is a former Joint Master of those hounds.

There is no secret so close as that between a rider and his horse.

R S Surtees from Mr Sponge's Sporting Tour

Foxhunting in the Shires

Michael Clayton

Leicestershire has been a magnet for generations of hard riding foxhunters since the late eighteenth century. Others have condemned it, and even today a few people profess to regard "Shires Hunting" as an abomination; too fashionable, and too crowded they say.

The truth is that Leicestershire offers far more variety of terrain, and therefore of hunting styles, than the detractors imagine.

Some of my own profession have not always been helpful; Nimrod (Charles James Apperley) the marvellous reporter of great Leicestershire runs in the early nineteenth century, delighted many but alienated others by his glorification of the Shires sport.

Robert Smith Surtees, the great novelist who created Jorrocks, visited Leicestershire as a hunting correspondent and 'crabbed' it most ungenerously. It must be said that he was not a top class rider across country and most spitefully lampooned Nimrod who most certainly was an excellent horseman.

Nowadays, Leicestershire still offers opportunities for thoroughly enjoyable cross-country riding in pursuit of hounds, but the best riding country is more confined to pockets, linked by wide, grassy verges.

Plough farming hit the great foxhunting county during the Second World War, and the former "sea of grass' has given way to a brown arable landscape in huge tracts of all the Leicestershire packs. Yet you could still forget this in the pastoral paradise of the wonderful Lowesby, Baggrave and Quenby estates in the Quorn Friday country. Swooping over the grass around Upper Broughton on a Quorn Monday is a reminder on the pre-war Shires, and the same applies to the best of the Belvoir's vale country, the Cottesmore's Tuesday country above Braunston, and the Fernie's lovely grass in the Laughton Hills.

Elsewhere, much hard work and expense have been devoted to making the country as crossable as possible, and there is immense fun to be had on the less grassy country.

Many who think they know the Leicestershire packs, having visited them on the more popular days, have experienced nothing of the foxhunting pleasures to be achieved east of the A1 main road, in the delights of the Quorn's Charnwood Forest – where stone walls sometimes divide cramped paddocks amid woodland – or the great enjoyment of the Fernie's less pastoral country.

It must be remembered that the science of hunting the fox in the open at speed was largely developed by Hugo Meynell, founder of the Quorn country in 1753. He perceived that the great swathe of undulating country, then largely grass, from Nottingham down to Market Harborough had wonderful potential as a foxhunting country.

Leicestershire has a subtle beauty, with wonderful miniature uplands, uncluttered hinterlands, unspoilt woodlands, copses and hedgerows, and miles of undulating old turf, best appreciated from the back of a horse.

Even today most Leicestershire villages are not fashionable as commuter bases, nor do they sprawl in the way that so many villages do in the south. It must be admitted that at night the street lights of Nottingham and Leicester cast an eerie glow over the surrounding countryside, and the pressure of Midlands commerce and industry is apparent on the rural fringes. Melton Mowbray, the historic centre of the Shires Hunts, has light engineering, makes pet food and pork pies, and has a huge, new coal mine on its northern edge.

The greatest legacy which Meynell's descendant foxhunters left us is the huge range of well-preserved, beautifully sited coverts, so cleverly positioned to ensure runs in the open over delectable vales, or well-drained wolds where the grass can rise like springs throughout most seasons.

I have not included in this brief survey, the Pytchley, nor the Atherstone, both excellent hunts with parts of their country in Leicestershire, since most of the former is in Northamptonshire, and much of the latter in Warwickshire and elsewhere. They are covered by David Reynolds in the chapter entitled *Foxhunting in the Southern Midlands* on page 146.

The thrill of Leicestershire hunting can be experienced in essence by finding a good fox in Clawson Thorns, above the Vale of Belvoir, of soaring down over the grass, taking the fly fences and timber as it comes, and if fortune smiles sweetly, by-passing Long Clawson village to take on the big, well-fenced pastures in the vale below.

Despite the depredations of so-called progress in the countryside, there are still choice coverts and stretches of country in each of the Leicestershire packs which provide remarkable riding after hounds hunting foxes found in historic coverts. It is advisable to ride a horse of some quality, which can gallop, as well as jump ditches toward in company, and the rider should concentrate and act decisively if he or she wishes to be "in the hunt" in a quick thing.

There is a competitive edge to riding to hounds over the grass in Leicestershire. If you wish to ride anywhere near the front of the field, you will position yourself and horse judiciously, and kick on with determination as soon as the Field Master gives you the office to move when a fox has gone away.

Mr and Mrs Michael Clayton

In recent years, specially constructed hunt jumps have become more common in Leicestershire, and barbed wire must be expected here and there. However, there are areas where you can choose your place in a fence – jumping timber or fly fences with ditches on a wide front. Alas, nowadays, I do not hear often enough the old cry "spread out!" as we ride up to the fences; the number of jumpable places has shrunk all too fast in recent years.

The key to knowing a foxhunting country is to learn the names and exact positions of the coverts. In Leicestershire they bear famous titles which have had special meaning for foxhunters during the past 250 years. For example, the Quorn's Botany Bay was so named because it was the furthest hack from the kennels, and therefore was likened to going into exile to the penal settlement in Australia.

Imagine Melton Mowbray as the hub of a wheel, with the hunting countries as its spokes. The Fernie country to the south is the exception, but it was originally an extension of the Quorn.

To the north-east of Melton lies the Belvoir; the Quorn is west, and has country north and south of Melton; the Cottesmore is to the south-east, with Oakham as its largest town; the Fernie, at the southerly end of the Quorn country, borders on Market Harborough.

Those who have merely swished through Leicestershire in a car on the M1 or hurtled through it in a train, tend to think of it as a rather flat, dullish Midland county. This notion will be dispelled by riding a horse up the hills to the south of the Vale of Belvoir, or up the slopes of Burrough-on-the-Hill in the Cottesmore country, overlooking the Quorn Friday country.

The Quorn continues to hunt its most pastoral, and therefore most popular, riding countries with a bitch pack on Mondays and Fridays.

The Monday country, north of Melton Mowbray, has smaller enclosures, a wealth of places to jump, but it is hit by modern road developments. The A46 road to Newark has become a four-lane highway, scything through much of the best of the Quorn country, and although fox, hounds and the mounted field have been known to cross it over a modern bridge near Willoughby, the road is not safe for horses nor hounds should the fox choose to cross the road itself.

Yet there is much fun to be had on Mondays, and there is always the chance of a dart eastwards across the famous boundary of the River Smite – in reality a meandering stream – into the neighbouring Belvoir country. The Belvoir has the same chance of a border raid if its foxes run west from such delectable coverts as Sherbrooke's or Hose Thorns.

The Quorn's Friday country below Melton is remarkably intact, with few problems caused by roads. There is some fine, wild foxhunting country around Great Dalby, as well as the three famous hunting estates I have already mentioned; all beautifully maintained and generously available to the Hunt.

The Quorn hunts its woodland and mixed farming areas to the west and north on Saturdays and Tuesdays, and smaller mounted fields enjoy a great deal of fun with the doghounds on these days.

The Belvoir hunts its famous Vale on Saturdays, inevitably a popular day, alternating between the grassier area above Melton and the more arable country below Belvoir Castle, but there are ample foxes to be found and much sport to be enjoyed throughout the Vale.

The Wednesday country mainly occupies the table of land southwards above the great Vale. It has much arable in patches, but some splendid grass and fences as well, and such famous coverts as Melton Spinney and Goadby Gorse still see the start of fine runs.

The Lincolnshire side is hunted on Tuesdays and Fridays, and offers more varied terrain, and a great deal more sport than you would imagine when driving through this corn growing county.

The Cottesmore, to the south-east of Melton Mowbray, has a delightful stretch of upland grass and fences between Oakham and Knossington in its Tuesday country, a reminder of the hunting county which abounded throughout Rutland, Britain's smallest county, which has been fighting again lately to regain independent status.

The large, well-stocked coverts of the Cottesmore ensure that there is plenty of sport four days a week (Saturdays, Mondays, Tuesdays, and Thursdays) throughout the season. The famous Owston woods always hold a multitude of foxes, but the deep going in the rides inside have earned this covert the reputation of being paved with "foxhunters' curses and lost horseshoes".

There is little problem from busy roads in the Cottesmore country, but the growth of arable farming has been immense. The Catmose Vale, between Oakham and Melton Mowbray, containing the famous Whissendine Brook, is largely down to plough nowadays, but is regularly hunted and provides a great deal of sport on Saturdays.

Land around the great reservoir, Rutland Water, east of Oakham and to the south of Uppingham, is supplied with excellent coverts and cooperative landowners and farmers, and there is hunting east of the A1 on the Lincolnshire side.

The Fernie has been reduced to a two-day a week country since the Co-operative Society banned it from its 5000 acre Stoughton estate, but the sport on Saturday and Wednesday benefits from some of the finest grassland remaining in the Midlands. Bounded to the north by the A47, the Fernie country runs down to the River Welland. Its coverts are cherished, its fences carefully maintained, and the Hunt enjoys remarkable continuity in its Mastership and staff.

Among the glories of the Harborough country are the coverts named John and Jane Ball on either side of the A50 road near Shearsby. The Lubenham Vale and the Laughton Vale are grand stretches of hunting country where the best of the old turf has a zing in it and you need a horse which can truly gallop.

Not only the countries, but the hounds and the atmosphere of the chase vary in the Leicestershire packs. The Duke of Rutland, owner of the Belvoir Hounds, adheres to the family tradition of maintaining a virtually pure pack of English-bred hounds, with none of the Welsh and other outcrosses which appear in most other foxhound kennels, except the Brocklesby, the York and Ainsty South and the County Limerick in Ireland, which had its pack transplanted from the Belvoir Kennel by Lord Daresbury after the last war.

The Quorn hounds have been bred by Captain Ronnie Wallace for some years, and therefore reflect modern lines popular in the Heythrop, Duke of Beaufort's and Exmoor kennels. The Cottesmore hounds have a noticeable infusion of Welsh blood, plus an excellent Irish line from the Carlow — introduced by their great amateur Huntsman, Captain Briain Fanshawe. The Fernie pack has Heythrop and Beaufort blood, but great care has been taken to preserve some excellent English lines from earlier breeding.

Leicestershire huntsmen, typified by the Quorn's brilliant Tom Firr at the end of the last century, have always had to be excellent horsemen as well as exhibiting high degrees of hound control. How otherwise could they show sport on farmed land, with large, hard riding fields close behind them?

Coolness under pressure is a hallmark of the huntsmen, all professionals, currently hunting the Leicestershire packs. Bruce Durno at the Fernie has been carrying the horn since 1966, and was Kennel Huntsman and whipper-in for four years previously; Michael Farrin has been Huntsman of the Quorn since 1968, and whipped in since 1963; Neil Coleman, previously Kennel Huntsman for Captain Fanshawe, has been hunting the Cottesmore hounds since 1992; and that same year Martin Thornton came from the Bicester with Whaddon Chase to hunt the Belvoir.

Watching Michael Farrin flit over the Quorn's big hedges and ditches away from Walton Thorns is a reminder that the art of jumping fences economically, always keeping the horse beautifully balanced, was invented in the hunting field.

The economic recession in the early 1990s saw some reductions in the size of Leicestershire mounted fields, but more foxhunters were returning to the Shires pack in 1994. Veterans as well as the eager young are to be found in the mounted fields.

An excellent way of tasting Leicestershire is to join the Melton Mowbray Hunt Club which since 1954 has been able to offer caps at reduced rates to its members all over Britain. The Hon Mrs Ursula ("Urky") Newton resigned in 1994 after 25 years as its Secretary, but the Club's work goes on – not least its great annual cross-country race over the cream of Leicestershire.

I should warn you that whatever you have heard about hunting in the county which generations of foxhunters have known as a paradise, you must take one risk which may affect the rest of your life – you may never want to hunt anywhere else!

Michael Clayton is Editor of Horse and Hound. *He lives in the Cottesmore country and hunts regularly in Leicestershire.*

Foxhunting in the Southern Midlands

David Reynolds

This part of the country has been subject to some major changes over the last 20 to 30 years, with more to come during the remainder of the century. It was, and still is, a marvellous, undulating part of England with some excellent hunting country. However, continual expansion of the major road and motorway system is having a marked effect as is the ever increasing spread of urbanisation. Very recently the A14 (A1-M1 link) road has been opened and, as it goes through the heart of the Woodland Pytchley and the Pytchley, both hunts must learn to live with it. Sadly it has taken a number of their best meets and coverts and they are learning from the Atherstone who have overcome many years of motorway developments. Farming, although wonderfully supportive, has become far more intensive, and the result in most of the region is that hunt jumps predominate over natural fences. These, combined with set aside, enable hunts to get around their countries remarkably well whilst continuing to show good sport.

Shooting has also become a very important and intensive industry throughout the hunt countries of the region. Relations between the sports, however, have never been better and they manage to work round each other very well. Most of the region is well foxed, although the urban spread means that there is often the risk of hunting a 'town fox', which, if he decides to go home, necessitates stopping hounds which is always unsettling.

Finally, support throughout the community in our region is substantial and still growing. The pressure of increasing mounted field sizes on all of the hunts is of concern, but it is something that is being managed well and must continue so to be. Hunting in the southern Midlands is very happy and healthy and looks forward to the next century with a great deal of confidence.

The Pytchley can be traced back many hundreds of years; in fact mention is made of the "Pitslea" in the Domesday Book during the reign of King Edward the Confessor when they hunted wolves, foxes and any vermin. However accurate records of both the Althorp and the Pytchley do not exist until 1634. In 1750 members of the Pytchley formed the Pytchley Club and were latterly known as the "White Collar Brigade". Lord Spencer of Althorp joined forces with the Pytchley Club in 1765 and he hunted hounds. It is thought that about this time both he and his Huntsman, Dick Knight, introduced the "flying method" of catching foxes which was then adopted by their then neighbours – the Quorn. Eventually the Althorp and Pytchley amalgamated. As the Pytchley country was then so large, a second pack of hounds were kept in kennels at Brigstock from 1873. This arrangement continued until 1881 when the Woodland Pytchley was formed and took over the hounds, the Brigstock kennels and that part of the country.

The Pytchley country, which is most of Northamptonshire, was famous for its huge hedges and big ditches. Whyte Melville said of it "I'll show you a country that none can surpass, with acres of woodland and oceans of grass". The famous Huntsman Stanley Barker bred the hounds smaller to go through the hedges instead of over and they still retain that size today.

However, the Pytchley country has altered greatly over the recent years due mainly to the continued construction of roads and motorways, Northamptonshire being the hub of the country's motorway network. This means that hound control is of the utmost importance and an exhibition of this can be seen by anyone watching Peter Jones, Huntsman for 23 seasons. The present Pytchley still has a strong following with fields of 100 and more of mostly local people. However, despite the country's changes, good sport can still be enjoyed with many good hunt jumps and hedges, in pursuit of those fast Pytchley bitches in full cry.

The Woodland Pytchley, as the name implies, was originally part of the Pytchley, and was hunted by the same pack of hounds until 1873. The following year a separate pack of Pytchley hounds was based at the present kennels to save travelling, hunting as the Pytchley until 1881. In that year Lord Lonsdale, the Yellow Earl, persuaded the Pytchley Masters to allow him to bring his own hounds and hunt the country and the name Woodland Pytchley was established. There have been some very famous Masters including Austin Mackenzie, George Belville, the Misses Wilson and Michael Berry (hunting correspondent of *The Daily Telegraph* and of "hunting by ear" fame). The present incumbent since 1981 is David Reynolds whose parents were both long serving Masters of the Pytchley.

The country is in Northamptonshire and the Leicestershire borders and consists of roughly one-third grass and valley land and two-thirds arable with, as the name implies, some very large woodlands. The hounds are mainly traditional English lines and in recent years a small infusion of Welsh blood has been introduced with quite a degree of success.

The present policy of maintaining the old Woodland Pytchley blood lines with occasional introduction of fresh blood appears set to take the pack very happily to the year 2000 and beyond. Support is very good, the farmers and landowners are, without exception wonderfully accommodating and relations with shooting are excellent. The country is well foxed, sport is good, and with the advent of set aside and hunt jumps, the field can get around very well and see a great deal of hounds.

The Atherstone country does not include as much of the old turf as it once did and the bullfinches that used to come thick and fast are now few and far between! Wire of varying descriptions is more plentiful so wirecutters have become an important accessory to some. However, although the odd motorway and railway occasionally give cause for a headache, the Atherstone gives plenty of fun over mixed country with numerous hunt jumps and it still has some good hedges. A fairly fit horse would be necessary as when the hounds, with their old English blood, go they take some keeping up with!

The Meynell and South Staffordshire Hunt was formed by the amalgamation of these two hunts in 1970. The varied country spans from Ashbourne in the Peak District, in the north, to Lichfield in the south.

The grass and small enclosures, with stone walls on the higher ground giving way to stout thorn hedges and ditches further south, give the Derbyshire country a certain reputation and a brave horse is required for the cream of this country.

Further south, in Staffordshire, the country is more open with some arable land and the inevitable hunt jumps. David Barker, who has carried the horn for eight seasons, shows great sport with his smart pack of bitches, bred largely on the "ST" line, back to the Carlow, and with a recent experiment of USA influence. As with many hunts, the pressure from shooting is constantly increasing.

David Reynolds is Master of the Woodland Pytchley.

....

We had some foreign visitors once who would have had a wonderful day if it was not for "those dogs in front" holding them up!

David Reynolds

Foxhunting in Central England

Ian Farquhar

The area of Central England from Bath in the south to Northampton in the north, the Severn in the west and Wallingford in the east, encompasses some of the most famous packs in foxhunting.

Dominated by the light, galloping land of the Cotswolds this region also includes the heavy clay of Warwickshire and Buckinghamshire and the loamier soils of Oxfordshire and North Wiltshire. In the main the packs are well supported, financially viable and well organised.

Major roads and urbanisation have taken their toll over the past two or three decades but no further boundary changes are in the pipeline in the foreseeable future. The communication between hunts is good and the support of the hunting fraternity to the cause had been as high as anywhere else in the kingdom.

The Duke of Beaufort's is one of the most celebrated hunts in the country and continues to run a top class four day per week establishment. It is a private pack and the management of the hounds and the stables is an admonition for anybody involved with the sport of hunting. Foxhounds have been kennelled at Badminton since the early 1700s, and are renowned throughout the world not only for their hunting ability but also for their propensity for breeding to type.

The country is varied with a predominance of walls in the north and fly fences and timber to the south, with the country around Badminton producing a mixture of them all. Good hill hunting can be enjoyed to the west along the Severn escarpment. Support in the country is of the highest order and large fields are not uncommon and can top 200 on a popular Saturday. In the main of the country the enclosures are large and a quality horse is advisable. The M4 running through the middle is well fenced.

The Joint Masters are the Duke of Beaufort and Captain Ian Farquhar who hunts the hounds. Badminton is also recognised as one of the centres of the eventing world and many top riders past and present can be seen following these hounds.

The Warwickshire in days past was famous for wet pastures and large fences and although much of the country has now been ploughed some galloping country is still available. The holding ability of the Warwickshire clay, however, cannot be underestimated especially in a wet year!

Having gained extra ground with the demise of the North Warwickshire due to urban sprawl, terrain is not a problem for this sporting pack and the Huntsman William Deakin does a good job from the kennels at Little Kineton. An enthusiastic Mastership is headed by the ebullient Mr Robin Smith Ryland and a great deal of time and effort is put into keeping the country open. The annual Warwickshire Hunt Pantomime is also a performance not to be missed.

The Bicester with Whaddon Chase, having undergone a successful amalgamation in 1986, found themselves as one of the larger countries in Central England. Although some country has been lost to major roads, there is still comfortably enough for this to remain a four day a week country. The old Bicester kennels are well situated at Stratton Audley in the centre of the country and Joint Master and successful national hunt amateur, Ian McKie, shares the horn with the popular Kennel Huntsman, Patrick Martin.

The country, now largely plough and in places heavy, nevertheless carries a good scent and on the eastern side and in the north there are still some very challenging grass areas. The hounds are fast and light and one of the best examples of recent Welsh outcrosses to be seen anywhere. The followers are keen foxhunters but in this case any outcross is almost certain to be Irish.

The Grafton, although somewhat dwarfed by the Bicester with Waddon Chase as their neighbours to the west and south, nevertheless is a friendly and well run country. Heavy and in places extensively ploughed the remaining grass areas can be as challenging to cross as anywhere in the Midlands – with the area of neutral country on the north shared with the Pytchley reminiscent of rolling Leicestershire. The kennels at Paulerspury are presided over by the Huntsman Tommy Normington who is commencing his 22nd season. No man is more popular than he. Sir Michael Connell, who heads the Mastership, has been in office since 1975 and as a high court judge sees that discipline in the country is not lacking.

The Heythrop is a large, well managed four day a week country which still maintains the high standard laid down during the Mastership of Captain Ronnie Wallace, and would rank as another of the most fashionable hunts in the country. It is now predominantly light plough interspersed with grass vale, part wall and part fly fences. The hunt staff wear the green coat of the Duke of Beaufort stemming from the days prior to 1835 when the country was hunted by the Beauforts. The hounds, kennelled at Chipping Norton, are a fine example of the best of the orthodox English and Heythrop blood appears in the majority of packs in the country. Anthony Adams, the Huntsman, a highly rated professional is no stranger to the area having been second whipper-in to Captain Wallace in the 1970s.

Although a heavily shot area, the landowners and farmer are great supporters of the chase and large fields, mostly residing within the hunt boundaries, are normal. An experienced team of local masters control a hard riding field famous for its forward bound females and a quality horse is advisable to cope with the big enclosures.

The North Cotswold is a charming if smaller country with a strongly fenced vale and a well walled hill area bordering on the Heythrop. A long tradition of amateur huntsmen is presently upheld by Mr Nigel Peel who moved in 1988 from the Chiddingfold, Leconfield and Cowdray after a lengthy and popular Mastership. Support in the country is strong and the hounds kennelled in the centre of the country at Broadway are on the up having experienced a lean time in the mid-1980s. The best of the bloodlines made famous by Captain Brian Fanshawe are again in ascendancy. Market gardening flourishes in the Evesham Vale and it is not uncommon to see hounds drawing a covert of brussel sprouts. The North Cotswold has long been known for its tight sporting community who enjoy stealing a march on some of their more fashionable neighbours.

The Cotswold country situated mainly to the east and south of Cheltenham is predominantly a hill country with extensive woodland on the east side and pockets of open country in between. Largely unaffected by main roads, it suits the 'hound man' and the kennels at Andoversford boast a good hunting pack with a strong recent injection of Fell blood. Both the senior Master and Huntsman, Mr Tim Unwin, and Roland Sheppard, the Kennel Huntsman, have been in office together for over a quarter of a century and a wealth of knowledge predominates. The Cotswold is not a hard riding country but a delightful terrain in which to see a carefully bred and effective pack of hounds going about its business.

The Berkeley: In the sixteenth and seventeenth century the Earls of Berkeley hunted the stag from the Severn to Berkeley Square in London and the Masters and hunt staff still wear the distinctive yellow Berkeley livery – the only other pack to do so being the Vale of Aylesbury. This tradition dates back to that time. The kennels are situated close to Berkeley Castle, the home of Major John Berkeley who owns and breeds the hounds which are famous as a fine pack of orthodox English foxhounds. The present Huntsman, Chris Maiden, comes from one of the best known families of professional huntsmen in England.

The country today has sadly been affected by both the M4 and M5 and some of the best of the vale has been lost. However, a good day can still provide one of the most challenging rides to be had anywhere in England and it is particularly renowned for the size of the rhines or big ditches.

Captain Ian Farquhar, Master and Huntsman of the Duke of Beaufort's hounds

The hill country on the edge of the Severn escarpment is particularly attractive and can provide some wonderful hound hunts in the wooded valleys. The present Mastership is headed by Mrs Buster Daniell who joined in 1976 and she, with her husband John Daniell, a renowned amateur steeplechaser, are famous for crossing the country. The Berkeley are well known for their friendly outlook and hospitality.

The Vale of the White Horse (VWH) is another four day a week pack in the area. It formed from an amalgamation in 1964 of the Earl Bathurst's and the Cricklade. The country is varied with a predominance of pasture in the south, fairly wired with some heavy plough, but with a much lighter and more easily accessible stone wall country to the north. Extensive woodland around Cirencester Park allows protracted spring hunting and the country is generally well managed and maintained.

The kennels, situated at Meysey Hampton, are those of the old Cricklade and the Huntsman, Sidney Bailey, is one of the most experienced in the land having hunted these hounds full time, except for six years jointly with Mr Martin Scott, since 1966. The hounds are bred by Mr Scott, one of the world's greatest exponents of the stud book, and now have two interesting outcrosses to Fell and American. The Mastership is headed by Mr Bill Reid who has done much for public relations and the country boasts a modern outlook to the problems for foxhunting at the end of the twentieth century.

The Old Berkshire covers three different areas; light Cotswold brush to the north, heavy loam in the centre running into the chalky Berkshire downland in the south. Much of the centre of the country is plough but areas of grass are to be found throughout. The kennels are situated near Faringdon and John Smith is the current Kennel Huntsman. Until recently the hounds were bred for nearly 30 years by the late Mr Colin Marsh and are neat and active. The present Mastership is headed by Miss Allsopp and Mr Tony Carter hunts the hounds.

Ian Farquhar is Master and Huntsman of the Duke of Beaufort's hounds. Previously he was Master and Huntsman of the Bicester.

....

Warwickshire 1965

Telephone conversation during busiest period of cub-hunting.

10.35 pm Senior Subscriber,

"Sorry to bother you old boy, can you tell me where the meet is on Saturday?"

Brian Fanshawe answers from deep sleep,

"Can't quite think just now – let you know in the morning."

4.30 am Brian Fanshawe to Senior Subscriber,

"Golden Cross 6.15 – don't be late."

Senior subscriber,

"Uumrr....."

Brian Fanshawe

Foxhunting in East Anglia

Ted Barclay

Anybody who passes to or from London along the major roads in the Eastern counties might be forgiven for thinking that it is an unattractive area for foxhunting. He will imagine himself toiling across an endless flat landscape, huge fields of winter wheat and oil seed rape, divided, not by hedges, but by motorways, railways and new towns. He would be suffering from a serious misconception.

It is true that modern development has a had a detrimental effect on East Anglia, as it has on most other parts of the British Isles. The proximity of London, and its overspill towns has swallowed up a good deal of hunting country, but this is a process which has been going on for a long time. The Hon Grantley Berkeley, writing in the mid-nineteenth century complained of the growth of London, "The very place is now covered with suburban villas where my father shot the highwayman." Sporting activities were thus being curtailed by development even then.

The spread of London to the north has, however, tended to follow the main roads and has left large areas of relatively unspoilt country in between. Thus the kennels of the Puckeridge are only 35 miles as the crow flies from Charing Cross, and yet there remains another pack, the Enfield Chase, between them and London. Sadly it is no longer possible to reach meets of the Enfield Chase by London Underground.

Some countries have been affected by motorways. The M1 through the Oakley country, the A1 through the Fitzwilliam, the M11 through the Puckeridge and Essex, although as these partly follow the existing railway lines much of the country lost was already not regularly hunted. In addition much of East Anglia, situated as it is with The Wash to the north and the North Sea to the east, is not on the way to anywhere. There remain therefore, large areas, particularly in Norfolk and Suffolk with no major roads at all. Even in North Hertfordshire there are villages whose population has actually declined over the past hundred years.

Modern agriculture has had its inevitable effect on the countryside. In places, woods and hedgerows have been removed and a prairie landscape created, but this is by no means general. The twin interests of hunting and shooting have ensured the survival of the majority of these features. It is easily forgotten that in many areas the great age of woodland destruction was not in the 1960s but in the 1860s. Driving through East Anglia today one is tempted to think that the 1980s will be regarded as a great age of woodland and hedgerow planting.

The change to winter cropping has made getting across country more difficult in the early part of the season but has, if anything, improved scenting conditions. Compulsory set aside has certainly improved one's ability to get about, and we look forward to the probability of many headlands being permanently set aside. Newcomers are warned, however, of the perils of galloping across set aside in the wet. It rides very heavy and will bring your horse up very short.

Contrary to popular belief, there are areas of old grass in East Anglia and there are even jumpable hedges. It would, however, be only fair to admit that these are not common, and in some countries one could hunt for many days without actually discovering such delights. There are, however, advantages to an arable country, for there is little use for barbed wire, and queuing up at gateways is most unusual. The many trackways and "green lanes" make crossing the country far easier, and faster than one might expect. A man who expects to leap a long line of well laid hedges and is not prepared to negotiate some very deep ditches is advised to seek his sport elsewhere.

A tricky ditch!

The going can vary tremendously. Much of the area is heavy clay; rock hard when dry and bottomless glue when wet. The Puckeridge variety is particularly adept at pulling the shoes off horses, whilst much of the West Norfolk is a light, sandy soil. The latter is preferable when it comes to cleaning one's coat at the end of the day, and a good coat is required.

Sportsmen from the north should not be taken in by talk of the "Soft South" especially when the east wind blows. There is no higher point between the East Anglian Heights and the Ural mountains, and those parts which are rumoured to be below sea level are not much warmer.

None of the East Anglian packs can be said to have a good scenting country. In general, the wetter the country, the better scent will lie. Hounds have therefore tended to be bred more for nose than speed, and it is in watching hounds work that one of the great joys of East Anglian hunting is to be found. The large, unenclosed fields are an advantage as being able to see what is going on is much easier for the follower, mounted or on foot, than in many more fashionable areas.

Being a bad scenting area is an additional test of the skills of both Huntsman and whip. On days when hounds can hardly own the line of a fox at all, the success of the day lies squarely on their shoulders, for they must outguess their fox. For this reason East Anglia is a very good training ground for amateur and professional huntsmen, and many of the more successful ones have served their time in East Anglia. The great Tom Firr, Huntsman of the Quorn was born and brought up at the Puckeridge Kennels and the late Major Bob Hoare of the Cottesmore came from the West Norfolk to name but two.

Many of the oldest packs of hounds are found in East Anglia. The Puckeridge dates from 1725. It has always had a history of long masterships which some, quite unfairly, attribute to the stickiness of the mud. The current Senior Master, Captain C G E Barclay's family took over the hounds in 1896.

The Fitzwilliam (Milton) date from 1769 but hounds have hunted the park at Milton since the time of Richard II. The West Norfolk claims to date back to 1534 but it is questionable what, or who, they were hunting then. They have the distinction of having had a Prime Minister as a Master (Robert Walpole), but it is feared that they are unlikely to have another. King Edward VII often hunted with them as Prince of Wales, before progressing to the Shires. He seems to have learnt well for on his first visit to the Pytchley, the Huntsman, Charles Payne, was asked his opinion of the Prince of Wales. "Make a capital King, my Lord" he replied, "Sits so well!".

The Essex was once known as "The Shires of the East". It would no longer warrant this description, but retains some excellent and quite wild plough country in Roothings area.

The East Essex is another heavy plough country but has some old grass towards the coastal marshes. Both the Essex and Suffolk have good, wild countryside with few roads of any size. They would be the envy of far more fashionable hunts if only they were down to grass!

The East Anglian hunts have shown remarkable resilience over the years, but there have been inevitable changes. The Essex Farmers and Essex Union have amalgamated their two small countries to form the Essex Farmers and Union. The Puckeridge amalgamated in 1970 with the Newmarket and Thurlow but have recently reverted to their former boundaries, whilst a new pack, the Thurlow, hunts the Newmarket and Thurlow country. The Thurlow have, arguably, some of the best East Anglian hunting country.

The Downham foxhounds were disbanded in 1934 and their territory reverted back to the West Norfolk. The Hertfordshire amalgamated in 1970 to form the Vale of Aylesbury and are thus no longer a subject for this chapter, but some of their territory went to extend the diminishing country of the Enfield Chase.

The Cambridgeshire has been somewhat cut about by roads and the overspill from Cambridge but still have some good sport. The Oakley still retains its boundaries of 1800 and has some good country, particularly on the Northamptonshire side.

All hunts in this area are pestered by saboteurs on occasions but the situation is no worse, and in many cases much better, than in other parts. This is another problem that has been going on a long time as illustrated by the diaries of Mr E E Barclay's Harriers for 1881 "Met at Cromer – Poor Day – Beset by a mob of cads".

The make up of an East Anglian hunting field is as varied as it is in any other part of the Kingdom. Sadly there are fewer hunting farmers partly because it is more difficult to keep a horse on an all arable farm than one geared for stock rearing. Many packs still attract subscribers from London as they have ever since the coming out of the railways, which opened up the sport to a wider following. Sadly the railways have not improved things lately for the London hunter as they no longer accept your horse on a train. The improvement of roads has meant that it is almost as easy to get to the Shires from London as it is to get to East Anglia, and many people who start hunting in this part of the world decamp to the Shires when they feel bold enough.

A large Saturday field is normally about 80 strong with half that number on a weekday. Numbers tend to decline as the season progresses, due to the opening of the point-to-point season, and casualties normally caused by skiing.

Some hunts only venture out on weekdays, notably the Thurlow who hunt on Mondays and Thursdays. For those with time available weekday hunting can often be the most rewarding, especially during the shooting season. Saturday shooting often restricts the huntable country available. After the end of the shooting season (1 February) more of the country is open for hunting, and often the best sport is shown.

Subscription rates vary between hunts and are often complex. Most hunts will offer much reduced rates for children and young adults. However, the age at which a child becomes an adult also varies. It is always best to contact the secretary to get the full details. Many hunts do not charge at all during autumn hunting.

In general visitors are welcome but it is essential to contact the secretary beforehand as meets may have to be changed, or restrictions put on numbers in very wet conditions.

A newcomer to East Anglian hunting should not expect to have to jump huge upright obstacles, as there are not very many and there is normally a way round. The ability to negotiate ditches is, however, important in most countries. It is also inadvisable, until you know the country and the Field Master well, to take your own line. The ability to recognise growing crops and avoid riding on them is also appreciated, so until you are certain, follow the Field Master, and you can still have a lot of sport hunting in East Anglia.

Ted Barclay farms in the Puckeridge Country where his father is Master.

....

It was a particularly dry early March. All day tractors had been working down the land ready for spring drilling. Hounds had met at 12.00 and had not done much, as one might expect in this part of the world when dust is blowing out behind the harrows. It was late by the time we drew back to our home farm, and almost dark when we found our last fox in Laundry Gorse. And on this fox they fled. A big circuit through Reaches Wood and Oxbury before turning back toward Laundry Gorse. By this time it was quite dark, as I galloped along a wide trackway, looking out to my right through the gloom for the hounds, which I could hear but not see. At this moment my horse gave a huge, and quite unexpected leap. I was quite taken aback. Indeed I was very nearly on my back.

I managed to stop and readjust my position and ride back to see what we had jumped. It was a four metre wide double set of disc harrows. We had cleared it, draw bar and all.

Ted Barclay

Foxhunting South of the Thames

John Robson

South of the Thames, where traditionally the young man has been advised not to hunt, has probably as much claim as anywhere in Great Britain to being the birthplace of foxhunting, with records of two packs of hounds having been maintained at Charlton, near Goodwood, in the mid-seventeenth century for the purpose of hunting foxes. By 1720, when the Duke of Richmond had acquired Goodwood, it was considered to be the "Melton Mowbray" of the day, with visitors, male and female, coming from far and wide, even across the Channel, to stay at Charlton for the foxhunting. It even provoked the neighbouring Duke of Somerset, who owned Petworth at the time, to set up a rival establishment.

The Old Surrey and Burstow hunting in the early autumn

It was the open country of the Downs emerging from the wooded Weald that provided the attractive venue for this new branch of venery. Traditionally hares were hunted in the more open parts of the country and deer in the wooded areas. At about this time many of the aristocratic packs, such as the Belvoir in the Midlands, were switching from deer to fox. Also many of the nobles, who had property close to London such as the Earls of Berkeley, north of London, and the Earls of Derby, south of London, realised they could start hunting establishments on the open Chilterns or North Downs. Thus the area round Croydon became an attractive centre for hunting and it was not long before the merchants and businessmen of London saw the attraction and Croydon soon replaced Charlton as the "Melton Mowbray" of the south, with packs like the Old Surrey and Surrey Union, supported by London tradesmen rather than landowners, becoming well established.

In between the North and South Downs, as the forest became cleared and fields became enclosed, local packs of harriers owned by small landowners and squires proliferated throughout the Weald and on the marshes until, by the end of the nineteenth century, in excess of seven packs of stag-hounds, 15 packs of foxhounds and 30 packs of harriers existed in Kent, Sussex and Surrey.

Inside the boundaries defined by the Thames in the north, and the English Channel on the east and south, was as wide a variety of terrain and scenery as could be found in the rest of England. Running parallel east and west are the two great chalk ridges of the North and South Downs which offered great vistas over steep valleys and hills of wonderful grass going interspersed with hanging woods and gorse brakes; between them lay the heavily wooded Weald out of which emerged sandy ridges and hills supporting large tracts of heathland in Surrey and in Ashdown Forest. To the east it gave way to the fertile Medway and Stour valleys which supported much fruit and hop growing and whose edges merged in with the north Kent marshes along the Thames, and the marshes of Pevensey and Romney along the south coats. Between the World Wars this part of England offered as big a variety of hunting as could be found anywhere, the main drawback being the holding nature of the extremely heavy wealden clay and the lack of drainage in the pre-War agricultural depression made it extremely hard going for the horses.

Today the market towns, large or small, have turned into urban centres attached to which may be airports, such as Gatwick, or seaports such as Sheerness. New towns have been planted and the coastal strip covered with concrete, but in between there are still many unspoilt pockets, and to look at the many extensive views over the wooded Weald, little seems to have changed. These pockets however have been marred by the installation of the ground electric rail on the railways and nose to tail traffic to and from the coast on both the A roads and the newly built motorways. The dwellings about the place, previously 90 per cent occupied by countrymen, professional or manual, whose work and recreation depended entirely on the countryside, are now owned by people whose attitude to the country is somewhere between Disneyland and a theme park.

Nevertheless there is enough real country left in Kent, Sussex and Surrey to support 10 packs of foxhounds, six packs of beagles and two packs of mink hounds and more than enough people to ensure that by enjoying the sport provided they can play their part in maintaining the traditional country life of England.

For those not inconsiderable numbers whose work confines them to an urban background, but whose heart still beats and yearns for the countryside, rural recreation on foot or horse is still available. An afternoon in the summer, meandering along a Sussex stream with the mink hounds; a wild winter's day on the Kent marshes with the beagles, in the sight of thousands of wild geese on their winter feeding grounds; or the feeling of elation galloping over the old downland turf on a spring days foxhunting with the sea on one side of you and the glorious Weald laid out like a map to the other side of you, are moments that are still available to the hunter and which obliterate the many hideousities of modern times.

Starting at the western end of the country we find the Chiddingfold, Leconfield and Cowdray, one of the biggest hunting countries in the British Isles, which extends south from Guildford to the coast and, while largely wooded in the north, it has an attractive vale country by the River Rother, near Pulborough, before running up into the South Downs. This pack is, of course, a direct descendant of the old Charlton Hunt, and hunting with them on the hills means that you are hunting with history.

Next to them to the east are the Crawley and Horsham whose country extends from Horsham to the coast. They too have an attractive bit of hill country on the South Downs embracing the training gallops at Findon and such well-known landmarks as Chanctonbury and Cissbury Rings. Their vale is attractive and, in places, testing, and to the north they have woodland hunting with its own charm.

North of them lies Surrey Union which again is predominantly a woodland country but has the advantage of the greensand ridge and heathy outcrops of Leith Hill and Holmbury Hill and, while the northern part of their country still embraces the North Downs, areas which they can hunt are becoming restricted. However, there are still days to be had within sight of the urban sprawl to the north.

Moving east from the Surrey Union, there is the Old Surrey and Burstow who stretch from the outskirts of Croydon to Haywards Heath and are split from their neighbours by the spine of the M23 and A23 running from London to Brighton, via Gatwick. Starting in the north, their country embraces the North Downs and like the Surrey Union there are still days to be had within sight of London, and, in fact, the Old Surrey is probably the only hunt left who meet inside the ring of the M25. South of the M25 the Old Surrey still have a vale country where some formidable fences can be encountered but which sadly has been split in half by the addition of ground electric rail to the track running from the Tunnel via Tonbridge and Redhill. South of the vale beyond the heathland of Ashdown Forest there are the woodlands of the high Weald which provide much sport.

Moving south we find the Southdown and Eridge, the north part of their country being much like the Old Surrey and Burstow's southern woodland country, before coming to their vale, which stretches through the farmland which embraces Plumpton Racecourse and gives way to the escarpment signifying the start of the Downs which provides much of their hunting country today. This stretches from above Brighton, embraces the old Lewes Racecourse and Firle Beacon and reaches the Cuckmere valley at Alfriston.

Still moving eastwards, we come to the East Sussex and Romney Marsh who extend along the coast nearly to Rye and go northward in Kent to Appledore. This is probably the wildest of all the south-east countries, again with the great variation from the Downs above Eastbourne to the marshes, both Pevensey and Romney. Marsh hunting has its own appeal which does not demand a great deal of jumping, and they are lucky to have enough downland country to add to the variation from their primarily wooded terrain where, as in most south-eastern countries, timber fences are in the preponderance.

To the north of them lies the Ashford Valley, who, like the Romney Marsh Harriers, switched from hare to fox between the Wars and hunt a typical bit of heavy Kent clay country and the Medway Valley running out of Tonbridge which bounds its eastern territory. The north of this country is cut off from its neighbours by the motorways and railways, extending from the Channel Tunnel.

To the north of the Ashford Valley running up to the Thames Marshes lies the West Kent, a hunt of considerable antiquity, which in the past had the benefit of the North Downs round Brands Hatch, today severely curtailed by motorways but there still are the advantages of the north Kent Cooling marshes to give a change. The south of the West Kent country is very like the Old Surrey vale and there are extensive woodlands in the middle of the country.

Next to the eastwards, running right up to the coast at Margate, lies another pack that was established back in the eighteenth century, the Tickham, who have recently joined up with a pack to their east, the West

Street, whose country runs down the Kent coast as far as Dover. As one would expect, the country is interspersed with orchards and woodland, and the inevitable arable. But the marshland, including the Isle of Sheppey, gives this Hunt elbow room and a chance to see hounds hunting, which is so valuable for beginners in the sport.

To complete the list, the East Kent are established south of the West Street Tickham and are bounded on their west by the Ashford Valley and the Romney Marsh, while to the south is the coast between Dover and Rye. The north of their country has some large stretches of cultivated downland and there are big wooded areas in which hunting can freely continue, but unfortunately the M20 motorway and the electric railway to the Channel Tunnel split the country in two.

So far as all the foxhound packs are concerned in the south-east, the modern world is sadly only too restrictive. The lack of country available for hunting is probably more noticeable in the south-east of England than in any other region outside the major urban centres. This means that all the foxhunts in the south-east have to take the greatest care of the interests of the farmers and landowners, and make sure that they do not put excessive pressure on the land or the patience of their hosts in welcoming the sport. Therefore anybody wishing to visit a pack in the south-east should go to immense pains to contact the Secretaries of the Hunts they wish to visit, and ensure they are welcome and on what terms. Those who are able to get a taste of hunting in the south-east will find foxhounds as good-looking and as well up to their tasks as any in England and as many foxes as will ever be needed in a day's hunting.

John Robson lives in the Old Surrey and Burstow country where he was Master from 1974 to 1986. He has also been Master of the Crowhurst Otter Hounds, whipper-in to the Ramle Vale Hunt in Palestine and hunted his own pack of hounds in the Old Surrey Country.

Foxhunting in Hampshire, Berkshire and Wiltshire

Simon Clarke

Urbanisation, busy roads, railway lines and serious shooting are amongst the problems the Masters have to cope with in this area. However, there are still some marvellous wild pockets where real good sport can be enjoyed. In many countries, shooting has gone hand-in-hand with the foxhunting for more than a century, and the cooperation is outstanding. Good communications and a high population, in the main, bring a large following, both mounted and on foot, and the economics, in spite of a difficult climate, are sound and consequently standards are maintained. As with most things in life, the more you put in, the more you can take out – hunting is no exception and enthusiasm and dedication can still produce sparkling sport on restricted pitches.

Taking the countries of the area alphabetically, the Avon Vale has a strongly fenced, good scenting grass vale, but the country is interspersed with numerous towns. However, they have a great tradition of sporting farmers who make the hounds very welcome. George Hyatt, previously Master of the South Devon and Huntsman of the Curre and the Tipperary, is the professional Huntsman. He has a great reputation across the country, having been a prominent point-to-point rider and he produces good sport for the thrusters.

The Garth and South Berks is one of several celebrated packs near London which have amalgamated. The M4 runs through the country, but Ian Langrish, in his 25th season as Huntsman, knows the difficulties well. There are many large woodlands, which ride deep but carry a scent. They are a particularly good looking pack of hounds, going back to those of Colonel Rodney Palmer. The Colonel was a brother-in-law of the late Sir Peter Farquhar and had access to the very best blood. Mr Bob Phillips carried on the lines during his Mastership and the present breeders have a very sound base to build on.

The HH (Hampshire Hunt) is a well-run country and probably the best supported in the area. A very strong Mastership is headed by Mr John Gray, who farms widely and is a leading figure in the countryside – he is in his 30th season. Hopper Cavendish is a top class hunter judge and takes charge of the hound breeding, while Mr Andreae is a landowner whose family have been involved over many years. The country has large woodlands, but the open areas are well provided with jumping places. There are some very good shoots, but first class cooperation exists between the two sports, which has been built up by diplomatic Masters and huntsmen over a long period. Bob Collins is the enthusiastic and popular Huntsman. His brother is at the Seavington, while another brother is a gamekeeper. They spring from a Somerset family of sporting farmers.

The Hursley Hambledon perhaps has more problems than its neighbour, but the Huntsman, Douglas Hunt, is in his 30th season, having started under the celebrated Colonel Frank Mitchell. Mr and Mrs Peter Humphrey, who have large agricultural business interests locally, have been Senior Masters for 12 seasons, and Mrs Humphrey takes great trouble both in the country and breeding the hounds. There is some lovely open downland to the west of the kennels at Droxford, and this experienced team produces a lot of fun.

The Isle of Wight has little trouble with invasion by its neighbours, but does have a very strong local following. There are plenty of thick, good, holding gorses, interspersed with rolling, galloping country, while there is some intensive vegetable protection on the low ground. Mr Michael Poland, after a long spell as Master of the Hambledon, where he still resides, has been Master for 12 seasons. A studious and successful hound breeder, he has recently also turned his attention to the turf, and bred and half-owned Kings Theatre, only just beaten in the 1994 epic Derby and winner of the George VI Diamond Stakes at Ascot. Henry Cecil has judged at the Puppy Show, which is a particularly hospitable event, with many visitors from the mainland being entertained by Mr and Mrs Poland, and his Huntsman, Giles Wheeler, who previously whipped-in at Badminton.

The New Forest hounds are hunted by the writer, but thanks to Sir Newton Rycroft's breeding, they are a good working pack with an above-average cry, which is useful in the Forest. The country is 60 per cent woodland and the remainder open heath, with bogs and plenty of heather, bracken and gorse, and also people! There are over nine million visitors a year, but the area is hunted by the foxhounds, the buckhounds, and the beagles. With careful organisation and great cooperation from the authorities it is still a fine country to see and hear the hounds. Being very good scenting, all three packs run at a good pace. There are plenty of hirelings and visitors are very welcome.

The Royal Artillery are enjoying a very successful time. Colonel John Jago had nine good seasons, and the new Master, Major Jonathon Seed, showed splendid sport last season. The hunting is mainly on Salisbury Plain, with plenty of opportunities to see the hounds without too much inconvenience from having to jump. However, the Plain produces its own hazards and a handy horse is desirable. Support for this pack has increased of late and there are often over 60 riders out.

The Tedworth are fortunate to have the services of Captain Rupert Inglesant as Master and Huntsman. His father was a distinguished Secretary of the Quorn Hounds, and Rupert is an accomplished race rider. David Jukes, ex-Huntsman of the Zetland, is Kennel Huntsman and 1st Whipper-In. The country is mainly arable, with some downland and plenty of shooting. The present incumbents have produced good sport, and morale in the country is extremely high.

The Vine and Craven are hunted by Mr Richard Hill, who formerly hunted the Spooners and West Dartmoor – quite a contrast. He has the assistance of Mr Robin Mackenzie as Joint Master, whose local knowledge and public relations skills must be invaluable. It is, for the main part, light galloping downland, with some fine country about Kingsclere. The racing community around Lambourn are very supportive.

The Wilton are enjoying a 'golden age'. Mr James Bouskell, a keen shooting man, gained the confidence and support of the shooting community during his Mastership 1983-1991, and created a first rate organisation. To the delight of everyone, he has rejoined the Mastership; meanwhile his wife is also a Master and has bred a good pack. Lady Traill, an elegant former Lady Mayoress of London, completes a Mastership of the highest quality. Peter Barker is well established as professional Huntsman and, although this is a cold scenting chalk down country, he gets his hounds to run well. The country is very well jumped.

The South and West Wilts is a very large country with tremendous variety, stretching from Salisbury Plain, over the Wiltshire Downs, to the Knoyle Vale on the east end of the Blackmore Vale, with some big Somerset woodlands and the very deep Witham Vale to the north-west. David Herring, a very experienced Master and Huntsman, is in charge. There are no large towns and plenty of elbow room, and fields tend to be small. Both vales are strongly fenced and need a bold horse with stamina. The lines created by Ikey Bell flow strongly through the blood of the present pack, who take some keeping with when the vale or downs are wet.

Simon Clarke is currently Master and Huntsman of the New Forest: he has previously hunted the South Dorset, the Cottesmore, the Duke of Buccleuch's and the South and West Wilts. He is a well-known hound judge.

Foxhunting in the South-West

Biddy Wingfield Digby

Hunting in the south-west has fewer problems than in most other parts of the country. Primarily it is a very rural area with the main industry being agriculture. There are no large industrial towns, and really all those who hunt in these countries derive their income from the land.

There are a number of large estates and a fair amount of shooting syndicates. A tremendous number of farmers hunt, and in most cases enjoy being hosts to their hounds.

Every hunt has a strong hunt supporters club. The "urgency" may not be so great as in the Shires or Midlands but the atmosphere and genuine friendliness of the hunting people, combined with the marvellous varied countryside with its vales, hills, woodland, forests and coast line make it a very special place to be and to enjoy hunting amongst such a sporting fraternity.

A fall with Blackmore and Sparkford Vale

The most northern of the south-west hunting countries is the Mendip. The country lies between the outskirts of Bristol, Cheddar Gorge and Shepton Mallet, where the fields are divided by dry stone walls which are the main feature of this country.

Many point-to-point horses, including Double Silk, are qualified here and there is a contingent of business people from Bristol who hunt. The going in most parts is good, but they do suffer from more than their share of fog. The average size of the field is 30.

The Blackmore and Sparkford Vale is the best known pack in the south-west; in pre-war days it was known as "The Meynell of the West". People in most parts of England will have heard of its big fences. It is virtually a totally Vale country which stretches from Shepton Mallet in the north to Sturminster Newton in Dorset in the south. There are no hills, and only one large wood called Penselwood which is where the last meet of the season is held in early March.

The pack hunts three or four days a week and a large proportion of the field are farmers. The average size of a field is 75. Visitors are welcome but should apply to the secretary. The Vales ride deep, which makes jumping the big fences quite formidable and the Blackmore Vale produces bold horses and bold riders with strong characters!

The Taunton Vale is also primarily a vale country and has few woods or hills. Hunting finishes in the middle of March – it is a two-day-a-week pack, hunting on Fridays and not Saturdays. The average size of the field is between 35-40. Unfortunately the M5 motorway goes through part of the country and also the A358 eats through a large section. There is also quite a lot of arable land, but it is well organised with hunt jumps. Visitors and children are welcome if it is not too wet, and the hunt is renowned for it's friendly atmosphere and strong Hunt Supporters Club.

The Seavington country is long and narrow, stretching from Langport in Somerset to Bridport in the county of Dorset. It is 40 miles long, and eight miles wide in most places. They have Masters for either end of the country and a professional Huntsman. There are no real hills – only the soft undulating West Dorset downs. The Marshwood Vale has big fly fences on banks and the country is well served throughout with hunt jumps. In the north of the country the main characteristic is the rhines – which are bottomless brooks! The A303 dual carriageway running through the country is a menace to those going hunting.

The Seavington is totally a farmers pack, and fields average 25. Although very well turned out, ratcatcher is most welcome. It is a very happy, friendly hunt with a lovely pack of hounds. It has a reputation for having no hunting politics, and visitors are welcome at all times.

The Portman Hunt, which borders the Blackmore Vale and South Dorset is a famous country with vales and big woods. It also has a largely hilly country where hunting goes on into April. The going in the vales is deep clay, and the fences as big as you will find anywhere. There are, however, many hunt jumps through this well-managed country, with its friendly and fun atmosphere. The average size of the field is 45-50. They have a first class pack of hounds which hunt equally well on the hills or in the vales.

The South Dorset Hunt is well renowned for taking on young inexperienced Masters to hunt the hounds. Most of these have risen to great heights. Simon Clarke and Alastair Jackson both started their hunting careers here. It is basically a farmers pack, with a very happy, friendly atmosphere. Subscribers' children can hunt free until they are 16 years old. The field is always strengthened and enlivened by a few young soldiers stationed at Bovington Camp. The country is tremendously varied, running from the sea and the Purbeck Hills in the south to adjoin the famous Blackmore Vale in the north where they have a delectable piece of vale. Hunting continues well into April in the hills, by the Poole Estuary in Wareham Forest and on the Tank Tracks near Bovington Camp. Visitors and children are always welcome. The average size of the field is 50.

Lastly, although they are harriers, no description of foxhunting in the south-west would be complete without including the Cotley. This famous private pack of West Country harriers belongs to the Eames family, who founded them in 1797 and a member of the family has been Master ever since. Although the hounds are registered in the Harrier and Beagle Stud Book they only hunt foxes, and show great sport in their beautiful, hilly country on the border of Devon and Somerset. Vyvyan Eames has hunted the hounds since 1974. They meet on Wednesdays and Saturdays. Visitors are welcome by prior arrangement.

Biddy Wingfield Digby lives on the border of the Blackmore and Sparkford Vale, South Dorset and Portman countries. Previously she was Master of the Blackmore and Sparkford Vale.

Foxhunting in Devon and West Somerset

Claude Berry

My earliest hunting recollections date from 45 years ago when I started to hunt with the Mid Devon during the second of Major A C Arden's three Masterships of that pack. "The Major" had kept the pack going through the war and was a man with a nice turn of phrase – on one occasion, when his whipper-in had committed some minor misdemeanour, instead of the usual "get the gun" I heard him roar the less flattering "get the humane killer". The sound of the Master and his hounds homeward bound in the dusk was music to the ears of many a Dartmoor publican.

Since those days hunting in Devon has changed but not, perhaps, as greatly as in many other parts of Britain. Now, as then, Devon hunting can be divided into two categories: moorland hunting and "in country" ("in-bye" as a Northerner would say).

Dartmoor and Exmoor provide the opportunity to gallop for miles and to watch hounds work unhindered by trunk roads, railways or sprawling towns. The difference between the two is neatly summed up in the old saying: "On Exmoor you can ride anywhere except where you can't; on Dartmoor you can't ride anywhere except where you can". The visitor needs to keep a look out for bogs – it is often wiser to follow someone who knows the moor – and, on Dartmoor, hidden rocks. On Exmoor there is no jumping; on Dartmoor the occasional stone wall. Those who dislike getting wet should not consider hunting here, particularly in mid-winter. Because of the unspoiled nature of the country, this type of hunting has changed relatively little in my lifetime.

In country change has been more noticeable. The area under trunk roads has increased but the railways have decreased. Devon, however, remains an agricultural county best suited, due to its high rainfall, to the growing of grass. The greatest curse, from the point of view of those who hunt to ride, has been the advent of the mechanical hedge-cutter. Until about 1960, many of the in-country packs had a fair amount of jumping. In west Devon, in particular, there were banks which, though not big by Irish standards, required a clever horse and a bold rider. Today, however, due to the hedge-cutter, most of these banks are unjumpable.

It also has to be said that since farming has become more intensive, farmers are less keen on seeing holes knocked in their fences by members of a large field jumping one bank in the same place. A well-known former Master of the East Devon used to solve this problem by jumping the easiest part of the bank and then calling over his shoulder "Don't all follow me!"

Farming in Devon consists mainly of small family units. On the better land, dairy farms are found; with beef and sheep on the colder, wetter clay. The land tends to be heavy although in the south and east of the country the soil is lighter and more grain is grown. One of the joys of hunting in Devon is the abundance of grass. In the whole of last season with the Tiverton, I doubt if I went through as many as ten ploughed or sown fields. This should fill any East Anglian with envy.

From the visitor's point of view, the moorland packs are the most attractive and indeed the Exmoor packs, in particular, draw huge fields, mainly in the spring. Hunting on the moor continues longer than elsewhere and the old practice of killing a May fox is still observed in one or two places.

Three packs of foxhounds hunt on Exmoor, the most famous being the eponymous pack whose Master and Huntsman since 1977 has been Captain R E Wallace. Ronnie Wallace has bred an outstanding pack of hounds and Exmoor blood now features predominantly in many kennels throughout the foxhunting world. The Dulverton (West), where that superb horseman Bertie Hill has been a Joint Master since 1975, hunt a lovely stretch of south and west Exmoor and the Dulverton (East) hunt, unsurprisingly, to their east.

Dartmoor is hunted by four packs: the South Devon, the Dartmoor, the Spooners and West Dartmoor, and the Mid Devon. The South Devon, among whose former Masters was the extraordinarily gifted hound man George Templer of Stover (1781-1843), hunt a small but attractive part of the moor around Haytor and Widecombe. The Dartmoor have long had a strong naval connexion due to the proximity of Dartmouth, Devonport and Plymouth and one of their most famous Masters (from 1919 to 1940) was Commander Davy, who is shown with his hounds crossing the West Dart in the well-known print by Lionel Edwards. The Spooners and West Dartmoor hunt the western part of the moor from their kennels at Sampford Spiney, and the Mid Devon, who are kennelled at Chagford, hunt the north-east.

These Dartmoor packs have often proved stepping stones in the careers of young men who have subsequently moved up country after gaining their early experience of hunting hounds in the demanding environment of a Dartmoor winter. Willie Poole, now best known as a writer, hunted the Dartmoor for three seasons and Adrian Dangar, now Master of the Sinnington, cut his teeth with the Spooners and West Dartmoor. By contrast Bernard Parker, the popular Huntsman of the Mid Devon, has been in service with that pack since 1958.

Two former hare-hunting packs, the Modbury Harriers and the Dart Vale and South Pool Harriers, hunt foxes. Both hunt in the south of the county and the latter, unusually, also pursue hares every other Thursday.

Four packs of foxhounds cover West Devon. To the north, the Stevenstone hunt the country immortalised by Henry Williamson in *Tarka the Otter*. South of them, three packs – the Tetcott, the South Tetcott and the Lamerton – straddle the Tamar, which forms the boundary between Devon and Cornwall. This is an area of high rainfall and wet land, much of it permanent pasture, where hunting flourishes thanks to the strong support of the local community.

Between the Stevenstone and the Dulverton (West) lie the Torrington Farmers, again in Tarka country. This is another pack with strong local support whose main income comes from their point-to-point. Held near Umberleigh, it traditionally ends the season and attracts a huge crowd each year. No chapter on hunting in Devon would be complete without reference to point-to-pointing. In no area of Britain are more meetings held or is enthusiasm for the sport greater.

Adjoining the Torrington Farmers to the south lies the Eggesford. This pack has a very large, almost square, country measuring 18 miles east to west and 20 miles north to south. It occupies the land between Exmoor and Dartmoor and marches on the east with the Silverton and the Tiverton.

The Silverton have the misfortune to contain the largest human population in Devon because Exeter, Crediton and Cullompton all lie within its boundaries. The land, much of it lying in the Exe valley, is lighter than in most parts of the country and much effort has been put in recently to building hunt jumps. An advantage of hunting with this friendly pack is that, if you are unlucky enough to be injured, you will be in good hands. One of the Joint Masters is Andrew Knox, an Exeter surgeon, for whose skill with the knife I have reason to be grateful.

The East Devon and Tiverton form the eastern boundary of the county. The former country takes in an attractive stretch of land from Exmouth nearly to Lyme Regis and north through Honiton. This is good farming land with more arable than is usual in Devon but it has become less easy to cross in recent years.

The Tiverton used to be considered the smartest pack in Devon in the days when it was virtually a private pack run by the Heathcoat Amory family but they have now been superseded in the matter of sartorial elegance by the South Devon. The Tiverton name is familiar to hound breeders through the influence of Tiverton Actor '22, one of the most influential stallion hands of his era, who was used with great success by the Duke of Beaufort and in the Cattistock kennel. A record, believed to be unique, is held by the Tiverton – they are the only pack to have been hunted by a man who subsequently became Chancellor of the Exchequer. He, Derrick Heathcoat Amory, used to tell the story of how, when he was hunting hounds beside the Taunton-Exeter railway line, the pack lost the scent just south of where the recently built Tiverton Parkway station now stands. At that moment, a train came by. The driver, on seeing the Master and his hounds, slammed on his brakes and came to a halt several hundred yards further on. He then reversed the train back to, and beyond, the pack, indicated to the Master where he had seen the hunted fox and, having seen hounds hit off the line, continued his journey.

Although they lie outside Devon, I have been asked to include the West Somerset and West Somerset Vale in this survey. The West Somerset country included the area now hunted by both packs until 1946. In that year, the country was divided and the eastern half, known first as the Quantock Farmers', became the West Somerset Vale in 1954. These two packs hunt that beautiful stretch of north Somerset running from the Brendon and Quantock Hills north to the Bristol Channel.

What should visitors expect if they decide on a foxhunting trip to Devon? The first thing to be said is that a warm welcome awaits "foreigners" (ie non-Devonians) both on the moor and in-country. Devon hunting is extremely un-smart. Red coats, other than those worn by Masters and hunt servants, are seldom seen; top hats are also rare – although the South Devon boast a few swells who turn out in full fig. The usual garb is a black coat – preferably one worn in earlier times by a parent or even grandparent – surmounted by a bowler hat or hunting cap. The latter gains ground each year at the expense of the former. That sensible but ugly contraption, the safety harness, is also on the increase but I have yet to see one attached to a bowler.

Most Devon packs are run on the proverbial shoestring and costs are kept to a minimum. Visitors will be surprised how little they are asked to pay. The exception to this rule is with the Exmoor where things are conducted on a rather grander scale, as befits "the Stars of the West". This should not be a deterrent, however, because no-one's hunting education is complete without a day following Ronnie Wallace and his bitch pack across some of the most beautiful country in England.

Fields on Exmoor in the spring often top 100 but elsewhere 50 is considered a good turnout and, with the smaller packs, meets are often attended by fewer than 20 riders. The going in winter tends to be heavy but few days are lost to frost, although on Dartmoor and Exmoor, fog is sometimes a hazard. If your main delight is in jumping, Devon is not, I am afraid, the place for you. While a few of the in-country packs have made valiant efforts to build hunt jumps, it is by no means uncommon to come home without having left the ground – unless you are lucky enough to find a tree fallen across a woodland ride. There is a depressing tendency among the Field Masters of some in-country packs to gallop along the roads when hounds run. If this practice is not checked, today's youngsters will grow up to think that this is what hunting is about.

Finally, what type of horse is suitable for Devon? The old-fashioned idea was to have a three-quarter bred hunter, often with a dash of pony blood, who was clever, sure-footed and durable. On the moor, a little Dartmoor pony blood gave the hunter that second sight which enables him to avoid bogs, rocks and holes. On Exmoor, unless one is built like a rugby forward, a thoroughbred is best. However, here I must confess to a prejudice; in my opinion a clever blood horse, once he knows the country, is the ideal mount whatever the terrain.

Claude Berry is a former amateur rider who is now a director of The Tryon Gallery. He has lived and hunted in Devon for more than half his life.

It is always most exciting when you are hunting a horse you cannot quite hold! In the early 1950s I had a brilliant 15 hand mare, who, once you pointed her at a fence, could not be stopped. One day during a good hunt with the Mendip, when visibility was poor and I was taking my own line over a series of delightful little walls, a bigger one loomed up. In the last few strides going at a good pace, I saw to my horror a disused quarry on the landing side. My brilliant mare jumped well out and landed on a ledge and then sprang sideways over a chasm (not unlike a mini Cheddar Gorge) to land safely in another field – I notched it up as surviving one of my nine lives!

Biddy Wingfield Digby

Foxhunting in Cornwall

Benjamin Sparrow

There are two types of hunting in Cornwall, moorland on Bodmin Moor which dominates north and east Cornwall and "in country" to the south and west.

The county has a very wide range of agriculture with large arable farms to the east and small dairy farms in the far west which results in similarly contrasting hunting country; large enclosures in the east with turf banks, and small fields with stone faced banks in the far west.

Bodmin Moor is divided between the North and East Cornwall who hunt twice a week. The Bolventor Harriers operate on Saturdays sharing the East Cornwall country with a few days in that of North Cornwall. Mid Cornwall is hunted exclusively by the Four Burrow who hunt five days a fortnight.

The Western occupy the far west and the Cury hunt the Lizard peninsular. The South Cornwall hunt the china clay country around St Austell being one of the most modern hunts starting in the early 1980s.

Visitors will find that they are welcome and that hunting is carried on in a very relaxed manner. Fields are fairly small ie 10-40 people and hirelings are almost non-existent. The ideal horse to hunt anywhere in Cornwall has to be tough and athletic. Traditionally they were three-quarter bred from the light draught horses found on most farms but with the demise of working horses they are now difficult to find.

In learning to jump a wide variety of banks, horses learn to look after themselves and have been much in demand as hunters up country or as eventers. For example, Cornishman V who won a Olympic Gold Medal.

Hounds have to be prepared to draw acres of thick gorse all day and everyday. They also have to be extremely accurate and turn on a sixpence due to small enclosures.

Four Burrow blood lines are to be found in many kennels throughout England.

Benjamin Sparrow is Master of the Western.

Foxhunting in the Welsh Marches

David Palmer

Hunting in the Welsh Marches must be more varied than in any other part of the British Isles. Not only are there huge geographical contrasts, but also enormous differences in the hounds which Masters in the region employ to hunt foxes in their various countries.

The North Shopshire, Albrighton, Albrighton Woodland, Worcestershire, Ledbury and the Cotswold Vale Farmers hunt countries that are principally low lying, fertile and well-farmed, and capable of providing fast, hard riding, classic foxhunting. Sadly, most of these have become more restricted in recent years by the increase in road traffic or the building of motorways. Nevertheless, in each of them there is still a good deal of lovely, huntable country of which full advantage is taken to please hard riding fields.

The North Shropshire are unique in the area in that they hunt a very even pack of old English hounds, beloved by their Huntsman Martin Jarrett for their persistance and cry. Both the Albrighton and Albrighton Woodland hunt packs of mixed modern and old English hounds with, in each case, an infusion of Welsh blood mainly supplied from Ludlow, which their respective Huntsmen, Ian Starsmore and Austin James, have found helpful in improving overall accuracy. The Worcestershire hounds have just completed a very successful season but are at present undergoing a change from a few years ago when, although tremendous fox catchers, they were decidedly plain. Now they have moved much closer to the modern English type and it is interesting for the hound student to observe their Huntsman, Julian Barnfield, continuing the work of his predecessor Ian Higgs in moulding these new hounds into an accurate pack.

The Ledbury hounds are in splendid form and accurately and effectively hunt their beautiful little country which is known for its lovely vale and fly hedges. Nigel Wakly, their Master and Huntsman, and Robert Oliver, of showing fame, as Field Master, make an exciting and formidable pair to follow. The hounds, which were brought to such a high standard in Huntsman Nimrod Champion's day, still have a bit of Dumfriesshire in them and now have been blended with Cotswold and Berkeley to maintain their class. Berkeley blood abounds, too, in the Cotswold Vale Farmers' hounds whose breeding has been guided for years by Mr John Brown. This pack of extreme loveliness, which has had many show successes in recent years, hunt their fast, galloping lowlands in excellent style for their enthusiastic Huntsman, Nick Valentine.

By contrast, the other packs in the Marches region hunt countries of a much hillier and, in some cases, wilder aspect.

The South Shropshire hounds, hunted now as they have been for 26 years by Michael Rowson, are lovely quality English hounds well known for their successes in the show ring. They also hunt their Shropshire hills and plains beautifully and to see them spread out and draw their Long Mynd hills is an education. The Wheatland hounds, next door and great rivals to the South Shropshire on the flags, hunt, as their name implies, a heavy plough region as well as a ration of hills. Given only half a scent these thoroughbreds can really fly and Huntsman Richard Fisk needs to call upon all his skill as a horseman to stay with them in well fenced and deep riding country.

Just over the border, the United Pack make a fascinating contrast hunting a wilder and, in parts, hillier country where sheep farming forms the main agricultural enterprise. Here Rodney Ellis, sadly about to retire as Master and Huntsman, has blended his once predominately Welsh hounds with College Valley fell types to produce a thrilling and effective pack of hounds.

The Ludlow is a large country which has both hill and highly farmed lowlands within its boundary. On the whole, it is not a good scenting country and over the last decade an English-Welsh cross-bred hound has proved ideal, having the voice and deep scenting abilities of the Welsh allied to the athleticism of the English, the union being seasoned with a touch of hybrid vigour. Similar hounds have also found favour in neighbouring Clifton-on-Teme and North Ledbury countries. Here, of all characteristics, hounds need persistence as there are few large tracts of easy galloping and one tough bank of thorns follows quickly on the next. Both packs cope admirably with their problems, however, and both Roy Tatlow and Geoff Parsons show excellent sport.

The lush farming countries of the North and South Herefordshire are different again with low, undulating hills of rich soil replacing the bracken and sheep grazing of Shropshire. They provide enviable country to hunt over and the North Herefordshire do so under Harley Godsall with classic English hounds very largely influenced by the Cotswold. Similar hounds, but with Heythrop and Berkeley influence, are employed by the South Hereford under their Joint Master and Huntsman Dianne Jones, also sadly about to retire.

The one feature which all these packs of the Marches have in common is that the hunting is great fun. Whether the Marches sportsmen hunt to ride, and there is jumping and galloping to be had with all of them, or to watch their chosen type of hound work, there is an unpretentious pleasure evident amongst them all which, like the part of England that they hunt, takes some beating.

David Palmer lives in Worcestershire and is senior Joint Master of the Ludlow.

Foxhunting in North Wales and West Midlands

Robin Gundry

From the Cheshire plain in the east, across the River Dee in the centre, then up the Vale of Clywd onto the hills of North Wales in the west, lies what some would say is the finest hunting country left in the British Isles. Dominated by dairy and livestock farms and criss-crossed by stiff upright and beautifully maintained thorn hedges, a sea of grass stretches out as far as the eye can see.

Taking your own line – the greatest thrill of all

Look at a map showing hunt boundaries and the domain of Sir Watkin Williams-Wynn's hounds is vast, stretching from the west coast of Wales to Chester in the north, Whitchurch in the east and Oswestry in the south, making it the largest country in the British Isles. Today, however, the hounds hunt rarely west of the A5. The country is almost all grass, bounded by neat, stiff thorn and holly hedges of manageable proportions. The dairy farms are interlaced by steep-sided wooded dingles in which foxes abound. The foxes often run a 'twisty-turny' route and accurate hounds of the old English type have been bred by the Williams-Wynn family for 150 years.

Robin Gundry, the amateur Huntsman, has the strong support of the Joint Masters Sir Watkin Williams-Wynn and the Hon Peter Greenall, whose infectious enthusiasm will galvanise anyone to enjoy their day's hunting.

The Wynnstay people are passionate about their sport: 150 people attend the earth-stoppers dinner and the hounds are not banned from any farm in the country. They follow on horse, on foot, in cars and, in many cases, on motorbikes.

To the east of the Wynnstay and stretching across the Cheshire plain lies the stamping ground of another famous pack – the Cheshire hounds. Home of the world-famous Tarporley Hunt Club – "The Green Collars". The country over which they hunt is again dominated by dairy farms with immaculate hedges and ditches across which a man can still take his own line. The terrain is not so broken up by the steep valleys found further west.

In 1991, after 25 very successful years, Jonny O'Shea retired as Huntsman. A young amateur Guy Mather has now taken over the horn under the direction of a keen Mastership led by Sir John Barlow. The best country now lies around Wrenbury, Cholmondeley and Calverhall. Cheshire has a great hunting history full of characters and tradition and is rising to meet modern challenges as it did those of the past.

Tucked away on the Wirral Peninsula lies the Cheshire Forest country. This has been under the control of the Hunter family since 1947. Mr Peter Hunter is about to complete 25 seasons as Master. The hounds are hunted by the very able and colourful professional Dick Chapman, an excellent horseman. The Cheshire Forest is not for the faint hearted equestrian and those following should be prepared to take on any obstacle from a big "fly fence" to a bedstead including all wire in between.

Moving west back across the Dee and over into the Vale of Clwyd you find yourself in the Flint and Denbigh country. In some ways this is the odd one out being primarily a hill country with open upland, forestry and old woodland predominating. However, they too have their own patch of vale. In common with their neighbours at the Wynnstay, the Flint and Denbigh have close ties with Sir Watkin Williams-Wynn and his family which means, amongst other things, a close similarity in the breeding of the two packs. Again a very friendly country, well worth a visit.

We are lucky to enjoy some of the best hunting country in the United Kingdom – and some of the best sport.

Robin Gundry is Master and Huntsman of Sir Watkin Williams-Wynn's foxhounds.

Foxhunting in Wales

David Jones

Wales has some lovely hunting country, varying from rolling hills in the South to the rugged terrain of the North. It also has old lay grass and boggy uplands together with oak filled valleys where the music of the Welsh foxhounds resounds. Hunting has a long history in the Principality dating back to the ninth century AD when Prince Hywel Dda had a pack of hunting dogs which had all the characteristics of the Welsh foxhound today. Up until recently there had been a lot of speculation as to where these hounds had originated but records recently found in the National Library of Wales have proved that the Welsh hound originated in his day.

One of the oldest packs of hounds in Wales is the Gogerddan. The Pryse family have played an important part in the history of hunting in Wales since 1038, and it is known that hounds have been in existence there since 1600. The name Gogerddan derives from Bynedda, a Romano-British cavalry officer, who kept a large part of Wales for himself after the Roman Conquest.

Showing Welsh hounds at the Wales and Border Counties Hound Show, Builth Wells

Following hounds in Wales varies from four-wheeled quad bike, to horses, or to hunting on foot. In the North it is impossible to follow in any vehicle or on a horse, the terrain there being too rough due to the areas of jumbled rocks and boulders left after the ice age. Coming south into mid Wales, we still have some remote areas with the hills becoming much softer and containing bracken, gorse and rushy boglands. Moving further south again we have the Brecon Beacons, which is a large block of unspoilt hunting country stretching from Abergavenny almost to Swansea. This is open running country where hounds can really drive on. After the Beacons, we have industrialised Wales, where despite its large coal tips and vast tracts of forestry, hounds still manage to show good sport. There are many packs of hounds currently hunting in Wales.

Banwen Miners Hunt: Found in the early sixties, and as its name suggests its supporters were mainly coal miners. The hounds are kennelled in the old pit head baths of the colliery. Situated in West Glamorgan, the country varies from hill to vale stretching from the beautiful Gower Peninsula inland towards the Brecon Beacons.

Brecon Hunt: The hounds are both fine English and fine Welsh. The country is mainly mountainous and includes both the Brecon Beacons and the Effynt Range – all the very rideable country of South Powys.

David Davies Hunt: The country lies in North Powys, the old county of Montgomeryshire. Hounds are fine Welsh with some fine Fell in the pack. The terrain varies from hill country to vale. Being one of the most intensive sheep rearing countries in Britain, fox control is an essential way of life.

Eryri Hunt: This must be the hardest country to hunt in Wales, situated in Snowdonia. Its rugged terrain is a challenge to man, hounds and terriers. Hound are Fell Welsh cross.

Gelligaer Hunt: The country is situated in Glamorgan, which is becoming more and more difficult to hunt due to development, although there are still some very nice bits to the north. Hounds are mainly Welsh.

Gogerddan Hunt: Recently amalgamated with the Llangeitho, the Gogerddan are now kennelled at Tregaron. The country stretches from the famous Elan Valley to the coast, being one of the most unspoilt regions of Wales, and is thoroughly hunted by these fine Welsh hounds.

Irfon and Towy Hunt: This used to be some of the best country in Wales, but sadly forestry plantations have engulfed a great deal of it. The hounds are fine Welsh.

Llangibby Hunt: Situated in the old county of Monmouth, which is now known as Gwent. Hound are mainly old English lines.

Llangeinor Hunt: The country is well foxed, the hounds being predominantly Welsh. It is quite difficult country to hunt due to wire and one-third of it being forestry plantations.

Monmouthshire Hunt: Hounds are fine English, the country being varied from hill to vale including the lower reaches of the Black Mountains.

Pentyrch Hunt: Situated on the outskirts of Cardiff this was once a lovely area to hunt but it is now spoilt by the M4 motorway. Hounds are Welsh and still show great sport despite the motorway.

Sennybridge Hunt: Kennelled in South Powys, the hounds are mainly Welsh. It is one of the least spoilt hunting countries in Wales. A large part of it consists of the Effynt ranges and the Brecon Beacons stretching to the lovely hills running down the Swansea Valley.

Taf Fechan Hunt: A relatively new pack in Wales started in the late sixties. The hounds are mainly Welsh and the country is situated south of the Brecon Beacons.

Teme Valley Hunt: The hunt is situated in Mid Powys, which used to be the old county of Radnorshire. Hounds are fine Welsh and fine Fell and they hunt the desirable, unspoilt heather moorlands which cover part of the country.

Teme Valley Huntsman, Roy Savage

Ystrad Hunt: The hounds are based in the famous Rhondda Valley. It is a difficult hunting country due to the forestry plantations and old coal tips which surround this once beautiful area.

In the south west corner of Wales are three packs, who hunt the area known as 'Little England'. These are the Pembrokeshire, the South Pembrokeshire and the Carmarthenshire. All three packs are famous for their very well bred hounds and the Carmathenshire were used for many years as a source of Welsh blood for crossing with traditional English hounds. The South Pembrokeshire were for much of this century in the hands of the well known Mrs Evans of Cresselly. Her son and daughter now share the Joint Mastership with an enthusiastic amateur, Simon Hart, and they show great sport in their very attractive country. The Pembrokeshire have equally good fun in their lovely grass country to the north while the Carmarthenshire hunt in the country immediately to the north of Carmarthen Bay. All three packs enjoy some lovely coastline and hunting with them is a unique experience.

David Jones is Huntsman of the David Davies.

Foxhunting in Ireland

Michael O'Fox

All the adjectives that can be applied to hunting in Leicestershire, Cornwall or Surrey can be applied to Ireland at one time or another. Included in this litany would be exciting, amusing, uplifting or, to the other extreme frustrating and infuriating for that is the nature of foxhunting. There is, however, a timeless quality about the hunting in Ireland which can hardly be matched elsewhere. It is still possible to cross the spine of Mizzen Head from Roaring Water Bay to Bantry Bay behind the direct descendants of Edith Somerville's West Carbery Hounds. Undoubtedly some of your companions in the field are descended from those who enjoyed sport with that redoubtable lady and who followed her lead not only in the hunting field but in establishing the British Friesian herd to maintain the family fortunes. Perhaps the only difference noticeable between then and now is that there are fewer boats in the harbour at Bantry and the labourer's cottages of then are now holiday homes and empty during the hunting season.

Being an island, Ireland rejoices in island weather. Wait half an hour and it will change! The Gulf Stream maintains a temperate climate all year round and thus it is rare to lose many days to frost or snow. The past five winters have been particularly mild with 1993/94 also very wet. This creates its own problems as farming is in gear by early March with cows and sheep back out on the land. The average farm size is 60 acres and many farms are crossed in a day's hunting so most hunts finish the season before Cheltenham to accommodate their greatest supporters.

The Irish countryside like the weather is very variable. It is boggy, deep, light and stony in turn and the fencing in each area reflects the type of ground. There are several countries noted for the size and quality of their banks – Wexford, The Island, Scarteen, Limerick and Tipperary to name a few. Galway is well known for its stone walls, as is Clare and parts of Limerick. Meath rejoices in extra large ditches or dykes.

Urban sprawl has thankfully not affected too many packs and the roads, even the motorways, are still gratifyingly empty. Ribbon building on the roads from towns and villages has probably affected more hunting country than anything else except for the proliferation of stud farms in some areas. Farming has come into the twentieth century and in-country suitable for winter corn crops are more prevalent than previously. Electric fencing is taking over from barbed wire almost everywhere but good farmer relations generally ensure that it is inactive on hunting days and that places for jumping can be found.

The determination to go over, under or through is ever present

The fox population has rebounded since the fashion gurus ceased trying to convince the general public that fox fur was really stunning on any other that its original owner. In some areas the 'circular' fox is all too prevalent whether from lessons learned during snaring or from electric shock it is hard to know. In general, there is no shortage of quarry. Packs of hounds of all varieties can be found. The Limerick and Muskerry, Waterford, Louth and Duhallow maintain the Old English strains. The Scarteen is almost unique with their famous 'Black and Tan' hounds with their booming cry. Tipperary and Kilkenny are the leading proponents of the modern hound as developed directly with the renowned 'Ikey Bell' and continued since with blood from packs such as the Beaufort, Exmoor and Cheshire. In other hunts packs have been developed which combine all the above to cope with conditions in situ.

The mounted field can be anything in number from five to 155. Most hunts hope to have 40 to 50 following on a regular basis as that number is manageable and also pays the bills. As a general rule visitors are welcome but numbers of some are restricted. It is too much to expect that a hunting tour of more than about six persons could be accommodated together on the same day. Demand is such for places with the more popular hunts that bookings are being taken in October for January and early February.

As a general rule, visitors to Ireland should come prepared to appreciate fun. As in any foxhunting country, good sport depends on good management, proper tools (horses, hounds etc) and scent. The last variable can be absent as often as anywhere else but the visitor will find that regardless of scent, fun is always there to be found. In most countries whether trappy or huge, there is no disgrace in falling off and the variety of obstacles will astound many. The determination to go over, under or through is ever present. There is an egalitarian atmosphere which pervades and the cut of one's coat matters not one wit if you are able to make country and add to the general sport.

It was realised early on that children are the future of hunting in every country and visitors marvel at the number as well as the level of expertise of the children out hunting. Thankfully it is still possible to buy and keep a pony quite economically in rural areas and many of today's foremost jockeys, showjumpers and eventers started life with horses in the hunting field. It is not unusual to find Charlie Swan, Michael Kinane, Eddie Macken and John Watson in the same hunting field with 'Mouse' Morris and Edward O'Grady.

The horses and ponies of the followers come in all shapes and sizes with 'handsome is as handsome does' as the motto. No matter how beautiful the animal, if it will not cross country it goes to another home. In general, it is not necessary to have a very fast animal as most countries require jumping ability rather than speed. Banks are jumped from a trot at the fastest and a good hind end is all important.

The tradition of hunting goes back a long way in many Irish hunting countries. The Ryan family have been Masters of the Scarteen for more than 200 years. The third generation of the McCalmont family hold office in Kilkenny. George Briscoe, Master of the Tara Harriers in County Louth has been in office for the best part of 60 years. At the same time, many enthusiastic foxhunters from other parts of the world have made their way to Ireland and have stayed as Masters or ordinary members of the field after been trapped by the charm of the country. These visitors turned residents would include Evan Williams, Lord Daresbury and Bert Firestone.

There are 39 packs of foxhounds in Ireland and it is possible to hunt on seven days a week. The list of hunts that follows is divided into three sections – west, central and east – running from north to south for ease of planning on the traveller's part.

West

North Galway is a stone wall country which has a long association with Lady Molly Cusack-Smith who is well known for her unique style of hospitality. They meet on Sundays.

A frightening place to jump with the North Galway

Next comes the County Galway, the famous 'Blazers'. Michael Dempsey, Master and Huntsman since 1978, hunts their wonderful country three days every week. Well known for their stone walls (32 to the mile in places!) and their sporting hospitality. The East Galway have great fun hunting the country between The Blazers and the Shannon whilst to the south is the County Clare – a stonewall and hedge country known for its hospitable farmers. Sport guaranteed! They also meet on Sundays.

County Galway Senior Master and Huntsman, Michael Dempsey,
at Turloughmore

South again to the famous County Limerick who boast a wall and bank country and who have been professionally hunted by Hugh Robards since 1972. Long, quality Masterships have produced a very level pack. The hounds are English and bred from Belvoir lines introduced by Lord Daresbury during his long Mastership.

Adjoining the Limerick are the Scarteen – the 'Black and Tans' – who have a long association with the Ryan family stretching back over two centuries. The current representative is showing great sport over the most daunting bank country preceded by his unique black and tan hounds with their deep, sonorous cry. The hounds are Kerry Beagles.

To the south are the Duhallow, famous for their large banks. The oldest hunt in Ireland, it continues in a fine sporting tradition.

County Cork hosts a number of packs. Macroom, Muskerry, United, South Union and Avondhu provide sport in difficult conditions in some of the best dairy country in the world. The old Somerville and Ross country of Carbery and West Carbery is hunted in a pre-war time-lock but unfortunately visitors are severely restricted. The O'Driscolls have been Masters since 1914.

Central

The Westmeath hunt is a small, very sporting set-up and they provide great entertainment over a very varied country interspersed with bog. The old traditions are maintained at the annual Hunt Ball. Just to their north are the Ballymacad, who also have a mixed bank, ditch and hedge country. Further to the west the Ormond and North Tipperary have interesting and varied countries well hunted by two enthusiastic huntsmen. This was the schooling ground for the champion jump jockey Charlie Swan and their pony club also boasted Walter Swinburn as a member!

South of them the Tipperary rejoice in a four-day week over a most varied terrain. The hunt has produced a number of Peterborough Champions as well as good sport due to a continuity provided by long masterships. They have some formidable banks, lots of support and lots of fun.

The West Waterford was home to the Morgans who had champion horses as well as hounds. The new men are making bold strides to reopen hilly country with limited resources, whilst the Waterford have a long tradition in testing dairy country and have recently increased momentum with a new Huntsman and are now breeding some most attractive Old English bitches to assist them.

East

The Louth hunt an old English pack of hounds bred by the Filgate family in an open country near Dublin, where they reap the benefit of long Masterships.

West and south is the Meath which is a most exciting country to hunt with large banks and its famous ditches (in which many visitors have come to grief) enclosing extensive fields of grass.

The Kildare continue to provide great sport and their open country allows great viewing of hounds. The Master's enthusiasm is infectious.

To their west the Laois hunt a heavily wooded country. It is home to the famous Lawlor family who do their best to generate sport in difficult circumstances. South of the Laois are the Kilmoganny, the North Kilkenny and the Kilkenny, where the McCalmont family took great trouble to produce a beautifully bred pack of hounds which can be seen sailing over their lovely open wall country.

The Carlow Farmer's were formed in 1979 to resurrect Mrs Halls's famous pack. They show sport in a daunting, trappy country with the enthusiasm of a youthful committee. Between the Carlow and the sea are the Island, a renowned horse producing country where the tall, narrow banks flanked either side by gorse-filled ditches inspire palpitations in both rider and steed.

The Wicklow hunt the coastal strip north of the Island on Sundays with the occasional Wednesday whilst the Wexford hunt the south-east corner of Ireland in a very sporting fashion. The Shillelagh, now run as a limited company, hunt their famous hounds, originally bred by the Fitzwilliam family, over their entertaining bog and woodland country.

North

There are two packs of foxhounds hunting in Ulster. The Dungannon hunt the country south of Londonderry and in County Tyrone. It is a mountain and hill country with big forestry blocks and peat bogs but great sport is to be had. The East Down hunt a small country north of the Mountains of Mourne on the east coast with a variety of obstacles. They have a fair share of plough and wire but still have a good crack!

Michael O'Fox has been Master and Huntsman of four packs of hounds in Ireland and is still serving.

....

The natives do not always provide entertainment for the visitors. Sometimes the reverse is true as on a day in Ballyluskey when a visitor from the Duke of Beaufort's sporting a very smart topper lost it on top of a very big double. He showed a great deal of form in jumping back on the bank to retrieve it. He dismounted from a very well known hireling, Nellie, who waited until he was bent down with hat in hand to move her hind leg about two inches. It was just enough to send him head first into a very deep and gorsy ditch to a howl of laughter from the attendant field who had been watching intently.

Michael O'Fox

191

Hunting with Harriers

Betty Gingell

Hunting with harriers is the most pleasant way of pursuing the hare avoiding the masochistic exertions of running across ploughed fields. This does not mean that following on horseback does not require a substantial degree of fitness both on the part of the rider and the horse since harrier hounds are extremely fast across country. Harrier packs which hunt hare exclusively are found mainly in East Anglia and the north-west of England. The hounds in these packs are usually tri-coloured; they are bright, busy and active animals with the doghounds measuring up to 21 inches at the shoulder whereas the bitches are smaller, some standing at only 19 inches. These hounds are often referred to as 'Stud Book' harriers as opposed to the lemon and white West Country Harrier; the latter are a slightly larger hound and hunt fox as well as hare. The light colour of these hounds makes them easy to see on the hilly country that they hunt, being very different from the large fields and open spaces of East Anglia.

The origins of the harrier hound are uncertain. Undoubtedly the Norman invasion of 1066 brought hounds to this country but the lapse of records between then and the Holcombe's documented association with James I in 1617 and a record of the Cambridgeshire in 1745 can only leave the interim period open to intelligent conjecture. The premier hound shows are Peterborough, Honiton and Rydal.

Mounted falconry probably became too dangerous with the coming of enclosures, and the wild boar became extinct. Hunting hare was at one time second only to deer, reserved for royalty, and pursuit of the fox was left to the 'lower classes'. Somehow the foxhunters have now inveigled their way into the senior status. Much harrier country is shared with foxhounds by invitation so that Masters of Hounds now have to plan the season around the adjacent or overlapping foxhound packs which becomes increasingly difficult with agricultural diversification, expanding urbanisation, development of new road systems, shooting and the proliferation of golf courses. Communications to local beagle and basset packs also sharing the area have been known to fail with consequent 'joint meets' ensuing.

The Brown Hare in East Anglia is large and can give a good pack of hounds excellent sport. The coursing fraternity value it equally; some 'unofficial' coursers up before the magistrates have been heard to remark that they were happy to pay their fines and would be back again since the hares were the best in the country. The hare population is mobile within a season, often migrating to the lighter land in the wetter weather, and the numbers also fluctuate over the years. Surveys by hunts, conservationists and game interests are gradually providing information on the numbers and diseases of the hare and some explanations are gradually coming to light for the discovery of dead and dying hares in certain areas in the late summer; it seems likely that quite severe afflictions have struck the population in the past from time to time as many old records speak of 'hare plague'.

Betty Gingell with the Cambridgeshire Harriers

Pressure from conservationists and inadequate rebuttal information on natural population fluctuation has led to the curtailment of hare shoots which could account for several hundred hares in a day. Farmer hosts will often apologise that they have not shot before hounds came because they were fearful of failing to provide enough hares for a day's sport, yet still hounds will find that there are too many for a really enjoyable day. It is often not appreciated that such controlled and constant culling of the population enhances the vigour of the survivors and their progeny. The adage of three hares to the parish is frequently exceeded to the detriment of the day's sport. Unlike our foxhunting friends, we can often see the changes of hare and the number afoot and it can take a talented Huntsman and active whips to keep a pack steady when hunting conditions are only moderate. The speed of the harriers leaves little time for the hare to practice some of the diversionary tactics romanced by beaglers, but sometimes it seems as though the baton is passed from a tired hare to a fresh one though this may well be a matter of chance rather than intent.

Given the right scenting conditions a well matched pack will sweep fast across the country where a blanket would cover them all – an exhilarating gallop and a marvellous sight to behold. Being mounted and thus able to stay with hounds throughout a chase, and to watch them draw, hear them speak, see them hunt, check, cast and go on again is an experience which is probably the greatest pleasure of hunting with harriers.

Although there is a considerable amount of hedgerow replanting, the size of the fields is still relatively large in the arable areas over which many East Anglian packs hunt. With the large expanses under corn by the start of the hunting season, drawing heavy land on horseback becomes an exhausting task if wet and is ungrateful thanks for permission to go over land. Hounds have to learn to cast and work themselves whilst the Huntsman and hunt servants observe and follow on better going chosen to permit rapid response once a hare is found. With the large open spaces there is often a relatively poor network of roads which, with the speed of the harrier, makes it extremely difficult for car followers to assist in policing some of the roads of which even the minor ones are carrying increasing amounts of faster moving traffic. Crop varieties have become more resilient to adverse winter conditions and so the old traditional farrow has disappeared; this used to provide some relief from the plough until cultivation started with the January frosts. The furrows created in diagonals and squares by the old type of plough then facilitated relatively rapid movement across country until spring drilling heralded the end of the season. Tramlines are now an easy route – providing they run the right way! This system of cultivation together with the reversible plough or minimal cultivation practice has seen the loss of the traditional headlands which have become increasingly narrow and the space between corn and dyke can become hazardously reduced.

The introduction of oil-seed rape has meant that has much as 25 per cent of some farms are down to this early winter foliage; it is a crop which requires regular attention and this often causes disturbed hares to move away, and the spraying and fertilising leaves the land foiled at least as far as hounds' noses tell us. Many greeted the prospect of set-aside as a bonus for hunting; perhaps the short-term set-aside now available will prove better, but the longer term cessation of cultivation led to land becoming poorly drained and developing large cracks in the summer which did not readily close with the winter moisture. Galloping over set-aside has proved the ruination of many good horses. Whereas with livestock, outbreaks of foot and mouth disease occasionally restricted hunting activities, now serious diseases of arable crops such as rhizomania can be equally disruptive.

A good hare will usually follow a wide circuit until hounds get on terms, but once into the New Year some jack hares will start to run much straighter from the outset. Hunting over relatively flat land may cause some disappointment to those who like to jump fences, but many dykes will prove a testing challenge to visitors from more undulating and well-stocked country with smaller fields and hedges. Unless it has been experienced, few realise the speed with which harriers move across country – they tested the fitness of any horse when there was plough to steady them, but the increase in autumn drilling seems to have made them keener still. To stay with the hounds often requires right decisions guided by experience tempered with a little luck, but it is even better if you are well mounted and can just go without thinking!

As to the future, no doubt those who are ignorant will try to dictate how we may use and enjoy the countryside but there are more insidious dangers encroaching on our sport. The modern car has the capability of attaining incredible speeds down minor roads and many drivers never think about hounds or horses, and do not expect to find them around the corner or coming through a gap in the hedge. As part of the promotion of hunting as a reasonable country sport it is beholden on all of us to show responsibility towards other road and countryside users as well as to our farming hosts. Therefore the onus is placed on the Master to consider whether hunting is safe to continue at a meet that has been held traditionally for years but the country has overtly changed – a hard but not defeatist decision; hunt servants have to be with and safeguard their hounds far more than in the past – with the speed of the harrier this task requires good horses, a good nerve, and a few years of experience, anticipation and knowledge of the country. Our sport depends on our hounds – we improve them through careful breeding and we owe them a duty to care in the field and to bring them home safely to kennel at the end of the day. If we succeed in this, then pursuit of the hare from horseback will continue to be an exceptional pleasure.

Betty Gingell has been Master and Huntsman of the Cambridgeshire Harriers for 52 years.

Hunting with Beagles

Jonnie Andrews

The start of the 1994/95 hare hunting season sees the sport as popular as it has been for very many year despite the attention of unwanted visitors on occasions.

There are currently 22 packs of harriers and 80 packs of beagles in Great Britain registered with the Association of Masters of Harriers and Beagles.

During the past few years the defence of hunting has had to change direction and with the formation of the Campaign for Hunting in December 1991 prior to the McNamara Private Members Bill in February 1992, it became obvious that there must be greater publicity, explanation and justification for all hunting including hare hunting. Harrier and beagle packs have played their part in providing the necessary funds from the hare hunting world which have been used in the defence of hunting by the Campaign for Hunting, now fully incorporated into the BFSS. For small packs with mainly amateur hunt staff working on a very small budget (in comparison with some of the larger foxhound packs) it has not been easy to raise the necessary finances. However, nearly every pack has realised the necessity to raise money for the defence of our sport. The Joint Committee of the Association of Masters of Harriers and Beagles is extremely grateful to all the packs who have made considerable efforts to raise the necessary funds.

Over the past decade there has been a considerable improvement in the standard of harriers and beagles now being shown at the major hounds shows throughout the summer. More time and thought is now being given to the breeding of hounds. A well-known professional Huntsman once said to a young Master, when discussing hound breeding, "study the pedigrees long and hard". How right he was.

The limitation for many packs of beagles and I suspect some harrier packs, is one of cost when considering the extent of the breeding programme. It is probably only possible to breed two or three litters a year. This therefore means that there can be no room for mistakes when selecting brood bitches and stallion hounds.

There is a considerable number of different types of beagle throughout the country and there is not as much uniformity as is seen in the foxhound world. No one beagle kennel has been as dominant as the Beaufort, Heythrop, or the Exmoor Kennels in foxhunting circles. Latterly, we have seen the Dummer dominate to a certain extent with their well-bred bitches.

The size of hounds has always been a matter for debate amongst Masters of harriers and beagles. A height limit of 16 inches for beagles and 21 inches for harriers is applied by all the major hound shows throughout the country. Hounds in excess of these heights are not eligible to be shown. It has always been advocated that some countries need larger hounds to cross the terrain. The moors of the north or the hills of Wales, for example, will need a larger hound than the lowland countries of southern England. In some enclosed countries, with the hazards of main roads railways and urbanisation, a smaller hound with not so much drive is probably required if the pack are not to get into difficulties.

Many packs of beagles will go "visiting" other countries before or at the beginning of the hare hunting season in September and October. The Northumberland Beagling Festival is a very good example of this practice.

It is always very interesting to see how hounds used to hunting the ploughs of East Anglia adapt to the hills of the north or Wales. Sheep foil and to a lesser extent, cattle foil, will be one of the immediate problems hounds will encounter. However, a good pack of hounds usually adapt quickly to a totally different country from that encountered at home.

The handling of hounds is something which every Huntsman needs to consider very carefully and make up his mind about the best way to achieve the "invisible thread" between hounds and Huntsman. It is fascinating to study some of the different styles adopted by professional huntsmen. The Huntsman must have confidence in his hounds and the hounds confidence in the Huntsman. It is always more difficult for a

Huntsman of beagles when hounds riot, as his staff are all on their feet and not on a horse. It is therefore more difficult to get to the appropriate position to stop hounds in the shortest possible time. Hence, it is essential that the hunt staff are in the right position and know what to do if something is beginning to go wrong. This will prevent a disaster happening. If hounds do riot they must be stopped quickly as once they have really settled it will be much more difficult to stop them successfully. Quietness in handling hounds is essential. Too much noise or excessive horn blowing will only get hounds wild and confused. It will also probably confuse the hunt staff and followers as well! Beagles can be much more excitable than harriers (or for that matter foxhounds) and it is essential to realise this fact from the outset and act accordingly.

Rodney Cooper, Master and Huntsman of the Surrey and North Sussex Beagles

Those that go hare hunting do so for a variety of reasons whether it be for the excitement of the ride across country, the exercise in following foothounds, to watch hounds working, to enjoy the British countryside or the partake in the excitement of the chase. A well-known writer once said "hunting is the most exciting thing one does when one is fully clothed". How right he is and long may hunting continue in Great Britain.

Jonnie Andrews is Master of the Glyn Celyn Beagles.

Hunting with Basset Hounds

Rex Hudson

The basset hound to the uninitiated might seem an unlikely working hound when compared with the better known beagle, and particularly the harrier. Partly this is due to the well-known logo of a popular brand of footwear, which has tended to put in the minds of many the fact that the basset hound is of a type, broadly summed up as being long in the back and short on the leg, hardly attributes for getting across difficult country in pursuit of the fast and elusive hare. Thirty or so years ago, the hound was also in danger of becoming "fashionable" and worse "popular" as a pet or show bench animal, a fate which has sadly befallen now the traditional working terrier, and registrations with the governing body increased dramatically. This is not to say that the pure bred basset hound is not a perfectly agreeable household pet, but those of us who love him for his hunting attributes cannot suppress a twinge of regret when seeing him in surroundings far away from the sporting life he was originally bred to lead.

Basset Hounds

As with a lot of good things, like champagne, foie gras and Edith Piaf, the basset hound came to us from France, where he was and is bred in a number of forms, his conformation and other essential attributes depending upon the type of work for which he was destined.

Any working hound, as distinct from a standard-bred or show type "dog", needs to have five essential qualities – nose, drive, voice, constitution or stamina and conformation – and nose and voice are two especial characteristics of the working basset hound.

For those with sporting aspirations, hunting the hare with basset hounds is the greatest possible fun. It is in many ways similar to beagling, in that it is conducted on foot by a Huntsman and two (or occasionally more) whippers-in. Most packs hunt on a Saturday and some mid-week as well. The hunting season usually commences as soon as the harvest is in arable areas, or in September/October in grassland countries, until the end of the following February. Most packs consist of ten to 15 couple of hounds, which can broadly fall in either of two types, either the pure bred basset hound or the English basset hound. The former, as their title implies, are now of a slightly more refined and athletic type, somewhat long in the back and with the characteristic domed head and crooked or semi-crooked front legs familiar to many although soundness is insisted upon as with any other working hound.

The English basset hound, having had infusions of harrier blood and occasionally that of beagle as well, resembles at first sight a heavily built beagle. The type preferred depends, as with all other hounds, on the type of country to be hunted and the individual preferences of the Master or committee owning the pack. The English basset hound tends to be somewhat faster, but both types enjoy the two most desirable characteristics of the basset hound – great depth of melody when a pack is in full cry and deep-scenting qualities especially on a poor scenting day.

The "traditional" basset hound has been well-known in France for upwards of 200 years, primarily as a hound for pushing out game from cover to the waiting guns, when its superior nose and voice were valuable attributes. Not being over-fast, it pressed its quarry sufficiently to drive it into the open and then remain in cover. There is evidence that there were two packs, presumably from imported hounds, hunting the hare in Kent in the 1850s, but it was not until the 1880s that its desirable working qualities as a truly hunting hound were fully recognised and the basset hound was developed by the Heseltine brothers, with the formation of their Walhampton pack in Hampshire. The basset hound has never reached the heights of popularity enjoyed by beagles, the number of packs of the latter expanding dramatically about 100 years ago, tending rather to take over from the harrier packs, which had hitherto enjoyed greater prominence. There are, however, sufficient packs of basset hounds principally in the Midlands and south of England for people to go out and enjoy a day with these thoroughly sporting little hounds.

The Masters of Basset Hounds Association looks after the affairs of the hound, lays down a strict code of hunting to be adhered to by all member packs, publishes the Stud Book and conducts the Annual Show, which is held on the first day of the Peterborough Hound Show each year in July. Since the Second World War, the names of many personalities in the hound world who have been active in the affairs of the Association come to mind, and none more so than the late Lt Col E F S Morrison, MFH, who took over the Walhampton (renamed the Westerby) in 1932. Eric Morrison was instrumental in the re-formation of the Association in 1958 along with Mrs Jo Groom, herself an ex-Master of the Westerby, and they drew together the skills of many other people in the basset hound world, notably the late Miss Peggy Keevil, who had a keen interest in both basset hounds and other working hounds and dogs.

What to wear – comfortable and ideally water-proof clothing, which permits as much activity as the wearer intends to put in on a hunting day. Good stout shoes or, for the more athletic, the ubiquitous "trainer" or Rugby boots are often favoured, and ideally a light, warm, water-proof jacket, and some sort of similar head covering will be appreciated, especially in those misty and sometimes overly cold days of November and December. For members of the field after a few years experience of getting to know the ways of the hunted hare, a whistle carried in the pocket is a very useful piece of equipment, and avoids too much "holloa-ing" (which gets hounds heads up), on the part of all those who see a hare and immediately assume it is the hunted one. What should always be in the boot of the car, or the saddle bag on the bicycle, is a dry pair of trousers, socks, towel, etc as, in the sometimes unpredictable English winter weather, one is almost certain to get damp at some time during the day, and a change of clothing for the journey home is always very acceptable. Such other items like Thermos flasks, bottles etc containing refreshment of various kinds are largely up to the whims and tastes of the follower, but a bar of chocolate or similar carried in the pocket can be acceptable at four o'clock, when hounds are still running and the Huntsman is of the type that just does not know when to stop.

There are nine registered packs of working basset hounds in the UK, compared with over 80 packs of beagles; in the USA there are some 18 packs of basset hounds and 30 packs of beagles. There the quarry is either European hare, Kansas jackrabbit or cottontail. At the present time there is also a useful interchange of hounds between France and the United

States, as well as from this country and Ireland and the quality of the American working hound is such that some are likely to be imported back here reasonably soon.

Nearly a hundred years ago it was written that: "There was something so sporting in seeing these little hounds (to all appearances a first-cross between a turnspit and a foxhound) driving along in grass that almost hid them. Their music – as compared to foxhounds – was as a peal of church bells to a tune upon glasses. The roar of nine couple would have drowned the combined dog packs of Pytchley, Grafton and Warwickshire". This was written by a great foxhound man, seeing basset hounds hunting for the first time.

Lovers of the countryside, of wildlife and the dynamic nature of its environment know only too well that the object of all hunting is not "just to kill things". Nothing is further from the truth as any real hunting person knows and appreciates. Hunting the hare in its natural environment, with a good pack of basset hounds is the greatest fun, for both Huntsman and onlookers alike, and the latter can take as much or as little exercise as they wish to do. The friendship of other like-minded people and especially of the hounds themselves make harehunting on foot tremendous fun. Eric Morrison said that hunting the hare with basset hounds was the champagne of all field sports, and none of us who have had contact with these wonderful little hounds would disagree with that.

Rex Hudson has recently retired as Hon Secretary of The Masters of Basset Hounds Association and has now been elected its President.

Staghunting

Dick Lloyd

Staghunting in the West Country is of very ancient origin and goes back at least to the early 1600s, although there are detailed records of sport with the North Devon Staghounds from 1780 to 1825, when that pack was sold to Germany and that strain of hound was lost. After 25 years without a resident pack – the Dark Ages of history when the red deer almost ceased to exist, a new pack, the Devon and Somerset Staghounds was established by Mr Fenwick Bisset with kennels built at Exford in 1865. Today the Devon and Somerset Staghounds continue to thrive there with the Quantock hunting those hills and immediate surroundings, while the Tiverton, based near Chulmleigh, hunt the country south of the old Taunton/Barnstaple main road.

The season, on which the Deer Act 1963 was based, is divided into three parts. Autumn staghunting, August 1 to about October 25; hindhunting, November 1 to February 28; and spring staghunting, March 1 to April 30. In the autumn the aim is to hunt the oldest – not necessarily the finest (although the two may coincide) stag in the district. In hindhunting, any adult is suitable, while in the spring preference is for three and four year old stags and often those with one horn or other deformities. At all times of the season, priority is given to any lame or sick deer which may be found and the day's hunt will be interrupted until such a casualty has been accounted for.

As the red deer is essentially a herd animal, the method of hunting is different from that of a fox or hare and is adapted to the fact that a stag, or more particularly a hind, is unlikely to be found alone. For this reason, therefore, a few hounds known as "tufters", usually between four and six couple, are drawn from the pack kennelled in a horse box conveniently near the meet. On the previous day the "Harbourer", normally a part time hunt servant knowledgeable about the deer, visits the area to be hunted to discover the whereabouts of a huntable stag which he then hopes to see come out to feed in the evening. Next morning, he will be there before daylight to see the stag "go back to bed" in the wood or gorse or bracken where he is to spend the day. As a stag may be inadvertently disturbed by a walker, shepherd or stray dog, the prudent harbourer always tries to arrange for a helper to look out for a "second string" in case his first choice cannot be found by the tufters.

The Huntsman, guided by the "Harbourer", with a small number of experienced members of the field, then draws the covert until the right stag has been found and hunted into the open away from other deer. At this stage, the tufters are stopped and the pack, signalled by a special call on the horn and the waving of a white handkerchief, are brought on by one of the whippers-in assisted by the second horsemen. The main body of the field, which could only serve to block the paths and make the Huntsman's job more difficult, do not take part in the tufting which they should be able to watch from a convenient hill, when much interesting hound work may be seen. After the pack is "laid on" the hunt proper begins, the field join in and, subject to any essential restrictions by the Master, are free to stay as near hounds as they may decide.

When a stag or hind realises that it is being hunted, its first intention is to find other deer and confuse the hounds, and nine out of ten unsuccessful hunts come to an end in this way. The red stag – more so than the hind – is a lazy animal and at any time in the day, if satisfied that hounds have checked or lost the line, may lie down and rest even early on in a hunt. Other deer however, do not usually welcome the company of the hunted stag and can often be seen trying to drive him away, but if they do not succeed and the whole party disappear into a big woodland, the Huntsman may be presented with an insoluble problem, although smart whippers-in or skilful members of the field can frequently help with useful information. The deer's second line of defence is the use of the numerous streams and rivers of Exmoor and the Tiverton country although not so much on the Quantocks where water is scarce. On coming to a stream, the hunted deer will often follow it for a mile or more until reaching some obstruction which causes it to take to dry land again. The skill of hounds and Huntsman in sorting out such difficulties can be fascinating to watch. If hounds take the line upstream, it is almost certainly right, but downstream is another matter. It may be that the scent is being carried down "on the wash" while the deer has in fact gone upwards and many hunts have failed when the Huntsman comes to the wrong conclusion.

At the end of a successful hunt the deer "stands to bay" often in a river or stream, is **not attacked by the hounds**, and will then be shot by one of two different firearms carried by mounted followers:

1 The "hunt gun" of which there may be up to three on any one day, is a folding single barrel 12 bore loaded with a heavy SSG shot which is most often employed and is carried by well-mounted farmers, all expert shots and holders of firearms certificates.

2 For use at close quarters in surroundings unsuitable for a big gun, the hunt staff are equipped with 0.32 pistols firing a single shot.

Exmoor and the Quantock Hills still have plenty of space on moorland

and woodland where large fields can be accommodated so visitors are welcome. The Tiverton country, which is all enclosed, has never been as popular from a rider's point of view, because when hounds run it is imperative to use the roads a good deal to keep in touch. Nevertheless the visitor will find a warm welcome in all three countries, whether on horse or motor car. The mounted visitor, on his own horse or hireling of which there are plenty at most times of the year, need make no previous contact and should introduce him/herself to the hunt secretary at the meet and pay a cap which may vary depending on the pack and time of year. It should be noted that at popular times such as September and October or April, horses are in great demand and plans should be made in good time.

Dress for autumn staghunting is ratcatcher (tweed coat with black or brown boots and bowler hat, tie or stock as preferred). For hindhunting, a black coat and stock with bowler or today a hunting cap is permissible. Dress for spring staghunting is as for the autumn, although winter clothes are perfectly acceptable and often worn to the end of season in bad weather conditions.

A feature of modern staghunting which causes much comment is the very large number of cars, mainly four wheel drive, following the hunts on all popular days; 300 to 400 is commonplace with the Devon and Somerset Staghounds in the autumn and spring and there is no doubt that this can have an effect on the run of the deer. On the other hand, an old stag or hind having made up its mind, even if headed the first time, will often circle round and make its point in a slightly different place. Incidentally it is worth recalling that the first recorded serious car jam with the Devon and Somerset Staghounds was in 1922, so it is not a new problem. Modern farming in the shape of mesh wire fences also restricts movement and the huge increase in conifer plantations has undoubtedly slowed the pace of hunting and reduced the deer's inclination to make long points. However, unlike in the vast majority of England today, most of the staghunting country is basically unchanged and a good hunt in the 1990s can provide as fine a ride and long point as in any time of history.

Staghunting has a long tradition, fully maintained to the present day, of wonderful support from farmers and landowners throughout the hunting area and there are only a very few small areas where hounds are not welcome. Owing to the nature of the fences, there is no jumping, therefore no wear and tear on this account, but grassland in the spring is vulnerable and without due care damage can be considerable. In addition and more important, some farms suffer regular and intense damage by deer, herds of 30 or more grazing almost daily on the most favoured areas.

In past times, particularly in the depressed farming years between the wars, large sums (up to £50 000 in today's values) were paid annually in compensation to farmers for deer damage. Now, due to considerable tolerance on the long-suffering farmers, this demand has shrunk to a trickle, which, considering that a deer will eat as much as a yearling bullock, reflects extreme generosity on the part of those concerned.

Dick Lloyd is Chairman of the Devon and Somerset Staghounds and of The Masters of Deerhounds Association.

In 1932, Frank Freeman, famous Huntsman of the Pytchley, when taken tufting as a honoured guest to see a big stag roused, remarked to Ernest Bawden, the then almost equally well-known Devon and Somerset Staghounds Huntsman, "I can't see how you can lose such a big animal." The reply came, "Maybe, but when I have lost him, I can't stand over the nearest hole, blow my horn and pretend he's gone to ground."

Dick Lloyd

Mink Hunting

Patrick Wild

To many people, hunting is seen as a winter activity with the colder weather being more conducive to scenting conditions. The absence of stock in the fields and less risk of damage to growing crops makes access to farmland easier. The exception is mink hunting. The Masters of Mink Hounds Association was formed 14 years ago and is the governing body for all mink hunts, having a set of rules and a code of conduct observed by all its members. Each member registers its hunt country with the Association and is responsible for an area of several hundred square miles or a group of counties and the rivers in such an area.

There are 19 packs of mink hounds registered with the Association. The mink hunting season runs from April to October, taking place principally along river banks. Most of England and Wales is covered by a mink hunt. The quarry is the North American mink, introduced to the UK in 1928 to be bred for the fur trade. Many escaped or were deliberately released by animal rights activists and have thrived in the wild. They have no natural predators; mink are themselves predators of fish, small mammals, bird life, game, lambs and even piglets. Mink were featured in the BBC 1 programmes *Wildlife on One* and *Country File*, both shown in 1991, giving a balanced and informative view of mink and their effect on the rural environment. Two mink hunts cooperated in the production of each programme.

Followed on foot, mink hunts usually meet at 11 am on Saturdays or on weekday evenings with the Master and Huntsman, assisted by whippers-in (who control the hounds), drawing along the bank of a stream or river to find a mink. The hounds are often a cross between English foxhounds, Welsh foxhounds or pure-bred otterhounds. They are bred for their scenting abilities, stamina, obedience, voice and skill in locating and catching mink. When a mink is caught, it is either killed instantly by the hounds or a terrier or it gets clean away and therefore does not suffer a lingering death from possibly inaccurate shooting or other causes. In the wild, many animals do not meet their end in a peaceful old age, but are at risk from disease, injury or starvation. Most hunts date from the mid-1970s when mink began to be hunted on a regular basis; although, some of the otter hunts which ceased operation in the mid-1970s (when otters became a protected species – otter hunting ceased two years before this) also hunted mink. The Association expressly forbids drawing for, or using hounds entered to, otter. Mink can swim, climb trees, run up drains and are tough, fearless and resourceful.

A hunt can last up to three hours and all hunts employ terriers to work tight places such as willow trees and drains. The Code of Conduct, referred to above, ensures that a mink is hunted in its wild state with a pack of hounds under such Rules. This ensures that a hunt conducts its affairs properly and responsibly, thus helping to control mink and counteract the serious effect they have on the balance of nature. Thus, mink hunts play their part in the life and management of our countryside.

Before arranging a meet, the staff of a hunt will always obtain the consent of the landowner, farmer or river keeper to go onto his land and for the hunt followers to do so. If, for any reason, a landowner does not allow access, the hunt will respect this wish and do its best to keep followers and hounds off the land in question. People from all walks of life follow packs of hounds and the cost of following is modest. Anyone who wishes to see what goes on and likes to get into open country with an interest in working hounds is more than welcome to follow a mink hunt. Today, sadly, not all hunts are able to advertise their meets because those who disagree with the right to hunt or not, according to the choice of the individual, seek to disrupt and spoil what they make no effort to understand.

Whilst less colourful than that worn by the hunt staff of a pack of foxhounds or beagles, the uniform worn by the staff of a mink hunt is designed for practicality and to convey a sense of identity. Everyone must be prepared to cross ditches, wade streams and battle through the undergrowth – comfortable, sturdy footwear is important. A day's draw may only cover a few miles but the going can vary with the terrain.

Meets are often on a call out basis in response to demands for help in catching mink which are causing damage to wildlife, farm stock, game or fish. Hunts are always ready to assist keepers and farmers who report mink damage. Mink hunting is a good way to see hounds at work in the summer months, outside the beagling, foxhunting and shooting seasons.

Finally, articles on mink hunting often appear in country-orientated magazines. Individual hunts frequently parade hounds at game fairs and agricultural shows, at which they may also mount static displays, where knowledgeable hunt followers are on hand to answer questions from those who are keen to learn more about one of our newer field sports.

Patrick Wild is Honorary Secretary of The Masters of Mink Hounds Association.

Hunting in Canada

Bill Bermingham

The fox has been hunted in Canada for a very long time. The earliest record is in the year 1801. On a very cold day in January, a private pack of hounds (of unknown origin) hunted a fox to the edge of Lake Ontario, near Toronto. The lake was frozen over, so the fox ran out onto the ice, where the small mounted field was replaced by an enthusiastic crowd of people on ice skates.

In 1805, an entire pack of English hounds was imported to Hamilton, in what was then called Upper Canada. This must have been a very expensive undertaking, as the sailing ships of the day took six or seven weeks to cross the Atlantic Ocean, and the pack of hounds would have to be fed and cared for during the voyage.

In Quebec in 1807, a man called Matthew Bell owned a pack of English hounds which he hunted to the north of the town of Trois-Rivières. Mr Bell leased the Forges of the St Maurice. These were the famous iron works which were the property of the Crown, but the lease was the gift of the Governor. Matthew Bell grew rich from the operation of the Forges and he was a figure of power in politics, business, and social circles. Today the Masters of Foxhounds Association, on both sides of the Atlantic, frowns on the promotion of business interests through foxhunting. Mr Bell, however, was unencumbered by these righteous prohibitions, and he found it advantageous to maintain extensive stables and kennels, and facilities for keeping foxes! A large number of guests could be accommodated, and a set of apartments was always reserved for the Governor. This exotic establishment became a social centre known as the Tally-Ho Hunt Club. There every autumn, Mr Bell entertained his influential and sporting friends and the Governor, who all bucketed gaily about the countryside, after bagged foxes, to the mingled astonishment and delight of all beholders.

Another private pack of English hounds was kennelled at Trois-Rivières, and hunted by a Monsieur Outhet. This man was a sporting butcher, who hired out his hounds and himself, by the day. In the year 1826, a group of Montreal sportsmen decided to form the Montreal Hunt, and they purchased Monsieur Outhet's pack of hounds, and hired him to be the Huntsman.

Unfortunately, Mr Bell came under vigorous attack from the left in 1829, and an inquiry was demanded into his affairs. It is not without significance that the date of the inquisition, and the sale of his entire pack of foxhounds to the Montreal Hunt, are one and the same. It was a bit of bad luck, but the Tally-Ho Hunt Club had 22 years of outstanding sport.

The Montreal Hunt is the oldest organised pack of foxhounds, with an unbroken record of sport, in North America. The British Army had the responsibility of defending Canada before Confederation. The military officer's love of the sport of foxhunting led to the establishment of the Toronto Hunt in 1843. Much later in 1930, this establishment split and became the Toronto and North York Hunt, and the Eglinton Hunt, which is now called the Eglinton and Caledon Hunt. The Ottawa Valley Hunt was established in 1873, and the London Hunt in 1885. The other Canadian hunts were established as follows:

- Lake of Two Mountains Hunt   1946
- Hamilton Hunt   1958
- Wellington Waterloo Hunt   1965
- Frontenac Hunt   1966
- Fraser Valley Hunt   1968
- Bethany Hills Hunt   1974

Recently the Trollope Hunt, which was established in 1976, amalgamated with the Wellington Waterloo Hunt. Through the years, other new hunts have been established in several locations, including the Prairie Provinces, but sadly they have not survived the extremely cold winters and the very short hunting season.

All of the packs in Canada have English hounds, rather than the American or crossbred hounds found in some American hunts. Although the breed is English, some of the hound's pedigrees can be traced back over 100 years in North America. Eight of the packs are hunted by professional huntsmen. Seven packs hunt live foxes and coyotes, two are exclusively drag hunts, and the remainder hunt both live quarry and a drag.

Naturally the hunting countries vary considerably. The Montreal Hunt is famous for its big stone walls whereas the Ottawa Valley has many unusual fences made from whole logs a foot or so in diameter, placed one above the other like a rail fence. Horses don't brush these fences when they jump!

The Toronto and North York Hunt has a good deal of sandy ground, so it is unaffected by wet weather. The Eglinton and Caledon Hunt, the Frontenac, and the Bethany Hills, have a lot of hilly and stony ground which is not suited to farming so they are able to hunt in the spring.

Hamilton and London have first class agricultural land that is relatively flat, and of the holding clay variety. It is intensely farmed. The main crops are wheat, soya beans, and corn or maize. Huge equipment is used to cultivate the land these days, and this has resulted in many fences being removed so that the farm equipment can be used more efficiently. Very little livestock is raised today.

Most hunts have panelled their country with hunt jumps, or chicken coops as they are called. In some places rail fences still exist and they are great fun to jump.

The Fraser Valley hunts a country in southern British Columbia which lies along the border between the United States and Canada. This International Boundary is marked only with small concrete markers every mile. The hounds are not required by the authorities to recognise this as the border, and it is fortunate that there, at least, foxhunting knows no bounds.

Again with the exception of the Montreal Hunt, all of the hunting countries have a grid pattern road system, unlike England where the roads follow the natural contours of the land. The British Army Surveyors laid out this grid system in 1793. The military mind is very partial to grid systems, so the land in Ontario was laid out in parcels of one thousand acres which were subdivided into ten one hundred acre farms. Each parcel was then bounded on the east and west, by roads running north and south, and on the north and south, by roads running east and west. Like the Czar of all the Russians who laid out the Trans Siberian Railway in a dead straight line, the military seldom varied the direction of the road, regardless of what obstacle lay in its path. This was called military intelligence, and the happy result is that it is difficult to become lost when hunting, and it is easy to follow the hounds by car.

The Canadian packs meet two days a week during the season, and usually three days a week during cubhunting. The exceptions are Ottawa Valley and the Montreal Hunts, which meet three days a week. The season usually lasts from August to December, and April and May for those who hunt in the spring. Several of the packs meet on Sundays instead of Saturday. The fields would number about 15 to 30 people on weekdays, and perhaps 30 to 80 on the weekend meets, depending on the size of the hunt. Very few foxhunters have second horses, so the hunts tend to last about four hours. All Canadian hunts welcome visitors, and they charge a modest cap for the day. Hirelings are not normally available, but arrangements can usually be made through the hunt secretary.

There are no private packs in Canada. All are subscription packs. Most hunts are governed by a board of directors, and are self financing. The directors usually appoint the Masters, and the guarantee system is not used. Funds are raised in various ways such as hunt balls, horse shows, subscriptions, silent auctions, hunter trials, and recently through the sale of wine by the case, to hunt members. The wine is purchased wholesale by the hunt, labelled with the hunt name and crest, and perhaps a photo of the hunt or a hound and sold on at a profit to the followers. This has been found to be a popular method of raising considerable funds.

Many of the hunts have a club house at the kennels, which becomes the social centre of the hunt. Some of these establishments, like the London Hunt and Country Club, are very elegant indeed. All of them provide a place where the members, many of whom travel over 50 miles to hunt, can gather after the days sport, and have a drink with their friends.

Unlike England, the fox population does not need to be controlled. The foxes tend to be a wilder type of animal than their English cousins. The Ministry of Natural Resources in Ontario has done an extensive study of foxes in relation to their rabies program. The Ministry have used electronic collars and tracking devices to study the habits of foxes, and they have discovered that foxes will range up to 250 miles from home. Sadly, Ontario is the rabies capital of the world. No one knows why it should be, but there are more confirmed cases of rabies than in any other place. This fact has an adverse effect on the fox population, but there is hope for improvement in the future. The Ministry have developed an effective oral vaccine for foxes, which can be dropped from the air. By this means it is hoped that the amount of rabies in foxes can be reduced by 90 per cent in a few years.

Many farmers, orchardists and naturalists have learned that the fox is a valuable asset, because his diet consists mainly of field mice and other crop-destroying rodents. The United States Department of Agriculture has estimated conservatively that no farm land today averages less than ten field mice per acre, and that the loss due to field mice, on the 65 million acres of hay land in the USA, is not less than three million tons of hay per year. Consequently there is little demand by informed land owners for the destruction of foxes.

The proliferation of coyotes in recent years has also adversely affected the fox population. The western coyote has gradually migrated to the east, and has now reached the Maritime provinces. During this migration the coyotes have bred with wild and domestic dogs, to produce offspring which differ from the western coyote. These are called coydogs or brush wolves. They are about twice the size of a fox, and can run very fast at a steady, and apparently easy going lope, which allows them to keep just ahead of a pack of hounds that are running like the very devil. The brush wolves tend to disturb the foxes, and this also has an unfortunate effect on the fox population. There is also strong competition for food, because both the brush wolves and foxes eat rodents and groundhogs.

With all of these pressures on the fox population, Canadian foxhunters are anxious to preserve the foxes that survive, and foxes are very seldom killed by a pack of hounds. The chase is the object of the exercise, and 'the kill' in Canada is the exception rather than the rule. Earth-stopping is almost unknown in Canadian hunting; the groundhog holes and earths are so numerous that this would not be a practical thing to do. Most runs end through the failure of scent, or the fox or brush wolf is marked to the ground. Foxes are never dug out or bolted. It is said that a pack of foxhounds must have blood in order to keep them keen. This must be a false conception, because the Canadian packs of hounds are very keen, and just as enthusiastic, whether they hunt a live quarry, or a drag.

With so few foxes to hunt, some packs also hunt the native jack-rabbits. These animals are slightly bigger than a hare. When they are first hunted, they tend to run in quite small circles, but after they have been hunted a few times, they will get up and go, and often give the hounds a five mile point. Jack-rabbits are found in coverts like foxes, but they are just as often found lying in the furrow of a ploughed field, or in tall grass. This means that the hounds must be able to draw thoroughly in the open as well as in the covert.

The author remembers fondly a stallion hound called Portman Dalesman '63. He hunted a fox vigorously with the rest of the pack when he first went hunting, but when the hounds found a jack-rabbit, and went joyously off in full cry, Dalesman sat right down beside the Huntsman's horse, with a look of utter disgust on his face, and one could almost hear him saying, "these bloody colonials!".

Other than these differences, foxhunting is conducted in the same way as it is in England; the dress is the same, the rules, both written and unwritten, are the same – the foxhounds are the same outstanding and amazing animals. Foxhunting in Canada is a non-competitive sport, where the only competition is for politeness and common courtesy.

The typical Canadian foxhunter is out to enjoy seeing a good pack of foxhounds at work, hearing their music, feeling the thrill of a fast ride across natural country on a good horse, with the wind in his ears, and spending the day in the open countryside, in the company of congenial fellow foxhunters. If he is lucky enough to catch a glimpse of the fox as it breaks covert, or tops a hill, it gives the hunt an added zest and the foxhunter goes happily home at the end of the day.

For those of us who are not yet ready to live completely in a world of plastic, steel, and concrete, the fox is something of a symbol, a symbol of the wild. He reminds us that we haven't entirely turned to the artificial. The fox is a symbol of our Canadian heritage, and a symbol of freedom within our civilization. May he never vanish from our scene.

Bill Bermingham is a former Master of Foxhounds in Canada and a Director of The Masters of Foxhounds Association of America.

Perhaps the most extraordinary thing that has ever happened to me in the field, occurred when hunting with Ben Hardaway's Midland Foxhounds at Fitzpatrick, Alabama. We had gone for a visit and taken our hounds with us, and we were hunting both packs together. Ben and I, and my Huntsman, and a chosen few, were riding with the hounds while drawing a covert. A Midland hound called Anne started to speak, and Ben assured us, "that ol' Anne ain't never been wrong", so we followed cheering her on. She was on a fox all right, but unfortunately she was running heel way. Finally a member of the field came galloping back to tell us that the whole combined pack of hounds, (with the exception of "ol' Anne,") had burst the fox away from the far side of the covert, and had gone away in full cry, fiercely followed by the whole field.

Ben was very cross when he heard this, and set off at a mad gallop to try to catch up to the pack. It is wonderful galloping country, but I've never crossed any country as fast as we did that day. All the time Ben, who was white in the face and furious at being "throwed out of the race" was looking for tracks and signs of where the hounds had been. Presently we jumped another fence into a farm yard, and Ben pulled his horse to a screeching stop from a gallop.

There, lying in front of us was a dead horse. It had its saddle and bridle on, and it was in a lather, but it was obviously dead. After a few seconds examination, Ben shouted, "Come on, they must have come this way, and that ol' dead horse is pointing the way! Let's go!!"

Bill Bermingham

Hunting in the USA

James L Young

Into its third century of existence, organized hunting in America can best be characterized by both its vitality and its variety as it moves towards the second millennium. 150 recognized packs of foxhounds currently enjoy sport in 35 states spanning the country from Florida to California, and from Vermont in the far north-east to Washington State in the Pacific north-west.

Although the total number of active riders to hounds is small compared to Great Britain and Ireland (an estimated 12 000 out of a population of more than 250 million), it is the considerable diversity of demographics, countries, hounds, quarry and climate which lends American hunting its unique brand of excitement. Indeed, in order to sample even a small slice of this variety, an international visitor would have to hunt more than a dozen packs scattered the length and breadth of the nation.

To experience the oldest and more traditional hunting in America, one would head for the venerable packs amidst the mid-Atlantic and mid-Southern states: New York, New Jersey, Pennsylvania, Maryland, Virginia, the Carolinas and Kentucky. Packs such as Millbrook (New York), Mr Stewart's Cheshire (Pennsylvania), Green Spring Valley (Maryland), the Piedmont (Virginia) and the Iroquois (Kentucky) are renowned for their long heritage, quality hounds and lovely hunting venues. The state of Virginia boasts the largest concentration of recognized packs (20), and its northern country sports the sobriquet of "the Leicestershire of America."

New England, on the other hand, is beset by development, resulting in more drag hunts or limited country for live hunting. Given these exigencies, however, such respected hunts as the Myopia and Norfolk in Massachusetts provide excellent, season-long drag sport, approximating live hunting in its best traditions.

In the deep South, the hunting is charaterized by enormous plantations of open pine woods, quarry other than the red fox and wide-open galloping with occasional jumping panels. It is here that such famous hunts as the Midland (Georgia), the Live Oak (Florida), and the Mooreland (Alabama) provide superb sport. Since these plantations also cultivate quail, pheasant and other game birds, there is an imperative for the hunts to rid the country of any vermin inimical to those avian crops. While the coyote is the quarry 60 per cent of the time, grey fox and bobcat, as well as the occasional opossum or racoon may emerge in front of the hounds. It may only be in this part of America that there is a significant agricultural imperative to cull the quarry, as exists in England.

Midland Hunt, Georgia. Mr Ben Hardaway, Joint Master and Huntsman since 1950, with hounds at Midland.

When the visitor heads into America's heartland across the Ohio and Mississippi Rivers, not only the topography changes dramatically, but also the quarry. In the wide-open ranges of Texas and Kansas, the countries of such hunts as Col Denny's Cloudline or the Mission Valley are defined in thousands of square miles. On the fertile plains of Iowa's North Hills Hunt or the sometimes frozen fields of Illinois' Mill Creek, the hunter's pilot, as in Texas or Kansas, may more often be the infamous coyote as the fox.

Hunting in the far western states of California, Nevada or Colorado is invariably in pursuit of the coyote with an occasional wild boar roused, accounted for and then barbecued! While the cowboy spirit of the Old West may ride in the hearts of western hunters, the sport is conducted in traditional foxhunting manner. The most exhilarating aspect of western hunting may be the boundless terrain – dry, rocky ground where sparse grasses and sagebrush may be the only ground cover. There is no dearth, however, of steep hills, ravines and canyons which demand a rawhide character from hound, horse and rider.

America's hunting quarry, as suggested above, is as diverse as its country. The traditional red fox is still abundant, especially in the mid-eastern states where it is not unusual to rouse 10 to 15 foxes on a hunting day. Their longevity is prolonged, perhaps, by the plethora of groundhog holes into which they can seek refuge. Because much of the county is no longer broken up, but rather, left in pastureland for horses and cattle, there are more refuges for Sir Charles than a legion of earth-stoppers could eliminate in their collective careers. The resulting sport is characterised by many brilliant races of relatively short duration (20 to 60 minutes), over rolling grasslands.

The American grey fox, most prevalent in southern latitudes, tends to live in thick briars and heavy coverts and prefers to run in maddeningly tight circles (some would say – increasingly concentric) until they disappear, either to earth or up a tree. There is a certain perverse enjoyment in watching hounds' bafflement when their grey pilot literally "evaporates up a rope." Huntsmen love the grey fox, however, as a marvellous tutor for teaching young hounds to stay on their noses.

The coyote – ah, the coyote (ki-oat). Our western brethren have been happily hunting him with hounds for decades. Only in the past 20 years, or so has he invaded the sacred environs of east coast hunts, and he initially fomented fear in those hearts:

"He'll drive the fox into extinction!"

"He's an unworthy adversary!"

"Neither hound nor horse can stay with him in our tight country."

These laments, however, have proven to be overstated. After an initial season of providing severe consternation to hounds, the coyote has evidenced a decided propensity to show elating sport, albeit fast and straightaway. These three stone, brindle-coloured canines are capable of loafing just ahead of a pack of hounds, at whatever speed pressed, only to suddenly disappear by virtue of innate speed, cunning or satanic deviousness. When put to bay, some coyotes have survived by the lack of enthusiasm on the part of the hounds to dispatch what seems to be a close cousin.

After the first generation has settled a country, the coyote seems to run in large circles, similar to their vulpine kin, and fox populations have sustained themselves along the periphery of the coyote's feeding range. It is an uneasy alliance, but one which eases the foxhunter's fear of fox eradication. One hunting fact does emerge: the coyote's intense scent excites hounds to a frenzy, somewhat like deer riot, and it tests a Huntsman's mettle to discern the difference.

There are more than 44 000 hounds currently registered within the MFHA's Foxhound Kennel Stud Book of America. If one considers, as does the MFHA and the American Kennel Club, that the foxhound is a singular breed of hound, then one will find that there are four distinct strains of foxhounds in America. The English hound, American, Crossbred and Harrier are all eligible for registration in the MFHA Stud Book, provided they are the property of a recognised hunt or of the Master and are bona fide members of a hunting pack.

English and American foxhounds are regarded as purebreds if each are free from any outcrossing other than their breed during three previous generations. One-sixteenth outcross is permitted. Crossbred foxhounds are those which do not qualify under the fractional rulings as either American or English hounds, yet fully 50 per cent of American packs are made up of crosses between pure English and pure American hounds.

One registered strain, the Penn-Marydel is considered to be a discrete line of American foxhound, but the Penn-Marydel Foxhound Association maintains its own registry and stud book, in addition to the MFHA Stud Book. Sometimes compared to the Blacks and Tans of the Scarteen, this hound is characterized by its low-scenting ability over the sandy soil of its native *Penn*sylvania, *Mary*land and *Del*aware country and by its deep, bass voice reminiscent of the French stag or American bloodhound.

An inadequate, thumbnail definition of each strain of pack hound would be as follows:

- The American hound: a lighter, racier hound than its English cousin, it is known for its independence in hunting style; its exceptionally low-scenting ability; a thinner, greyhound-like conformation, and its notable speed in the open. These hounds descended, for the most part, from two "Irish Dogs", Mountain and Muse, imported from America about 1815 by Bolton Jackson, an Irishman who came to live in Baltimore, Maryland around 1810.

- The English hound is characterized by its substance and bone, animated bidability and tenor-like cry. Its classic conformation and progenitor typology (Belvoir-type, Fell, Welsh, and modern English) provides the American Master with a variety of type to suit his country.

While English and American strains share half of all foxhounds in America, the Crossbred hound is by far the emergent choice of American hound breeders. Aficionados of the Crossbred tout its substance of frame, intelligence and drive, bidability and stamina over time. It is significant to note that it is the Crossbred foxhound which is the overwhelming favourite of breeders who chase coyote.

Some of the foremost, all-English packs in America would be the Blue Ridge (Virginia), Mr Stewart's Cheshire (Pennsylvania) and the Arapahoe (Colorado). Forerunners with traditionally American foxhounds would include the Orange County (Virginia), the Potomac (Maryland) and the Essex (New Jersey). Crossbred packs with certain renown would include the Midland (Georgia), the Live Oak (Florida), and the Green Spring Valley (Maryland).

While variety may describe the panoply of foxhunting in America, simple enthusiasm and hospitality would define the spirit of American foxhunters towards their compatriots. Most hunting clubs are smallish affairs, with less than 100 members and subscribers, yet their welcome to visitors usually reflects a simple, down-home friendliness. Most hunts welcome visitors and only ask for an advance call to the honorary secretary to ensure a day's sport. Capping fees range from a paltry $20 to as much as $150 for a holiday hunt with a prestigious pack. Visitors should be forewarned, however, that hirelings are hard to come by and a fortunate guest may find himself on a member's favourite hunter. *Caveat equitor!* Another word of caution is advised, moreover, since there are hunts which accept visitors by invitation only. Thus, either *Baily's Hunting Directory* or the Annual Hunt Roster Issue (September) of *The Chronicle of the Horse* should be consulted before calling or writing to a hunt.

Spring hunting, the Golden's Bridge Hounds of North Salem, New York

Cub hunting begins at different times depending upon latitude. Northern hunts, particularly, begin early, usually in August and the opening date drops back as one moves farther south. Some states, such as Virginia, restrict live hunting until after September 1 in order to enhance young fox health. Formal opening meets, moreover, vary according to climate as well. Northern states may open as early as September, while more traditional dates such as late October or after the Feast of St Hubert in November apply to southern hunts.

Many hunts in the far northern climes must either close or suspend hunting during the winter months because of frozen ground and adverse weather conditions, but hunts below those tundra-lines end their season in early spring – March or April. At least one pack in the deep south hunts whenever its Master wishes.

Jumping fences in America is not usually a high-risk venture requiring double-indemnity insurance policies. The average fence panel probably will be in the three foot to three foot six-inch range with occasional obstacles soaring to four feet. It all depends on which height salves the farmer's fears for his livestock.

There are no banks, and only the random ditch over a stream. Those delightful drag hunters oftentimes provide a series of constructed jumps along trails which provide some impediment to flat-out galloping. Usually there are side-by-side jumps of varying heights, as well as "go-around" paths, thus allowing options to the discerning rider.

Because of the paucity of jumpable line fences, there exists the damnably-modern feature of jumping panels which requires queuing-up before such constructs as the ubiquitous "chicken coop", a triangular-shaped panel of boards laid over wire. It is one of the safest obstacles in the hunting field, but it certainly doesn't enhance "thrusting" by rangy, hell-for-leather devils.

Foxhunting in the United States continues to grow and flourish despite enormous pressures brought upon it by urban and suburban sprawl. Whereas our brethren in the United Kingdom must face the daunting assaults of the anti-bloodsports and the class warmongers, Americans consider their primary foe to be the bulldozer and its desecration of open landscapes.

This is not do say that we do not contend with misguided animal welfarists and eco-terrorists. We do, and we are conducting an ongoing campaign against their attempts to anthropomorphize all living creatures and their rural habitats. In this regard, we are one with our compatriots in the United Kingdom, and we will continue our support, as we did during the dark days of the McNamara Bill.

Foxhunting in the USA is vibrant, vigorous, varied and vivacious. It needs only its friends of kindred spirit to enhance its magic. We welcome you to join us in our devotion to the Meynellian Science.

> *"This is the game of our hearts!*
> *Foot to the stirrup! Away!*
> *Care with the night departs*
> *Joy comes in with the day.*
> *A good horse tossing his rings,*
> *A light rime decking the thorn:*
> *And the heart of a horseman sings*
> *For the love of a hunting morn."*

Will H Ogilvie

Good hunting!

Jimmy Young is a third-generation foxhunter who has followed in his father's hoofprints as Master of the Orange County Hunt in Virginia. A Doctor of Education and a published author, Jimmy Young is the current President of the Masters of Foxhounds Association of America.

Hunting in New Zealand

Philip Langdale

Hunting in New Zealand is very much alive and well, though little is known about it in the United Kingdom. In historical terms, New Zealand is a very young country. In the very early days the country was found to be desirable by itinerant whalers and subsequently by shipwrights, who found the timber called Kauri growing to the north of the North Island to be of the very best for repairing sailing ships. Naturally, some of these people settled on a permanent basis, but were soon to have their troubles with the indigenous Maoris despite inter-marriage. Britain ruled the waves and did not like any of its subjects wherever they may be to be molested by the locals. Troops were sent from India in order to calm the situation. Some of these soldiers liked the country and they too stayed.

Countryside was cleared of scrub and bush and farms were established. As the settlers position became secure, their thoughts turned to recreation and hunting was not far from the top of the list. Beagles were brought to the Auckland area by Governor Sir George Grey in 1868. The first hunt to be formed was the Pakuranga near Auckland in 1873 and with the Christchurch in 1880, others soon followed. A governing body, the New Zealand Hunts Association, was formed in 1900 from nine packs that were hunting regularly. Others followed so that today the tally of recognised hunts stands at 29, the most recent being the establishment of the Central Otago in 1989.

Sam Nelson, Master of the Hawke's Bay

Heat and dry ground conditions prevent the hunting season commencing before late March or early April. This continues until early July for most hunts when lambing activities curtail it. There are a few hunts who are able to continue longer because of their altitude and consequent later lambing dates or merely lack of sheep. All hunts will hunt for two days per week and some will have weeks when three days are available thus 25 to 35 days of hunting per season are achieved. A hunting day is rarely cancelled except in cases of extremely wet ground conditions out of respect for the landowner. The emphasis of support is changing from that of the countryside to the town and with this in mind, hunts are trying very hard to have one of the weekend days carded and all public holidays that fall within the hunting season. The size of fields varies from a mid-week meet in a small country of 20 to the weekend meet of a hunt close to a large urban population which may exceed 150. Membership of all categories (senior, junior, family etc) for each hunt varies from 80 to 600.

Rainfall and terrain dictate farming patterns. The east coast of the North Island has a dryer climate with rolling hills, some of which may be steep. This is more suited to grazing sheep and cattle. The western side of the North Island is better suited to dairying with consequent smaller farms and paddocks (fields do not exist in New Zealand and everything is a paddock whether two acres or 200). There is no hunting at all on the western side of the South Island. On the eastern side of this island the country varies from the flats of the Canterbury plains with some arable cropping to the wide open spaces of Central Otago where paddocks of 500-1000 acres are common and some, in the high country, so big as to be unfenced.

New Zealand has no foxes. Practically all mammals were introduced by Europeans and infuriated local sheep farmers drowned the foxes that some homesick Huntsman had imported to hunt in Christchurch harbour. The hare provides the only suitable alternative. There are a very small number of packs that have to hunt the occasional drag, owing to a shortage of hares. Hounds are all harriers and as such were originally imported from England. Occasionally stallion hounds are still imported. The New Zealand Hunts Association has established a stud book for all hounds within all packs. The New Zealand harrier hound is firmly established and there is plenty of good genetic material within the country for the continuation and improvement of the harrier.

Needless to say, horses and ponies ridden by participants vary greatly. Adults are mostly carried by thoroughbreds. There are still a number of farm bred station hacks used. After all, a horse that has been developed to carry shepherds and used to muster stock with sheepdogs over a particular country must have attributes. It should not be forgotten that Charisma, Mark Todd's dual Olympic Gold Medal Winner, was station bred.

Tim Wellwood, Huntsman of the Taupo

Like the horses, the jumps that are encountered vary considerably. All hunters must be able to jump a wire fence. This is of paramount importance for many farms are fenced entirely with eight strand wire fences, supported by permanent concrete or wooden posts, with the wires spaced by wooden battens which are placed about two feet apart. Within this type of fence, there are usually one or two barbed wires which serve to maintain the battens spaces and prevent the cattle rubbing. Hunt jumps are created in suitable places by lowering the top wire and inserting more battens in order to make it more visible for the horses. These are called spars or rickers. Remarkable though it may seem, the tighter the wires, the better, for should a horse hit a wire, it will break and render little damage: whereas a slack wire will "take up" and then cut the horse. Most cuts to horses repair quickly so that it can return to the hunting field, but the occasional bad cut will render it out of action for the rest of the season. Dairy country contains more hedges, usually of barbary, where hunts establish jumps by cutting them down to the right size but they have to be careful as these hedges are required to grow upright in order to provide shelter. In the South Island more fences of wire netting topped with two strands of barbed wire are encountered. Here, the barbed wires are lowered to the level of the netting and a rail is placed between the posts. The Canterbury plains have many shelter belts of pine trees. These are protected on each side by a wire fence. Hunts have to create their jumps by pruning the branches to a suitable height and lowering the wires on either side, thus creating "doubles". Very few ditches coupled with a fence are encountered. An often forgotten attribute of a wire fence is that the rider knows that height and width never vary and he can always see what lies on the far side.

Horses are rarely stabled for the hunting season. They live in a New Zealand rug, hence the term. These canvas rugs may be in the form of unlined "sheets" or woollen lined "covers". This lack of stabling has one very distinct advantage for after the horses return from a day's hunting, they are released into a paddock where they can move about all the time, thus preventing filled legs or any other infirmity associated with standing in a stable. The only disadvantage is that hunters always seem to find the biggest and dirtiest cow pat in which to roll immediately prior to a hunting day!

The format of a hunting day varies greatly from that in England. The meet is held in an area where there is plenty of parking for motor vehicles of all types. This is often beside a hard farm road near a building for which the road was built. This avoids obstructing public highways and gets all the participants together. As hounds move off at the appointed time, it has the advantage that the Master is able to announce any local conditions. At the end of the day, riders will wash or brush off their horses and then feed them. Tables are carried in the hound van which are erected for the "hunt breakfast". Everyone will gather around these tables bringing prepared food for all to enjoy. Landowners and their staff are encouraged to be present and at a suitable moment, the Master will make a speech to thank them in public for their generosity in allowing the hunt to cross their land. This is also a good opportunity for him to announce any future plans or alterations to the card. At the conclusion, people can make their way home. New Zealand hunting countries are very much larger than their northern hemisphere counterparts resulting in greater distances to be travelled, therefore these tea parties perform a very useful function, satisfying the hunger and thirst of hunters and horses alike.

Very few Masters hunt their hounds, a Huntsman being employed to perform this function. He will have to mount himself and look after his horses and hounds alike. He will be wearing a red coat and is assisted in his task of hunting the hounds by amateur whippers-in. They will be dressed in the particular uniform of the hunt. Each of the 29 hunts in New Zealand has a different colour. The only other person to wear the red coat will be the Master. He will almost certainly be Field Master for the day. The presence of only two persons wearing red coats on a normal hunting day makes it easier for the field to recognize the officials – the Huntsman with his hounds and the Field Master who they must follow and obey. Members wear normal riding clothes with coats bearing their hunt's colours. Visitors can wear anything appropriate that is comfortable and safe. Hard hats are obligatory and approved safety hats encouraged. On wet days, all manner of gear is worn to exclude the weather.

Each hunt organises its own social and fundraising functions. These may include hunter trials, dances and balls. All hunts endeavour to invite their farmers and landowners to a function which is usually in the form of a cocktail party. These people are collectively the most important, for without them there would be no hunting. Some 18 hunts are entitled to hold public race meetings which are held under the rules of racing on regular racecourses. Until recently, these race meetings have made a significant contribution to hunt funds. They are also yet another opportunity for hunts to return some hospitality to their landowners. Annual hound shows rotate around the hunts of each district – Northern, Central and South Island. Every four years a National Hound Show is held to encompass all the hunts of the country.

New Zealand is a country with a land area greater than that of the British Isles and a population of slightly over three million. Hunts are very fortunate for they only hunt land where the owners and farmers make them welcome. Hunting's profile remains low, but nevertheless it affords great pleasure to some 6000 members of all categories. Its basics are founded on its older counterparts in the northern hemisphere, but there the comparison stops. It is a field sport in its own right and, although somewhat different, is run to a high standard and gives many people considerable pleasure. Overseas visitors have commented that some parts of New Zealand enjoy the very best hunting country in the world.

Those visitors who wish to hunt and lack the necessary contacts will find all hunts and the New Zealand Hunts Association listed in *Baily's Hunting Directory*. Time involved in a little research and enquiry prior to a visit will definitely not be wasted for many have indicated that they wished that they had had more time to see more hunting. It is a fact of life that the best way to see a country is to view it from a horse's back. Should that rider also be hunting, there is the added advantage that the host farmer will have cleaned up all his dead sheep immediately prior to the hunting day!

Philip Langdale lives in the Hawke's Bay area of North Island and has been Secretary and Treasurer to the Hawke's Bay Hunt. He used to be Field Secretary to the Duke of Beaufort's hounds.

Foxhunting in Australia

John Crosbie-Goold and Ray Willmott

Hunting with hounds began in the 1790s shortly after the initial settlement around Sydney and Hobart. Packs of hounds were formed mainly by officers of the garrison forces. This did not amount to established hunt kennels. In the 1850s the formation of the new colony of Victoria was to provide a new environment for settlement. Shortly after in 1853 the Melbourne Hunt was founded by George Watson, formerly from Ireland, the son of John Watson, Master of the Carlow Hounds from 1808 until 1869. This was the beginning of established hunts and the pack has continued until the present day.

Victoria is the mecca of foxhunting in Australia with 13 packs of hounds registered with the Hunt Club's Association in Victoria. There are a further ten packs throughout the country in New South Wales, South Australia and Western Australia.

The season runs from May to September. The best months are June, July and August. The weather can vary considerably throughout this very large country. The price of horses and hunting is considerably less expensive than in the United Kingdom or the United States of America. Hirelings are limited but can be obtained. It is best to contact the hunt secretaries.

The Melbourne Hunt formed with Carlow hounds in 1853 have been the yardstick for breeding hounds. The last decade or so has seen a renaissance in hound breeding in Victoria with Ellerslie, Findon, Melbourne and Oaklands importing blood lines from the UK. Hounds have been drafted from the Duke of Beaufort's, North Cotswold, Cottesmore and Exmoor. The results to date have been most encouraging.

The main hound show is conducted in October at Sherwood which is the property of the Oaklands Hunt. This attracts large entries from all the hunt kennels in Victoria. Thady Ryan, former Master of the Scarteen, judged the foxhounds last year.

The early part of the season can be mild – 12-20°C. Mid-winter temperature range between 5 and 12°C. The going is generally very good, but, when it rains it really comes down. In some countries this can be dangerous. Many followers have a medium and a heavy hunt coat. Travelling is a way of life in Australia; meets can vary from 30 minutes to one and a half hours from respective kennels. Joint meets with hunt weekends are very popular. The established hunts all conduct their annual point-to-point meetings during the season.

Foxhunters have a great camaraderie throughout the hunting world. Following hounds in Australia is different in many respects. The availability of large parcels of natural countryside is unique. One can expect to spend the whole day on grass. There are no villages and very few laneways and roads. In fact, one rarely sees another person outside of the field except maybe just the odd farmer. The Australian countryside is truly spectacular. Fences are mainly hunt jumps constructed of post and rails in the wire fences; stone walls in some countries. Fields average 20 to 30 mid-week and up to 60 on Saturdays. The average day is four to five hours but be prepared for some of the legends that can last up to six to seven hours. Visitors are most welcome.

Victoria is the most heavily hunted state in Australia. It is about the same size as the United Kingdom with a population of 4.5 million. The country is mainly open grazing land and home to sheep and cattle properties. Estates of several thousand acres are joined to make a day's hunting over mostly undulating grassland. Coverts vary from large ravines with native grasses and tussocks, to creeks and river flats. The natural beauty is outstanding. The fox is hunted in the wilderness with all the advantages of nature. The following is a brief description of the main two day a week hunts in Victoria:

The Ellerslie (1983) are situated 120 miles from Melbourne in the Western District. The hunt country is 200 000 acres of pastoral land; open grazing with natural coverts and river flats. A feature is the superb lawn meets, enjoyed on the most picturesque estates. Hounds (40 couple) are the property of the Master, Mr John Crosbie-Goold. Kennels at Ballangeich, Ellerslie, property of the Master. Meet Tuesday, Wednesday and Sunday and some Saturdays. Best centres are Ellerslie, Mortlake, Camperdown, and Mt William.

The Findon Harriers (1871) were originally formed as a harrier pack by the Miller family and in later years changed to foxhunting. The country is approximately 50 miles north-east of Melbourne; open grazing and undulating to native bushland and high country. Best centres are Broadford, Seymour and Pyalong. Hounds (25 couple) property of the hunt. Kennels at Woolert. Meet Tuesday and Saturday.

The Melbourne (1853) hunt south of Melbourne up to 100 miles in Gippsland; undulating grassland and natural coverts, fences mostly post and rail; country is close to the sea in some areas. Best centres are Cape Patterson, Tarwon Lower and Rosedale. Meet Saturday and Wednesday. Hounds (30 couple) property of the Melbourne Hunt. Kennels at Cranbourne.

The Oaklands (1888) are 30 to 50 miles north-west from Melbourne. Meets up to one hour from the kennels. Country is mostly open grassland and very undulating with natural coverts of native grass and river flats. Some areas are quite hilly. Best centres are Lancefield, Pyalong, Knowsley and Heathcote. Meet Wednesday and Saturday. Hounds (30 couple) property of the hunt. Kennels at Sherwood, Greenvale.

The Yarra Glen and Lilydale (1900) are east of Melbourne up to 60 miles, mainly centred in the Yarra Valley. Heavy country in some areas. Open grassland to river flats and valleys. This is also some of Victoria's best wine growing country. Meet Wednesday and Saturday. Hounds (40 couple) property of the hunt. Kennels at Yering, Coldstream.

However, there are also several packs hunting outside Victoria. Prominent amongst these are the Hunter Valley Hunt. They are the most northerly of hunts in Australia, having country in the Upper-Hunter Valley, some four to five hours drive north of Sydney. The pack originated as a harrier pack in 1977 but changed to foxhounds in 1991 to hunt the fox exclusively. The country is undulating to hilly cattle lands. Hounds work well under less than desirable scenting conditions and fields of 20 to 40 are the norm. The hounds are now predominantly foxhounds with some foxhound/harrier crosses.

The Sydney Hunt Club is the oldest established pack in the state of New South Wales, but has had a turbulent career, with many breaks in its continuity. They hunt farming land on the southern side of Sydney. Fields of 20-30 are the norm. Currently they are only hunting a small pack of five and a half couple of English foxhounds.

The Southern Tablelands Hunt Club enjoys hunting over some of the best scenting country in the state with a diverse range of hunting country, almost all sheep grazing but from gently undulating to steep and rocky. Ideal hunting climate with cool, wet winters, and situated only 45 minutes from Canberra, the nation's capital. The hunt has one of the busiest seasons of all hunts in Australia and is well supported with fields of 20-50 hunting two days (sometimes three) a week. Hounds are all English foxhounds.

John Crosbie-Goold is Master of his own hounds, the Ellerslie, in Victoria, and Ray Willmott is Master of the Southern Tablelands Hunt in New South Wales.

Hunting in France

Pierre Bocquillon

In France there are:
  131 packs of hare hounds
  96 packs of fox hounds
  77 packs of roe buck hounds
  35 packs of stag hounds
  18 backs of boar hounds.

There are:
  6800 horses
  6500 hounds
  1300 people employed by hunting
  50 000 followers
  10 000 practicants
  6000 members of La Société de Vénerie
  2500 members of La Fédération Internationale des Trompes de France
  9000 to 10 000 days hunting each year.

Hunting in France takes place over 300 000 hectares of forest managed by The National Forest Office, 250 000 hectares of private forest and 250 000 hectares of open and fallow land. In all these areas hunting and shooting happily take place together.

Stag hunting (La Vénerie du Cerf) is the figure-head of French hunting and is the one sort of hunting which is guaranteed to provide a grand spectacle. It is for this reason that it tends to be the most admired but it also attracts more criticism. Stag hunts have considerable numbers of followers; riders, cyclists, foot followers, car followers – indeed some say that stag hunts have more, but better behaved followers than football teams! The selective method of hunting employed ensures that the population of bigger stags is maintained and protects their traditional qualities of vigour and cunning which have enabled the species to survive over the centuries. Hunts require a lot of skill to cover their widely spread out countries. Every year stag hunts kill about 700 to 800 stags.

Boar hunting (La Vénerie du Sanglier): Boar hunts are called "vautraits" (literally "wallowers"). The origin of this name comes from the hounds, called "vautres", used by the Gauls. The boar is an animal renowned for its fierceness and a worthy enemy of its pursuers whom it sometimes injures and for this reason the hunts are usually made up of country people. It is necessary for them to know where the boar live and what their habits are in the truly vast areas that they hunt. This is why preparation for the hunt, called "rembûcher" (literally to drive to cover), carried out by the "valets de limiers" (tufters) the same morning is essential. Boar hunting needs strong and brave hounds, hunted by people on fit horses capable of covering over 40 kilometres a day. Boar hunts account for between 350 and 450 boars each season out of a total of 200 000 killed in total – the remainder by shooting.

L'Equipage de Bonnelles: A French stag hunt

Roe buck hunting (La Vénerie du Chevreuil): Careful breeding of these hounds since 1800, and outcrossing to the English packs, has led, uniquely, to packs that are capable of killing roe buck. The roe buck is a fast, cunning animal that has a very indistinct scent. This is why hunting it requires fast hounds with an exceptional scenting ability, a good voice, a love of hunting and an intelligence that comes from centuries of breeding so that they do not charge deer. For these reasons, roe buck hunters take a passionate interest in their hounds. Hunting the roe can be a difficult, even thankless task, that is very dependent on the weather. Normally roe buck hounds will kill 600 to 650 deer each season as opposed to 9000 by shooting and 3000 run over by motorists.

Foxhunting (La Vénerie du Renard): Foxhunting, traditionally an English sport, has only developed in France since 1980. The preferred method of foxhunting is now to hunt with hounds and leave the guns in their rack! The hounds are a mixed type, made up with drafts from stag, boar and roe hounds crossed with hare hounds. They are, nevertheless, quick and resourceful and need to have the same skills. Nearly all French packs also have traces of English blood. Foxhunting is now seen as a very effective and ecological method of controlling foxes, who are carriers of rabies, and hunted foxes may be dug out and killed.

Hare hunting (La Vénerie du Lièvre): Hare hunting is excellent sport for the young! You really do need to be very fit to follow on foot (although there are a few packs who hunt hares on horses) and to be able to cross woods and fields in all weathers! It is not unusual for a follower to cover some 15 kilometres in an afternoon, sometimes walking, sometimes running and with boots heavy with mud. Because of the skill and effort required, it is an excellent education for those who will later go on to hunt other animals. Hare hounds are smaller than other hounds and need to have a very good scenting ability, to be very fast, very enthusiastic and to be as dedicated as their Huntsman for the challenges are both uncertain and difficult. Some hare hunts also hunt the wild rabbit, which is easier but just as thrilling to catch. Hare hunts kill about 600 to 800 hares each season out of the 1.5 m killed altogether.

Hunting underground (La Vénerie Sous Terre): This form of hunting, colloquially known as "chasse sous terre", is getting more and more popular in France with about 1000 packs kept specifically for this purpose and with 600 recognised by L'Association Française des Equipages de Vénerie sous Terre. It is a form of hunting that requires energy and courage because it is necessary to capture the animal, which the hounds will have localised and trapped underground, and to know how to use spade, pickaxe and biceps. Underground packs are principally composed of those keen and clever little hounds, the fox terrier. These packs are very selective as to what animals they hunt and they exercise a greatly preferable form of control to the use of gas or poison.

Horse (Les Chevaux de Vénerie): Hunting horses are athletes who must be as fit as the hounds which they follow in a wild environment. Nearly 200 mounted hunts are affiliated to La Fédération Equestre Française. About 3850 horses, owned by hunting people, are used permanently for hunting. A further 3000 horses are used for hunting and other activities such as riding clubs, equitation centres, etc. Horses used for hunting represent about 19 per cent of the riding horses in France and make, as such, a vital contribution to the agriculture of France.

The Hunting Trumpet (La Trompe de Chasse): The French Hunting Trumpet, known also as the Hunting Horn, is indistinguishable from hunting itself. Its origins, significance, and development are inextricably entwined. The earliest calls must be attributed to Philidor l'Aîné in 1705 but it was le Marquis de Dampierre who documented 2000 calls in 1723 and it is these that still form the core of the unique hunting horn tradition of France today. The horn allows huntsmen to communicate with their hounds and to notify each other of what is happening during the course of a hunt. Never have there been so many horn blowers as now and never have they played so well. 2500 hunting horn enthusiasts, being the keenest, are members of La Fédération Internationale des Trompes de France. French hunting horn societies also exist in Belgium, Switzerland, Germany and Canada. These associations take part annually in festivals and competitions, both in private and in public.

Hunting employs 1300 people directly in France. 300 are employed full time in kennels; 1000 are employed looking after hunting horses. In addition a further 1800 are employed in associated jobs such as forage merchants, veterinary pharmacists, horn makers, farriers, saddlers, boot makers, tailors, horse transporters, horse hirers, veterinary surgeons, insurers, builders, garages, and very importantly in France, restaurateurs.

Pierre Bocquillon is Le Délégué Général de L'Association Française des Equipages de Vénerie.

The Work of the Masters of Foxhounds Association and the Hunt Servants' Benefit Society

Anthony Hart

The cohabiting of these organisations in recent years has proved a happy and successful arrangement.

The Masters of Foxhounds Association was founded in 1881, as the Governing Body of Foxhunting. Masters of Hounds know very well of its role in the Hunting World, but many who follow hounds today have little idea about the Association, which in fact plays a vital part in the sport they enjoy.

Every Master has to be a Member and abide by our strict Rules. The Association currently recognises 191 Hunts and the areas they hunt over, and only recognised Hunts may hold a Point-to-Point and enter their hounds in the Stud Book.

The early Minute Books of the Association are fascinating and record boundary disputes in a colourful manner, which seems to have been the main business of all their meetings at that time. The Association has evolved into a unique institution concerned with every aspect of the sport. We have to achieve a balance of the strict enforcement of the Rules, coupled with an understanding of the many problems which face Masters, Hunt Committees and the Hunting World in general. This must encompass a back-up at all times and a lead when necessary. Our Committee meets three or four times a year and has to face long agendas with many perplexing problems that can affect Hunting and the countryside.

Much work is done in Parliamentary matters and in conjunction with the BFSS much has been achieved. Legal problems regularly arise and a great deal of trouble is taken by our Solicitors to assist the Committee to provide the right advice to Masters. In recent years political attacks by County and Local Councils have required considerable advice to those in the area concerned.

Public relations, of course, play an important part and this year there has been an expansion of this department in conjunction with the BFSS. Brian Toon has guided us wisely for many years and remains our consultant, with eight regional Public Relations Officers to provide a comprehensive team under the leadership of Peter Voute, Public Relations Director to the BFSS.

We maintain a vigilant lobby in the European Parliament where legislation affecting Hunting could eminate. Every year we organise a meeting of all Hunting Associations in the European countries and work has been done to establish reliable contacts in Brussels, where we have a special committee to deal with matters concerning "Hunting with Hounds".

From the Association office at Bagendon we operate the Hunt Servants' Registry which provides a service to Masters and Hunt Servants where jobs and staff are concerned. Point-to-Point racing comes under Jockey Club Rules and the MFHA is closely concerned on behalf of hunting both at the Jockey Club Point-to-Point Liaison Committee and through the various stages of administration. Hunter Certificates to ensure proper qualifications must be issued by Masters of Hounds. Cross-Country Team Events also come under our responsibilities.

The Foxhound Kennel Stud Book is an annual publication and is one of the leading breed records, dating from 1800. This book is edited in our office.

Since 1985, we have also had the Hunt Servants' Benefit Society under our roof, which is a natural inclusion. Through support from Hunts, legacies and donations, the HSBS can guarantee that Hunt Servants are amply rewarded for their many years of hard work. The Society is a Registered Friendly Society.

Hunt Servants with pension arrangements in our scheme are known as Benefit Members of the Society. They, or their employers, pay premiums and, thanks in great part to the generosity of many supporters of Hunting, these benefits are better than any comparable pension policy available from leading assurance companies and others in this field. This generous support comes from friends who are known as Honorary Members and all those who enjoy Hunting are asked to join the Society in this way.

Benefit Members, of which there are currently 195 contributing, must, at the time of joining, be employed as a Huntsman, Whipper-in or Kennelman of a pack of Foxhounds, Deerhounds, Harriers or Draghounds, or work with a pack of Hounds that is recognised by the appropriate association. Young men joining Hunt Service as a career are encouraged and advised to start their pensions as soon as possible.

During 1993 the Society's income amounted to £245 415. After deductions for benefits and running costs, £105 121 was invested for the future. A sponsored Race Day at Leicester Racecourse last March, which raised over £12 300 will boost this year's figures. This was the second fundraising event held by the Society and it is hoped that it will be repeated.

In addition to the HSBS there is the Hunt Servants' Fund which is a Registered Charity. Charitable money has been given from time to time and this is valuable for assisting in cases of special need or hardship.

Enquiries for this, the HSBS or the MFHA should be directed to The Secretary, Parsloes Cottage, Bagendon, Cirencester, Gloucestershire GL7 7DU.

Anthony Hart is Secretary of the Masters of Foxhounds Association and the Hunt Servants' Benefit Society.

Masters of Foxhounds Association
The Hunting Code of Conduct
Introduction

Foxhunting has been for centuries an integral and important part of the life of rural Britain. It is the most humane and natural way to control foxes and the beneficial part it plays in conservation of the countryside and in the rural economy is beyond doubt.

Hunting's detractors are largely ignorant of, or choose to ignore, these considerations. Any lapse from the humane and decent standards traditionally observed by those who conduct and take part in foxhunting is grist to their mill. Since hunting takes place in public, we must all assume that our activities will be observed by the public and must be prepared to be held publicly accountable for them.

This Code of Practice is aimed at ensuring that not only newcomers to hunting but all who hunt understand that it is their absolute obligation to maintain the highest standards of sportsmanship and good behaviour at all times.

Three Golden Rules

1   Foxhunting as a sport is the hunting of the fox in his wild and natural state with a pack of hounds. Nothing must be done which in any way compromises this rule. The MFHA have laid down detailed rules for Masters of Foxhounds to observe, the most important of which are:

   i   If, when a fox is run to ground, the decision is that the fox be killed, it must be humanely destroyed

   ii   When a hunted fox is run to ground there shall be no digging other than for the purpose of humanely destroying the fox

   iii   A fox which has had to be handled by a terrierman or his assistant must either be freed or humanely destroyed immediately; under no circumstances may it be hunted.

2   Hunting flourishes entirely because of the goodwill of landowners and farmers. No-one who goes hunting should do anything to jeopardise this goodwill. It should always be borne in mind that for much of any hunting day, you are a guest on someone else's land.

3   Masters of Foxhounds or their appointed deputies are solely responsible for conducting the day's hunting and are bound by the strict rules and instructions of the MFHA. Their authority is absolute and their instructions must always be cheerfully obeyed.

Mounted Followers

Because the Hunt meets by arrangement and is recognisable and therefore accountable, mounted followers enjoy access to large areas of countryside denied to other people. When you follow hounds mounted, you must:

1 Conform to local standards of behaviour. These are many and various. For example, in some countries it may be permissable to jump fences which elsewhere should not be attempted because of lack of fence-mending facilities. Find out what the local conventions are and observe them strictly.

2 Ensure that your turnout is neat, clean and safe.

3 Do not block roads.

4 Be punctual at the Meet.

5 Refrain from causing damage. If you break a fence or cause or notice damage of any kind, report it immediately to the Master or Secretary.

6 Close all gates.

7 Refrain from disturbing livestock.

8 Remember that a red ribbon on your horse's tail provides no excuse if it kicks.

9 Refrain from parking your horsebox or trailer so as to cause an obstruction. Obtain permission before parking on private land.

10 Above all, always obey the Field Master.

Car Followers

Many people follow hounds by car and motorbike. Such followers are welcome but they too must obey the rules, in particular:

1 Do not interrupt the flow of ordinary traffic. Every motorist or lorry driver whom you delay becomes a potential enemy of hunting.

2 Do not obstruct gateways or drives, farmland or open country unless you are sure that the permission of the farmer or landowner has been obtained.

3 Do not drive vehicles onto private drives, farmland or open country unless you are sure that the permission of the farmer or landowner has

been obtained.

4   Keep together as much as possible and try to avoid heading the fox or getting between the hounds and their fox.

5   If there is a car Field Master appointed, obey him implicitly. By doing so, you will both avoid interfering with sport and greatly increase your own chances of seeing it.

6   If hounds are near your car, switch off the engine. Exhaust fumes mask scent and irritate hounds' noses.

7   Please do all you can to help the Hunt. When you leave your vehicle, follow the Code for foot followers.

Foot Followers

Foot followers can be of enormous help to the Hunt both during a day's hunting and at other times. Please remember:

1   That if you leave the road, you too become a guest on someone's land and should behave accordingly.

2   Do not get into such a position as to head the fox; if you do you spoil your own and everyone else's sport.

3   Remain as quiet as possible.

4   If you see the fox, let it get well past you. Then as a signal to the huntsmen either give a holloa or hold up your cap or a white handkerchief.

5   Shut gates which have been left open and be ready to open gates for the hunt staff. Report any damage you see to the Master or Secretary.

Generally

1   Before hunting proper begins, traditionally on the 1 November, many farmers and landowners wish to see the new season's litters of young foxes dispersed and a due proportion of them killed. This is preferably done in covert to prevent disturbance to stock still out in the fields.

At such times therefore, it is permissible for those mounted and foot followers who have been appointed by the Master for the purpose to discourage a fox from leaving covert (the process known as 'holding-up') by traditional means, ie by voice, by tapping with a whip or stick or by whip-cracking. No other means are permissible.

The Master should make every effort to discourage members of the public from participating in this process. In particular, the assistance of the covert-owner should if possible be obtained to prevent incursion onto the fields adjacent to the covert by vehicles, including motorbikes, or by unrestrained dogs.

2   If when a fox is run to ground, the decision is that it be killed, it is usually necessary to use terriers. The terrierman charged with the duty of humanely destroying the fox should normally be accompanied by one assistant only and every effort should be made to discourage the presence of foot followers and members of the general public.

3   Terriermen, whether or not directly employed by the hunt, are to be regarded as hunt servants; they must be aware of the provisions of the Rules and of this Code.

4   Accidental trespass cannot always be avoided but the wishes of all landowners, no matter how small, must be respected. Every effort must be made to prevent hounds and followers from straying onto places where they are not welcome.

5   So-called hunt saboteurs frequently break the law. Hunt followers must resist the temptation to retaliate in kind, whatever the provocation.

6   Today, many people use the countryside, some of whom have no interest in hunting. We must make every effort to avoid giving offence to such people. Common courtesy, particularly in the form of a simple 'please' or 'thank-you' costs nothing. Strict observance of this Code, politeness and, when appropriate, reasoned argument are what is needed to ensure that foxhunting continues to flourish.

We are grateful to the Masters of Foxhounds Association for allowing us to reproduce their Code of Good Hunting Practice.

FACE-UK

The UK Branch of The Federation of Associations for Country Sports in Europe

Field sports and the European Union

Each country within the European Union has its own traditional field sports, but none has a richer heritage than the UK. Game shooting, wildfowling, fishing, falconry and hunting with hounds have their origins lost in time and yet are more popular today than ever before.

Increasingly, these pastimes take place in an environment regulated by European law. Legislation on subjects ranging from firearms to the environment and even the meat trade can all be relevant. Decisions taken in Brussels may fail to recognise the complexity of Europe's varied field sports. There is a need for constant vigilance.

What is FACE?

The Federation of Associations for Country Sports in Europe (FACE) was founded in 1978. With an office in Brussels and close contacts with politicians and officials, it monitors all European legal developments likely to have an impact on field sports – beneficial or otherwise. It lobbies actively for the sports on the basis of freedom of recreation and scientific knowledge. It is both well known and respected, and has fought and won countless battles to amend inappropriate legislation. It has even set up an Intergroup of the European Parliament to bring together MEPs of all parties who are interested in country sports and conservation.

FACE-UK

FACE is controlled and funded by the national country sports organisations within each member state. In Britain its affairs are handled by FACE-UK, a body comprising representatives from all the UK field sports organisations listed on page x. Each organisation pays a share of the costs, and FACE-UK ensures that the legislative proposals spotted in Brussels are screened for their likely effect in the UK. FACE-UK helps FACE to prepare appropriate arguments for amendment and assists in lobbying the UK's own MEPs.

What has FACE achieved?

It may sound complicated, but it works. FACE has been responsible for some remarkable shifts in European thinking and many key changes in relevant Regulations and Directives. For example:

- The Birds Directive (1979) allowed the continuation of shooting practice despite great pressure to stop it.

- The Firearms Directive was changed to permit sportsmen to travel around Europe with their guns.

- The Wild Game Meat Directive was re-written to allow traditional game management to continue. As originally drafted it would have crushed Europe's game meat trade.

- The Flora, Fauna and Habitats Directive, which at first threatened the very future of hunting, shooting and fishing, was turned into a real force for the conservation of quarry species throughout Europe.

What you can do to help

This important work must continue. All the time legislative proposals are emerging and often, in the small print, there are implications for sport in the UK. Through their cooperation within FACE-UK our national field sports organisations have recognised how essential it is to have an active and informed lobby in Brussels.

You can play your part by sending a donation in support of FACE to J R Greenwood Esq Honorary Treasurer, FACE-UK, Stone Hall, Balcombe, Haywards Heath, West Sussex, RH17 6QN. Cheques should be made payable to FACE-UK. Thank you.

Organisations subscribing to FACE-UK

- British Association for Shooting and Conservation
- British Field Sports Society
- Conseil International de la Chasse (UK)
- Country Landowners' Association
- Masters of Deerhounds Association
- Masters of Mink Hounds Association
- National Federation of Anglers
- Scottish Landowners' Federation
- Game Conservancy Ltd
- The British Deer Society
- Atlantic Salmon Trust
- British Falconers Club
- The St Hubert Club
- The Association of Masters of Harriers and Beagles
- Masters of Foxhounds Association
- The Game Farmers' Association

Useful Names and Addresses:
Hunt Associations

United Kingdom

Association of Masters of Harriers and Beagles
Hon Director J J Kirkpatrick, Horn Park, Beaminster, Dorset DT8 3HB. 0308 862212.

Central Committee of Fell Packs
Chairman: W Edmund Porter.
Jt Secs: Mrs Olwyn Barber, 33 The Millfields, Beckermet, Egremont, Cumbria. 0946 728076; Mrs Linda Porter, Sword House, Eskdale, Holmrook, Cumbria. 0946 723295.

FACE-UK, Stone Hall, Balcombe, Haywards Heath, West Sussex RH17 6QN

Masters of Basset Hounds Association
Hon Sec: D A Peacock, 20 St Catherine Close, Burbage, Hinckley, Leics. 0455 632237.

Masters of Bloodhounds Association
Chairman: C Keating Coyne.
Hon Sec: Mrs J Lucas, Croft Farm, Hook Norton, Banbury, Oxon OX15 5DB. 0608 737303.

Masters of Deerhounds Association
Chairman: Dick Lloyd.
Hon Sec: Dr J D W Peck, Bilboa House, Dulverton, Somerset TA22 9DW. 0398 23475.

Masters of Draghounds Association
Hon Sec: Mrs P J Hawksfield, The Maltings, Church Road, Steyning, West Sussex BN44 3YB. 0903 815204.

Masters of Foxhounds Association
President: Capt R E Wallace
Chairman: E H Vestey (due to retire 1995)
Sec: A H B Hart, Parsloes Cottage, Bagendon, Cirencester GL7 7DU. 0285 831470 (office) or 0285 831378 (home).

Masters of Mink Hounds Association
Hon Sec: P Wild, 8 Wilson-Valkenburg Court, Bath Road, Newbury, Berks 0635 44754.

Northern Ireland Masters of Hounds Association
Sec: (1959) Mrs A J Chittick, 53 Castle Street, Ballymena, Co Antrim. 0266 656087.

Ireland

The Irish Foot Harriers Association
Chairman: J Murray, 9 Rosewood, Ballincollig, Co Cork. 021 870609.

Irish Masters of Beagles Association
Hon Sec/Treasurer: Lt Col J O'Sullivan, Tipper Road, Naas, Co Kildare. 045 41534.

Irish Masters of Foxhounds Association
Chairman: Lord Harrington
Hon Sec: Nicholas MacDermott, Thornton, Dunlavin, Co Kildare. 045 51294.

Irish Masters of Harriers Association
Hon Sec: G Gleeson, Newtown, Crecora, Limerick. 061 355304.

The Irish Masters of Minkhounds Association
Hon Sec: D J Daly, Greenridge, Ballea, Carrigaline, Co Cork. 021 372358 or 0885 80355.

The Irish Masters of Otterhounds Association
Hon Sec: D J Daly, Greenridge, Ballea, Carrigaline, Co Cork. 021 372358.

Europe

Deutscher Reiter und Fahrerverband
Roonstraße 54, 33615 Bielefeld, Germany.

Masters Association of the Netherlands
Chairman: J J P Bakker
Hon Sec: Drs P Aalberse, Kastanjelaan 16, 6571 CG Berg En Dal. 08895 42698.

Nederland Bond van Rij en Jacht
Postbus 455, 3740 AL Baarn. 0-2154 21741.

Société de Vénerie de la France
Sec Gen: M Pierre Bocquillon, 10 rue de Lisbonne, 75008 Paris.

Australia and New Zealand

The Hunt Clubs Association of Victoria (Inc)
Sec: Ian Rough, PO Box 51, Bayswater, Victoria 3153. 03 729 4333.

New Zealand Hunts Association
President: C J Glynn, Eastern Bush, RD 2, Otautau. 03 225 58560.

Sec of the Hound Committee & Keeper of the Hound Register: P M Y Langdale, Stockgrove, RD 4, Hastings, NZ. Tel./Fax. 64 6 874 9732

United States of America

Masters of Foxhounds Association of America
Executive Director: Dennis Foster, Morven Park, Route 3, Box 50, Leesburg, Virginia 22075. (703) 771 7442.

National Beagle Club of America
Sec: J B Wiley Jr, River Road, Bedminster, New Jersey 07921. (201) 234 0245

Other Administrative Organisations and Useful Addresses

Animal Health Trust
Balaton Lodge, PO Box 5, Snailwell Road, Newmarket CB8 7DW. 0638 661111.

Army Beagling Association
President: Col D F Easten MC, Bowdens Cottage, Wormingford, Colchester, Essex.
Chairman: Maj Gen S Cowan, CBE
Sec: Col J G Aldous OBE, HQ Southern District, Aldershot GU11 2DP.

British Association of Homeopathic Veterinary Surgeons
Christopher Day, Chinham House, Stanford-in-the-Vale, Faringdon, Oxon SN7 8NQ. 0367
710324.

British Field Sports Society
Press & Information Officer: Caroline Yeates, 59 Kennington Road, London SE1 7PZ. 071-
928 4742.

British Horse Society
Chief Exec: Col T J S Eastwood, British Equestrian Centre, Stoneleigh, Kenilworth,
Warwickshire CV8 2LR.

British Veterinary Association
Miss C Nicholls, 7 Mansfield Street, London W1M 0AT. 071-636 6541.

Country Landowners Association
Tamara Strapp, 16 Belgrave Square, London SW1X 8PQ. 071-235 0511.

Horse and Hound
Kings Reach Tower, Stamford Street, London SE1 9LS. 071-261 5000.

Hounds Magazine
Rose Cottage, Hughley, Shrewsbury, Shropshire. 0746 36637.

Hunt Servants Benefit Society/Hunt Servants Registry
c/o Masters of Foxhounds Association, above.

Hunters' Improvement & National Light Horse Breeding Society
G W Evans, 96 High Street, Edenbridge, Kent TN8 5AR. 0732 866277.

National Association of Farriers & Blacksmiths
Sarah Jagger, Avenue R, 7th Street, NAC, Stoneleigh, Kenilworth, Warwickshire CV8 2LG.
0203 696595.

Peterborough Royal Foxhound Show Society
Sec: R W Bird, The Showground, Alwalton, Peterborough PE2 0XE. 0733 234451.

Point-to-Point Owners Association
Chairman: T P Tory, Crab Farm, Shapwick, Blandford, Dorset DT11 9JL.
Sec: Mrs Jeanette Dawson, 2 Little Fryth, Hollybush Ride, Finchampstead, Wokingham
RG11 3RN. 0344 778438.

Point-to-Point Secretaries Association
Chairman: Mrs C N Higgon, Newton Hall, Crundale, Haverfordwest, Pembrokeshire SA62
4EB. 0437 731239.
Vice Chairman: A M MacEwan, Urless Farm, Corscombe, Dorchester DT2 0NP.
0935 891327.
Secretarial Service: The Jockey Club, 42 Portman Square, London W1H 0EN.
071-486 4921. Registry Office of the Jockey Club (incorporating the National Hunt
Committee)

Messrs Weatherby & Sons, 42 Portman Square, London W1H 0EN. 071-486 4921 and
Sanders Road, Wellingborough, Northants NN8 4BX. 0933 440077.

Royal Agricultural Benevolent Institution
Shaw House, 27 West Way, Oxford. 0865 724931.

Secretaries of Foxhounds Association
Hon Sec Sir Geoffrey Bates, Bt, MC, Gyrn Castle, Llanasa, Holywell, Clwyd CH8 9BG.
0745 853500.

The Side Saddle Association
Sec: Mrs Maureen James, Highbury House, 19 High Street, Welford, Northampton NN6
7HT. 0858 575300.

Society of Master Saddlers
HC Knight, The Cottage, 4 Chapel Place, Mary Street, Bovey Tracey, Devon TQ13 9JA.

Ireland

Country Sports Association
Hon Sec: Aiden Kearney, West End, Magazine Road, Cork. 021 545747.

FACE Ireland (Federation of Field Sports)
Hon Sec: Mr Tourlough J Coffey, Weston, Spawell Road, Wexford. 053 24849.

Field & Country Sports Society
Hon Sec: Col D J McLoughlin, 20 Frenchfurze Grove, Kildare. 045 22152.

Glossary

"All On!"
A pack is "All on" when every hound comprising it is present. Upon leaving a covert, and at the end of the day's sport, a whipper-in counts ("makes") the pack, and, if all are present, reports "All on".

At fault
When hounds check, they are said to be at fault.

Babble
A hound is said to babble, or to be a "babbler", when it throws its tongue unnecessarily: for example, when it is far behind the leading hounds, or, in covert, without the line of a fox.

Benches
The wooden platforms upon which hounds sleep in kennels are known as "benches".

Billett
A billett is a fox's excreta or droppings.

Blank
A covert is blank when it does not hold a fox. A blank day is a day on which no fox is found.

Blowing away
A Huntsman blows his hounds away from a covert, with quick, pulsating notes of the horn, on to the line of a fox; "blowing away" is therefore the prelude to a hunt in the open.

Blowing out
A Huntsman blows his hounds out of a blank covert with long mournful calls of the horn.

Bolt
To bolt a fox is to force it out of a drain or earth.

Break
A fox "breaks", or "breaks covert", when he leaves a covert or woodland for the open.

Brush
The fox's tail.

Burst
The first part of a run.

Butcher -boots
These are plain, long, black boots without tops, worn with "ratcatcher" or with a silk hat, black coat and coloured breeches.

Button, Hunt
Every hunt has its own button, consisting of a black (worn on a black coat) or a brass (worn on a red coat) button engraved with the monogram or initials of the hunt, or some other design.

Bye-day
A extra hunting-day; an unadvertised hunting-day; a hunting day above the normal quota of the week (ie a two-day-a-week pack may hunt three days in one week; the third day is a bye-day).

Cap
The controversial head-gear worn by Masters, hunt staff, Field Master, secretary, visiting and ex-Masters, farmers, their several wives, and – apparently – anybody who knows no better. It is covered with black velvet.

A sum of money extracted by the secretary of a hunt from those persons, not being subscribers, visiting the hunt for the day.

"Car Please?"
Is shouted by the Master or Members of the field to indicate that a car wishes to pass the hunt, normally when they are gossiping on a road. Everyone should do their best to clear a way through as quickly as possible. Nothing gives a hunt a bad name as quickly as delaying other road users when going about their daily business.

Carry a scent
Good scenting land "carries a scent".

Carry the scent	Those hounds of a pack carry the scent which, at a given moment, are actually smelling the fox's scent.
Cast	The effort by the pack, or by the Huntsman with his pack, to recover the scent after a check.
Check	Hounds check when they are unable any longer to follow the scent trail of the fox. A check is the period of time during which the hounds are checked.
Chop	Hounds are said to chop a fox when they kill one asleep or surprise one before it gets away.
Close a cast	To close the cast is to make good all the ground in a complete circle round the spot at which hounds checked.
Country	The area in which a hunt may draw for a fox is said to be its "country"; it may run a fox outside its country, and may even kill outside, provided it does so without the use of terrier or without "breaking ground". Hunts do not draw outside their own country.
Couple	Two foxhounds. The size of a pack is spoken of in terms of couples – eg 22 $^1/_2$ couple. But one hound, all by itself is not "a half-couple" – or should not be – but is one hound; it only becomes a half couple when coupled with at least one other couple.
Couples	Two leather hound collars attached by links or a chain of steel, and used to join two hounds together so that neither can escape; couples are carried on hunt servants' saddles at all times.
Course	Hounds are said to course a fox when they run it in view, without heed to scent.
Covert	Any woodland (unless very big) or place that might hold a fox.
Cross-bred	A hound which contains some Welsh, as well as English blood, is sometimes spoken of as being "cross bred", "Curre bred", "Curre type" or "a bloody Welshman".
Cry	The music of a pack is its cry. To be in full cry merely means that the majority of the pack are speaking to their fox.
Cub	A young fox – becomes a fox on November 1st, after the opening meet.
Cur-dog	In the hunting-field, and at all times to a hunt servant, any dog other than a foxhound is a cur-dog, no matter how blue blooded it may be in its own inferior breed.
Dog fox	A male fox
Double the horn	A Huntsman "doubles his horn" when he blows quick pulsating notes on it: eg when a fox crosses a ride or is holloaed away. The horn is only doubled when a fox is a-foot.
Draft	To draft a hound is to separate it from the pack. "The draft" is therefore a collection of hounds which, because they are no good to him, the Master separates from his pack with a view to their being given away to another pack. The day before hunting, the Huntsman drafts the hunting pack away from the rest of the hounds, into a separate kennel.

Drag	The line of a fox leading to his kennel; to hunt *the* drag is to hunt this line up to the sleeping fox. This method of finding foxes is often used on moorland (cf drawing for a fox in covert, where the sleeping fox is actually winded by a hound). A drag is also an artificial scenting line, made by dragging an evil-smelling rag along the ground. To hunt *a* drag is to hunt such a line. The foxhunter should beware of using "a" when he means "the" – the mistake may mean a black-eye, or, in the barely civilised countries in which *the* drag is still hunted, a good old-fashioned horse-whipping!
Drain	An underground drain-pipe used as a sleeping-place or refuge by foxes. A large ditch, without fence. A small ditch draining moorland, into which a galloping horse invariably puts one foot, so breaking its rider's neck.
Draw	A covert is drawn by the hounds when the Huntsman puts them in it. The draw for the day is the country the Master intends to hunt. A hound is drawn when the Huntsman takes one away from the rest of the pack.
Earth	A fox's underground home.
Enter	Teaching young hounds to hunt a fox is to enter them.
Feather	A hound may own a very weak scent but be uncertain that he *does* own it. In that case, he will snuffle along the line, his stern lashing from side to side, but he will not throw his tongue. He is feathering along the line.
Feathers	A hound's feathers are the ruffled, long hairs on the under-side of the lower part of his stern.
Fence mender	Many packs now employ someone to follow the hunt in a vehicle to repair the damage done by the horses.
Field	The collection of mounted men and women hunting with a pack; the hunt servants and second-horseman are not members of the Field.
Foil	A fox who "runs his foil" is doubling on his own tracks. A smell which tends to disguise or obliterate the fox's scent trail is called "foil", eg manure, natural or artificial; the smell of horses, hounds, human beings, cattle, sheep, pheasants, deer, porcupines, etc. Foil is the arch enemy of the pack.
"Gate Please!"	Shouted by one person to another to indicate that the gate through which they have just passed requires shutting. Do check that there is actually somebody behind you before making use of this over used cry; it does not absolve you of responsibility for making sure that gates are shut.
Gate shutting	Many packs will detail two or more members of the Field as gate shutters for a particular day. They will turn out in scruffy clothes and carry copious amounts of binder twine. Their duties are to ride at the back to ensure that all gates are properly closed and gaps repaired. The presence of a gate shutter does not absolve other members of the Field from these tasks. They are really an insurance policy.
Given best	When a Huntsman decides that a fox has outwitted his hounds and that he will no longer be hunted.
Going	The nature of the ground as it affects a horse's ability to gallop; eg hard, heavy, deep, wet, or (rarely) good.

Gone to ground	When a fox has got into an earth or drain.
Good head	Hounds carry a good head when they are running hard on a broad front, instead of tailed out.
Guarantee	The sum of money which a hunt committee guarantees to pay the Master annually towards the cost of upkeep of kennels, hounds, horses, salaries etc.
Hack on, to	To hack on to a meet is for the foxhunter to ride on a horse to the meet.
Hackles	The hackles of a hound are the hairs along the ridge of its spine (sometimes known in the west as the "ridge-hairs"). A hound that is angry "gets its hackles up," or, in other words, is all het up.
Headed	A fox which is turned away from its original line is said to have been headed.
	To "Head" a fox in such a manner is a heinous crime – which you will not be in danger of committing if you stay behind the Field Master.
Heads up	Hounds are said to have their heads up when they no longer have their noses to the ground searching for the fox-scent.
Heel	Hounds run heel, or "run the heel-way", when they follow the line of a fox in the opposite way to that in which he was travelling.
Hireling	A horse which is let out on hire.
Hits the line	A hound "hits" the line of the fox when he first smells it after a check; so too, a Huntsman "hits" it when he causes a hound or hounds to strike it after a check.
Hold	A covert that contains a fox is said to "hold". To "hold" hounds on or round, or back, is to take them on, or round, or back.
"Hold hard!"	Shouted, sometimes rather crossly, by Masters when the Field are in danger of over riding the hounds. If you are told to "Hold hard" it is best to do so – quite quickly. A good tactic is to circle rapidly to the back of the Field.
Hold up	To hold up a covert is to surround it and prevent foxes (as a rule, cubs) from leaving it. To "hold up" a litter (of cubs) is to surround the covert in which they live.
Holloa, a	A scream, meaning the same as the spoken words "Tally-ho!" – that is, "I have seen a fox!" The words "Tally-ho!" are only used when they can be spoken – when the person for whom they are intended is within speaking distance; at long ranges, he is regaled with a holloa. Pronounced holler.
Hound pace/ jog	The pace at which horses jog when travelling with hounds on the road; about six mph.
Huic!	Also written "Hoick!" Pronounced "Hike!" "Ike!" "Hark!" or "Ark!" Means Hark!
Huic Holloa!	Hark (to the) Holloa! A cheer drawing the attention of the Huntsman or the hounds to a holloa.
Hunt	To hunt: to pursue a quarry. A hunt: the process of pursuing a quarry. The hunt: the whole caboodle – men, women, hounds, horses, servants – that pursue a quarry. The organization of the hunt.

Kennel	A fox's above-ground bed is his kennel; to unkennel him is to push him out of bed.
Kennels	The abode of foxhounds.
Kennel Huntsman	The individual, a professional hunt servant, who is in charge of the kennels. A professional Huntsman is his own Kennel Huntsman; where an amateur hunts the hounds it is usual for him to appoint someone, probably his first whipper-in, to be in charge of the kennels: this is the Kennel Huntsman.
Kennelman	Someone who works in the kennels under the Kennel Huntsman or Huntsman, but who does not also take the field (ie a whipper-in may work in kennels, but he is not the kennelman).
Lark	To lark over a fence is to jump it when hounds are not running, or on the way to or from hunting. It is a hunting field crime.
Lift	A Huntsman lifts hounds when he takes them, during the course of a hunt, across country without giving them time to try for the scent.
Line, a	The scent trail of a fox.
Mark	Hounds are marking to ground when they gather round and bay outside an earth or drain where a fox has gone to ground.
Mask	The fox's head.
Meet	The place designated for hounds to meet the Master. "A Lawn Meet" is at a private house, where refreshments ("stirrup cups") are provided for the Field.
Mixed pack	A pack comprising hounds of both sexes; care is taken to ensure that the party is strictly moral.
Music	The cry of hounds is also "the music of the pack," or, more prosaically, hound-music.
Mute	A hound runs mute when he follows the scent of a fox without throwing his tongue; a hound is mute when he never throws his tongue.
Nose	The smelling-power of a hound. A hound with a good nose has good smelling power, plus the mental ability to interpret what he smells in terms of the fox's actual movements.
Open	The hound which, winding a fox in covert, is the first to speak to it, is said to "open". An unstopped earth is said to be "open".
Own the line	A hound which is hunting on the fox's line is said to "own the line."
Oxer	Thorn fence with guard rail.
Pack	A collection of hounds.
Pad	The foot of a fox.
Pick up	A Huntsman is said to "pick hounds up" when he lifts them. See *Lift*.
Point	The point of a run is the distance between the two farthest-apart points of it, measured as the crow flies; it is not the distance between find and finish, which might be 12 miles whilst the point was six miles.

Point, On	To be asked by the Master or Huntsman to go on your own to watch a particular area of a covert which is being drawn and to let the Huntsman know if the fox goes away within your view – either by Holloaing, raising your hat, whistle or, in the future, I expect by mobile phone.
Quick thing	A very fast, short, gallop.
Rate	To rate a hound is to correct it by the voice for any act of ill-discipline.
Ride	A ride is a wide path through a covert.
Riot	Anything, from the proverbial cat in a kitchen to a wagtail in the wallflowers, which hounds hunt when they should only hunt fox. To riot is to hunt these other anythings: they include rabbits, hares, deer, pheasants, moorhens, cats and cur-dogs – in fact everything which moves.
Running	Hounds are said to be running when they are in actual pursuit of a fox. Thus, though they may be galloping to go to a holloa they are not technically running: but they are technically running when they are only walking after a fox on a very cold scent. They are not running when they are drawing or checked.
Second Horses	In many hunts the hunt staff will ride two horses in a day because one horse is not capable of the work asked of it. In the smarter packs many of the Field will also have a second horse and will "change horses" half way through the day. Packs where it is normal to have second horses will detail where they should rendezvous on their meet card.
Set	A place where a hare lies up.
Speak	Foxhounds do not "bark"; they "speak", which is, of course, far more refined.
Stale line	The line of a fox which has been gone a long time and of which the scent is almost non-existent.
Stern	Foxhounds do not have tails, only sterns.
Stopping	Or stopping out. Fox earths are "stopped" when they are blocked during the hours of darkness preceding a hunting-day. The fox is then out, and the object of the manoeuvre is to make him sleep out the next day, and so be available for hounds to find.
Tail-hounds	Hounds which, in a hunt, are some way behind the main body of the pack.
Tally-ho!	A hunting cry meaning, "I have seen a fox.' See *Holloa*!
Tally-over!	A hunting cry, meaning " I have seen a fox cross this ride (or road)".
Terrier-man	A man employed by a hunt to lead or carry terriers.
Tongue	The cry of hounds. To "throw the tongue" is to bark or "speak".
Tops	Top-boots. Long black boots with a few inches of coloured top above the black.
Tufters	Those hounds taken on by the Huntsman when staghunting, to separate the selected stag.
Unentered hounds	Hounds which have not yet learnt to recognize and follow the scent of a fox; normally, a hound which has not finished one cub-hunting season.
View	To see a fox is to view it; the sight of a fox is a view.
Vixen	A female fox.

Walk

Foxhound puppies, for the good of their souls and bodies – not least, the former – are sent out to farms and private houses from the age of about 2-3 months to the age of about 9-12 months; they are then said to be "at walk". This culminates in the annual puppy judging at the kennels, colloquially known as "The Puppy Show".

Ware!

A cautionary word used to tell the hounds or the Field to be careful – literally from Be-ware; ie "Ware Hole!" is shouted by one member of the Field to another when they spot a looming rabbit hole or similar death trap. "Ware Cur Dog!" is shouted to the hounds by one of the hunt staff when they pass a pedigree labrador which is likely to upset them. There are lots of other "Wares" eg "Ware-'Oss!" when a hound gets too near your horse, "Ware Motor" when a hound displays dangerous contempt for a motor vehicle, or "Ware Stranger" when a hound decides to be friendly with somebody undesirable such as an anti hunt demonstrator.

Whelps

Unweaned puppies.

Whipper-in An assistant to the Huntsman in both kennel and field.

Good night

Major Gerald Gundry was my stepfather-in-law. He was stubborn, charming, maddening and amusing; those who did not love him respected him. A great part of his life was devoted to the Duke of Beaufort's Hunt. He was Joint Master with the late Duke from 1951-1985 and for nearly quarter of a century he hunted the Doghounds. Everybody knew "The Major". The Beaufort Hounds and Foxes were his passion. He was indeed a "mighty hunter before the Lord".

On December 20, 1990 at 3.25 pm Major Gundry died, aged 79. On December 22, 1990, the Duke of Beaufort's Hounds met at Foxley Green. Little was done in the morning, but in the early afternoon they found a fox. At exactly 3.25 pm, hounds killed the fox at the Major's front door.

The man who told me this said "I am not an imaginative chap, but I do not mind telling you that I feel chills down my spine. There was a very strange feeling. Several people burst into tears."

So there you are; make of this what you will. Coincidence, some may say. Is there such a thing? I do not pretend to know. All I know is that at the end of the day's hunting it is customary to thank the Master and wish him goodnight, so it can do no harm to say "Thank you, Major and good night."

Willy Poole

This story first appeared in *The Daily Telegraph* and is reproduced by their kind permission.